THE HARMONY OF REASON

The Harmony of Reason: A Study in Kant's Aesthetics

Francis X. J. Coleman

University of Pittsburgh Press

Copyright © 1974, University of Pittsburgh Press
All rights reserved
Feffer and Simons, Inc., London
Manufactured in the United States of America

Library of Congress Cataloging in Publication Data

Coleman, Francis X. J.
The Harmony of reason: a study in Kant's aesthetics.

Bibliography: p. 205
Includes index.
1. Kant, Immanuel, 1724–1804—Aesthetics. I. Title.
B2799.A4C63   111.8'5   74–4520
ISBN 0–8229–3282–2

Quotations from Immanuel Kant, *Critique of Judgement,* translated by James Creed Meredith, are reprinted by permission of The Clarendon Press, Oxford. Quotations from Kant's *Critique of Pure Reason,* translated by Norman Kemp Smith, are reprinted by permission of Macmillan, London and Basingstoke, and St. Martin's Press, Inc. Material from *Art and Illusion,* by E. H. Gombrich, no. 5 in the A. W. Mellon Lectures in the Fine Arts, Bollingen Series XXXV (Copyright © 1960, 1961, 1969 by the Trustees of the National Gallery of Art, Washington, D.C.), is reprinted by permission of Princeton University Press.

For Robert Killam Churbuck

Cras ingens iterabimus aequor

*. . . the antinomies, both here and in the Critique of
Practical Reason, compel us, whether we like it or not,
to look beyond the horizon of the sensible, and to seek
in the supersensible the point of union of all our
faculties* a priori: *for we are left with no other
expedient to bring reason into harmony with itself.*

—The Critique of Judgment

Contents

Preface

Although Kant's first two *Critiques* have been widely discussed and commented upon during the last two hundred years, Kant's *Third Critique*—the *Critique of Judgment*[1]—has been largely neglected by both the general reader and the student of Kant's philosophy. Nonetheless, Kant's aesthetic philosophy, as contained especially in Part One of the *Critique of Judgment*, has exerted considerable influence upon writers as different in their philosophical persuasions as Schiller and Hegel, Schopenhauer and Nietzsche, Goethe and Coleridge. A number of modern critical articles and commentaries on certain aspects of Kant's aesthetics exist, but there is no book-length critical study in any language devoted solely to Part One of the *Critique of Judgment* and to Kant's other writings on aesthetics. In this study, I have attempted such a commentary.

My aim has been to expound and sometimes to expand upon Kant's aesthetics, but never explicitly to defend or argue in favor of his views. Whether Kant's aesthetics represents a living philosophy I leave entirely to the reader's judgment. With the exception of the aesthetic writings of E. H. Gombrich, I have not drawn upon the theories of any other writer to defend or to expand upon Kant's own views. Once again I believed it wiser to let the reader bring his own aesthetic interests and predilections to bear upon the texts. Moreover, I have rarely engaged in criticism of other commentaries on Kant's aesthetics, not because I believe my own interpretation to be definitive, but simply because of lack of space and time. Philosophy is not greatly advanced, I believe, by passing in review all the critiques of a philosophical text or system, with observations concerning their shortcomings or strengths. A prudent commentator should naturally be acquainted with the other works written on his subject, but he should not weary the reader with glosses upon glosses.

I have not attempted to give another line-by-line commentary of Part One of the third *Critique* because, in this capacity, H. W. Cassirer's *Commentary on Kant's Critique of Judgment* suffices.[2] Only rarely have I tried to set Kant's aesthetic theories into the historical setting of the Enlightenment; several excellent studies already exist on this subject, for example, Ernst Cassirer's *Philosophy of the Enlightenment*.[3]

There is the temptation in expounding the thought of any great philosopher for whom one has some degree of sympathy to make his ideas one's own and to try to defend him against latter-day attack. The result of this temptation is often anachronistic and usually blurs the commentator's ideas with those of his subject. I have tried to be scrupulous in keeping Kant's doctrines distinct from my own reflections on problems similar to those dealt with in his aesthetics. Though I have tried to complement certain of Kant's doctrines, I have done so only when I believed my own expansions would throw his intentions into better relief.

Along with providing an exposition of Kant's aesthetics, I have also sought to correct what I believe to be the most frequently encountered misinterpretation of Kant's position. In histories of aesthetics and in the majority of articles, Kant's aesthetics is represented as an extreme example of aesthetic formalism. There is a similar stereotyped view of Kant's ethics as based solely on the barren formula of the Categorical Imperative. I hope that my own study will show that though form plays an important role in Kant's theory, it is a mistake to describe his aesthetics as "formalistic."

What makes it especially difficult to expound Part One of the *Critique of Judgment* is its intimate connection with the themes of Kant's *Critique of Pure Reason* and the *Critique of Practical Reason*. Consequently, wherever it has been of value in explaining Kant's aesthetics to turn to the first two *Critiques*, I have done so.[4] Moreover, I have also drawn upon Kant's shorter writings, such as the *Foundations of the Metaphysics of Morals* and *Religion Within the Limits of Reason Alone*, for parallels between Kant's aesthetics and ethics which I hope will prove helpful.

Perhaps I have been too ambitious in this study, for I have also attempted to show what I believe to be internal inconsistencies in Kant's argument, as well as mistakes of a broader and external nature. For example, I found it necessary to inquire into the hedonic underpinnings of Kant's entire aesthetics. I am therefore doubly vulnerable in regard to such external criticisms; for not only must they be relevant to Kant's own aesthetics, but they must have some philosophical merit of their own.

Acknowledgments

Scholars tend to have a keen sense of territorial rights; it is therefore inevitable that some scholars of Kant will charge me with poaching on their preserves. Earlier versions of this book were read by some of the best-known Kantians, both in Europe and in America; their criticisms and suggestions have been invaluable to me. But because I should not like to imply that my own interpretations of Kant's aesthetics agree with theirs, I must leave them unnamed. Nonetheless, I should like to express my appreciation to Monsignor Abelard Dichter for his aid and encouragement in seeing this book to its completion, as well as to Professor John R. Silber and certain other of my colleagues at Boston University: Professor John Findlay, Professor John Lavely, and Professor Marx Wartofsky. I also thank Ms. Karen Reeder for preparing the final version of the typescript. My final note of thanks, which I must confess to be the strongest, is to Ms. Beth E. Luey, who edited the final typescript.

THE HARMONY OF REASON

CHAPTER 1

Introduction

The General Bearings of Kant's Third *Critique*

The *Critique of Judgment* may be broadly viewed as a work of philosophical diplomacy in which Kant attempts to reconcile the laws of Nature, as described in his first *Critique*, with the laws of freedom, as described in the second. Kant holds that the deterministic laws of physics can be brought into harmony with the unconditional commands of morality only if reason has the right to presuppose an underlying and fundamental purposiveness behind Nature.

Part One of the *Critique of Judgment* attempts to show how purposiveness is presupposed by aesthetic judgment. According to Kant, the beautiful, either in art or in Nature, must be conceived as if it were preadapted to bring about a certain kind of pleasure in persons constituted like ourselves. Part Two of the *Critique of Judgment* attempts to give a case for purposiveness in biological organisms. For Kant, the physical sciences employ a mechanistic model of Nature, whereas the biological sciences employ a teleological model. Assuming that an organic product is "one in which every part is reciprocally both end and means,"[1] Kant argues that the principle of teleology must be employed as a heuristic rule, though not as a rule productive of empirical knowledge.

Before turning to the details of the *Critique of Judgment*, Part One (with which my study is primarily concerned), I shall attempt to show how Kant intended the third *Critique* to complete his "Critical philosophy," or the analysis of the a priori elements in human experience. Kant himself regrets that "the difficulty of unravelling a problem so involved" led him into "a certain amount of hardly unavoidable obscurity in its solution."[2]

Beginning with the assumption that human cognition is composed solely of three broad realms—understanding, judgment, and reason—Kant holds that three faculties respectively correspond to them: the thinking faculty, the feeling of pleasure and displeasure, and the faculty of desire. By "faculty" Kant does not intend anything psychological, other than the traditional or scholastic conception of "faculty psychology." Understanding, which works in accordance with its own rules, supplies the a priori laws of Nature, by which knowledge of the empirical world is made possible. Although for Kant knowledge of the world is exclusively based upon the world of appearances, or phenomena, he holds that knowledge is both objective and public, and in no way illusory or deceptive. It is at least logically possible, so Kant argues, that there exists something behind, or other than, the world of appearances. For reasons that will shortly become apparent, Kant holds that there must be presupposed something other than appearances—or in his term, a "supersensible substrate"—in order to bring the cognitive faculties into reciprocal harmony. Describing the "antinomy of taste" in Part One of the third *Critique*, Kant says that "the antinomies . . . compel us, whether we like it or not, to look beyond the horizon of the sensible, and to seek in the supersensible the point of union of all our faculties *a priori:* for we are left with no other expedient to bring reason into harmony with itself."[3]

The faculty of understanding leaves the supersensible undetermined; that is, by definition, understanding can have no empirical acquaintance with it. When the understanding tries to determine the supersensible or to give a positive description of it, the road is opened to the vanities and sophistries of metaphysics. According to Kant, the supreme a priori principle in accordance with which understanding functions is conformity to law: no knowledge is possible unless it be presupposed that all events in the phenomenal world, or in Nature, are determined by law.

Kant holds that the faculty of desire is as intrinsic to what may be broadly called human nature as the faculty of understanding. From the phenomenal point of view, human beings are wholly determined, like any other object in Nature. Yet human beings sometimes blame, sometimes praise, each other's conduct, as well as their own. Kant assumes that as an ethical agent acting out of a pure sense of duty, a person must be construed as belonging both to the supersensible and to the phenomenal, empirical realm. Moral responsibility and moral worth cannot be explained, so Kant argues, in a deterministic or mechanistic world. Consequently, just as the supersensible lies behind the world of Nature, so the "supersensible substrate" is at the basis of the moral agent.

Although the understanding cannot give a positive or scientific determination to the supersensible, reason must nevertheless give a practical or moral determination to the "supersensible substrate" of humanity. The chief "Idea" of reason, according to Kant, is the freedom of the moral agent, that is, a self-determining agent acting in accordance with the universal principles of morality. Just as the *Critique of Pure Reason* concerns the systematic explication of the a priori elements of the understanding, so the *Critique of Practical Reason* attempts to explicate the presuppositions of morality, or in Kant's terminology, of "freedom."

With the *Critique of Judgment*, Kant announces that he is ⟵ bringing his "entire critical undertaking to a close."[4] In his transcendental explication of judgment and of the faculty of pleasure and displeasure, Kant means to bridge the "broad gulf that divides the supersensible from phenomena."[5] Kant himself finds judgment "a strange faculty,"[6] especially in its capacity of aesthetic judgment. Acting as the middle term between understanding and reason, and between the faculties of cognition and desire, judgment prescribes an a priori rule to the feeling of pleasure and displeasure. Although judgment is sometimes employed by the cognitive, and sometimes by the desiderative faculties, if there is a rule peculiar to judgment which will guarantee its autonomy and independence as a faculty, then the rule must not be derived from a priori concepts, for these are exclusively the province of understanding. To show the possibility of aesthetic judgment involves explicating its a priori rule; what makes judgment especially difficult to explicate is that it must furnish a rule which is "neither a cognitive principle for understanding nor a practical principle for the will,"[7] but an a priori rule for the feeling of pleasure and displeasure. Such a rule must regulate affectivity without contributing anything positive to knowledge.

The a priori laws furnished by understanding leave the supersensible *undetermined*. Reason, in its practical use in moral judgment, gives a *determination* to the supersensible by postulating the possibility of God, freedom, and immortality. The faculty of judgment joins the other two faculties, or effects the "transition from the realm of the concept of nature to that of the concept of freedom,"[8] by supplying a general a priori principle of the *determinability* of the supersensible.

It is not an exaggeration to say that pleasure, in the most inclusive sense of the term, keeps the edifice of Kant's three *Critiques* from crumbling. Not only is pleasure "necessarily combined with the faculty of desire";[9] not only is "the attainment of every aim . . . coupled with a feeling of pleasure";[10] but pleasure can also "effect a transition from the faculty of pure knowledge, i.e. from the realm of concepts of nature, to that of the concept of freedom."[11] For Kant, pleasure supplies the key to both human motivation and desire; what Kant calls "disinterested pleasure" supplies the key to aesthetic judgment. Later in this study it will be necessary to examine Kant's theory of pleasure in detail; for now it might be helpful to notice that Kant observes, in the Second Introduction to the third *Critique*, that pleasure also arises from comprehending how various empirical laws fall under a larger principle. Yet he concedes that "it is true that we no longer notice any decided pleasure in the comprehensibility of nature."[12] Moreover, according to Kant, it appears that aesthetic judgment is itself pleasurable because it involves what he calls the "free play" of the cognitive faculties. When judgment is neither purely conceptual, as in cognitive experience, nor bound to the realization of the good as such, as in moral judgment, the cognitive faculties are not employed in a determinant manner.

Kant links the pleasure of aesthetic judgment to the great underlying theme of the *Critique of Judgment*: the purposiveness of Nature. Aesthetic judgment "alone contains a principle introduced by judgment completely *a priori* as the basis of its reflection upon nature. This is the principle of nature's formal finality for our cognitive faculties in its particular (empirical) laws—a principle without which understanding could not feel itself at home in nature."[13] The pleasure of aesthetic judgment arises from estimating or reflecting upon the forms of objects, either of Nature or of art. Such pleasure can be nothing other than subjective; yet, Kant claims, because aesthetic pleasure arises from the free play of the cognitive faculties, it must possess a kind of intersubjective validity.

The purposiveness of aesthetic pleasure, moreover, supplies Kant with the two major headings of his "Critique of Aesthetic Judgment"—"The Beautiful" and "The Sublime." For insofar as judgment reflects upon the forms of objects and their purposive adaptability to the cognitive faculties, the result is a "judgment of taste" or a judgment concerning the beautiful. Insofar as judgment reflects upon an object that violates the sensibility because of its immensity or even formlessness, judgment is reminded of its own finality as a free moral agent; the result is a judgment of "higher intellectual feeling," or of the sublime. Thus, the "Critique of Aesthetic Judgment must be divided on these lines into two main parts."[14]

Though both the beautiful and the sublime are based upon the feelings of pleasure and displeasure, the beautiful is linked to the understanding, while the sublime is linked to reason. Just as the harmony between the faculties in aesthetic contemplation is universally communicable, so, Kant holds, the moral feelings engendered by the sublime are also independent of cultural conventions and universally communicable. It is clear that Kant intends his analysis of aesthetic judgment to hold for any culture or epoch. Whether he makes good his claim against aesthetic relativism would be premature to judge at this point. Kant claims that his analysis is of "pure" judgment, that is, of judgment insofar as it is a faculty legislating a priori.

Kant defines "judgment" as the "faculty of thinking the particular as contained under the universal."[15] Judgment is "determinant" if a rule or law is given, under which the particular is subsumed. Judgment is "reflective" if the particular is simply given and a covering rule must be found. Determinant judgment poses no philosophical problems, because it simply avails itself of the pure concepts of the understanding. Judgment as determinant is the intermediary between particulars and universals, guided by the understanding. The variety of the world and the number of empirical laws of Nature are so immense that though laws appear merely contingent to the human knower, they must be considered necessary from a higher point of view. Reflective judgment thus furnishes itself with its own a priori principle that can be simply stated: All empirical laws of Nature must be ultimately construed and unified as if they were designed for human comprehension. Kant calls this principle "the finality of nature"; it cannot be empirically proved, for it is presupposed by all experience. To try to prove it metaphysically leads to ensnarement in illusion and sophistry. Yet to deny the principle would leave man in a fundamental disharmony with himself, and, in Kant's nostalgic phrase, "understanding could not feel itself at home in nature."[16]

According to Kant, reflective judgment must employ the principle of purposiveness, or teleology, solely in a regulative or heuristic way; it is an epistemological tool for guiding investigation of organic life by means of a remote analogy with man's own purposive behavior.[17] Although the principle of teleology is not on a par with the principles of natural science, neither must it be ascribed to speculative theology, of which Kant was consistently suspicious throughout the three *Critiques*. Indeed, part of Kant's motive for arguing that the beautiful is not an objective property of objects, such as their chemical properties, was that the beautiful must not be cited as support for arguments from design for God's existence.

Because of the fundamental harmony between the knower and the known, which is essential to Kant's entire philosophy, the principle of purposiveness is as legitimate a tool for understanding reality as the mechanical principles of the physical sciences. With an undeniable air of paradox, Kant argues in Part Two of the *Critique of Judgment* that both principles belong to "reflective judgment," and that therefore neither has priority over the other. Yet Kant describes aesthetic judgment as estimating or reflecting upon form, as opposed to giving cognitive explanation. It would seem to follow that both "The Critique of Aesthetic Judgment" and "The Critique of Teleological Judgment" involve a reflective use of the principle of finality. Kant's position is made more difficut by his statement in the Second Introduction to the third *Critique:*

On these considerations is based the division of the Critique of Judgment into that of the *aesthetic* and the *teleological* judgment. By the first is meant the faculty of estimating formal finality (otherwise called subjective) by the feeling of pleasure and displeasure, by the second faculty of estimating the real finality (objective) of nature by understanding and reason.[18]

In the first *Critique*, Kant argues that the principles of physics, or of Nature as mechanism, possess constitutive value. Such a doctrine appears incompatible with his claim in Part Two of the third *Critique* that both mechanical and teleological principles belong to reflective judgment. However this might be, Kant implies that the principle of purposiveness must not be confounded with mechanical principles. His reasoning seems to be that though man readily constructs mechanisms and investigates Nature in the light of such models, he cannot create life, or an organism capable of reproducing itself and replacing its own parts. Consequently, so Kant argues, the principle of judgment is *sui generis.*

Kant's principle of finality, however, might be more generous than is required by knowledge of the empirical world. The laws of physics—which for Kant apply only to the phenomenal world—state correlations between events that hold with a high degree of probability. Although it is conceivable that Nature might have been so varied and ill adapted to human cognition that no prediction about the world could ever have been made, science can well survive if correlations hold with a high degree of probability. If Nature were entirely ill adapted to the "cognitive faculties" of any species, the species would doubtless perish. Yet to conclude, as Kant does, that Nature must be intrinsically rational and purposeful seems more an affirmation of Enlightenment faith than a statement of the presuppositions of empirical science. Kant's principle marks his adherence to certain ideas widespread in the eighteenth century concerning the rationality of the universe, the perfectability of man by means of humanistic education, and the moral harmony of man with the universe.

Aesthetics and Kant's Philosophy of Law

The word *aesthetik* or "aesthetics" does not occur in Kant's first essay on the subject, *Observations on the Feeling of the Beautiful and the Sublime.*[19] A literary and rather facile treatment of the differences between the sublime and the beautiful, this essay is far removed from his attempt in Part One of the third *Critique* to show that "judgments of taste" legislate a priori.

When Kant introduces the word "'aesthetics" into his own public philosophical vocabulary, he assigns it a meaning quite different from that given by A. G. Baumgarten, who coined the word.[20] Baumgarten used the term to designate what he called "sensory cognition" and, by extension, "criticism of taste." In a footnote in the *Critique of Pure Reason* appended to "aesthetic," Kant appears to dismiss aesthetics, as criticism of taste, as an idle and unilluminating subject:

The Germans are the only people who currently make use of the word "aesthetic" in order to signify what others call the critique of taste. This usage originated in the abortive attempt by Baumgarten, that admirable analytic thinker, to bring the critical treatment of the beautiful under rational principles, and so to raise its rules to the rank of a science. But such endeavors are fruitless.[21]

Kant further states that because the so-called rules of taste are empirical, they cannot serve as a priori laws of judgment. Anticipating the essential theme of Part One of the third *Critique,* Kant says that "our judgment is the proper test of the correctness of the rules" rather than the reverse.[22] Although Kant never explicitly speaks of a Copernican revolution in taste, parallel to his Copernican revolution in knowledge announced in the preface to the second edition of the *Critique of Pure Reason,*[23] his philosophical logistics are fundamentally the same. Just as objects must conform to our categories in order to be possible objects of experience for us, so too the forms of objects must conform to our feelings of pleasure and displeasure to be objects of aesthetic judgment for us. A similar "revolution" is implied in Kant's ethical writings.[24]

In the same footnote on "aesthetic," Kant states that "it is advisable either to give up using the name in this sense of critique of taste, and to reserve it for that doctrine of sensibility which is true science . . . or else to share the name with speculative philosophy, employing it partly in the transcendental and partly in the psychological sense."[25] In the first *Critique*, Kant uses "aesthetic" as the title for his own treatment of the pure forms or intuitions of sensibility—space and time. These are the pure conditions of sensibility; all external appearances must be subject to the form of space, and both external and internal appearances must be given under the form of time.

Kant introduces the phrase "aesthetic quality" only in the Second Introduction of the *Critique of Judgment:* "That which is purely subjective in the representation of an Object, i.e. what constitutes its reference to the Subject, not to the Object, is its aesthetic quality."[26] But he quickly distinguishes such a quality from the pure forms of sensibility. Whatever serves to determine the representation of an object for knowledge has logical validity; consequently, although space is a purely subjective form of the sensibility, it is "still a constituent of the knowledge of things as phenomena."[27] The supersensible, therefore, is not determined by the forms of space and time. Kant also holds that qualities of sensation, such as color and sound, belong to objective knowledge: "*Sensation* (here external) also agrees in expressing a merely subjective side of our representations of external things, but one which is properly their matter (through which we are given something with real existence)."[28] For Kant, "aesthetic quality" designates exclusively the affective side of a representation, insofar as the object is referred to the feelings of pleasure and displeasure. Thus, not only agreeable sensations—like odors, titillations, and the like—but also the beauty of objects of art and of natural objects have "aesthetic quality":

But that subjective side of a representation *which is incapable of becoming an element of cognition,* is the *pleasure* or *displeasure* connected with it; for through it I cognize nothing in the object of the representation, although it may easily be the result of the operation of some cognition or other.[29]

Yet if both ordinary sensuous pleasure and Kant's "disinterested pleasure" possess what he calls "aesthetic quality"—or to state the matter crudely, if both the pleasures of the table and the pleasures of listening to a Mozart piano concerto are "aesthetic"—then two alternatives present themselves. Either it can be argued that the difference between the two sorts of pleasure is a mere matter of degree, and that consequently so-called aesthetic judgment is as private and relativistic as judgments of personal preference; or it may be argued that the difference is one of kind, and that though aesthetic judgment is based upon the feelings of pleasure and displeasure, it is in some sense, to use Kant's phrase, possessed of "exemplary validity."[30] Kant, of course, claims that there is a difference in kind between the agreeable and the disinterested sort of pleasure, or between what he calls "judgments of sense" and "judgments of taste." The former state mere likes and dislikes and make no claim upon other persons' sensibility; the latter are based solely upon the form of an object and are universally legislative.

It would also be premature to judge whether Kant presents a convincing case for the fundamental distinction he draws between judgments of sense and judgments of taste. What I believe might be helpful is to observe that Kant's mature views on aesthetics are strongly legalistic in tone. The parallel between Kant's legal philosophy and his aesthetics might provide a key to a broad understanding of Part One of the *Critique of Judgment*.

Kant's underlying concern is to determine who has the right to say that a given object is or is not beautiful. Such a question would not arise, Kant implies, with the merely agreeable or sensuous. Yet simply because everyone's verdict concerning the beautiful is not taken on the same plane, and because some persons are said to be better judges of the beautiful than others, the question concerning the qualifications of the judge naturally arises.

A number of legal words and phrases occur systematically throughout Part One of the third *Critique*. One such expression I have already referred to: in the Introduction, Kant states that the entire critical endeavor consists of three parts: "the Critique of pure understanding, of pure judgment, and of pure reason, which faculties are called pure on the ground of their being legislative *a priori*."[31] The title of the immediately following section carries the heading: "Judgment as a Faculty by Which Laws Are Prescribed *A Priori*."[32] Later, in the "Analytic of the Beautiful," Kant writes: "Where, however, the imagination is compelled to follow a course laid down by a definite law, then what the form of the product is to be is determined by concepts."[33] In the same context, concerning the free play of the imagination in aesthetic judgment, Kant says: "Hence it is only a conformity to law without a law . . . that can consist with the free conformity to law of the understanding . . . and with the specific character of a judgment of taste."[34] Later, in the "Deduction of Pure Aesthetic Judgments," he writes that "taste would further be presented as a link upon which all legislation must depend."[35]

Even if Kant's usage of the language of law were only a rhetorical device in Part One of the third *Critique*, it must be admitted that it is extremely pervasive. In the first pages of the Introduction, Kant speaks of "territory," "realm," "jurisdiction," and exercising "legislative authority . . . over one and the same territory of experience."[36] The judgment of taste "rightly lays claim to the agreement of everyone."[37] In the final pages of Part One, Kant writes: "In our general estimate of beauty we seek its standard *a priori* in ourselves, and, that the aesthetic faculty is itself legislative in respect of the judgment whether anything is beautiful or not."[38]

I suggest that such language is not merely a rhetorical device, but reveals Kant's basic conception of aesthetic judgment. His distinction between "judgments of sense" and "judgments of taste" seems to parallel the common distinction between "de facto" and "de jure." His claim that judgments of taste must be universalizable seems to indicate that only by making one's aesthetic judgment open and public does one take a risk. Kant seems to claim that just as the law must hold for everyone, and self-exception must be ruled out, genuine aesthetic judgment requires putting oneself into the position of any rational and sensuous being like ourselves. The demand of universal agreement is a means by which the capacity of aesthetic judgment is strengthened by coming into conflict with the aesthetic judgments, or verdicts, of other persons. Thus, the "ought" of aesthetic judgment involves risk:

Accordingly we introduce this fundamental feeling not as a private feeling, but as a fundamental sense . . . experience cannot be made the ground of this common sense, for the latter is invoked to justify judgments containing an 'ought'. The assertion is not that every one *will* fall in with our judgment, but rather that every one *ought* to agree with it.[39]

Kant's "ought" states an ideal of unanimity in matters of taste. Though both the laws of the land and aesthetic taste are correctible and improvable, Kant implies that both require ideals. Just as aesthetic education requires study of what Kant calls "exemplars," or great works of art, so legal education requires the study of precedents. In neither case, however, is judgment constrained or determined by precedents or by exemplars. The examination of precedents affords a more nuanced understanding of the case at hand.

Kant's conception of a common sense, or *sensus communis*, reveals his strongly humanitarian interest in the aesthetic, as well as further parallels between aesthetic judgment and law. The *sensus communis* comprises feelings of universal sympathy and the power of communicating one's inmost feelings. Just as the aesthetic judgment of the individual must fit into the network of the *sensus communis*, so the rights of the individual must fit into the just claims of all other members of society. "Justice is therefore the aggregate of those conditions under which the will of one person can be conjoined with the will of another in accordance with a universal law of freedom."[40]

What Kant calls the a priori legislative capacity of aesthetic judgment parallels his general conception of right and of natural law. "All justice and every right in the narrower sense (*jus strictum*) are united with the authorization to use coercion."[41] Natural law requires no external legislator, but is founded upon its own a priori necessity; positive law requires some external authority. Kant's conception of the free play of the cognitive faculties is described as spontaneous and natural, and valid for all persons.

Freedom plays an important role in both Kant's aesthetics and his moral and legal philosophy: "Every action is just [right] that in itself or in its maxim is such that the freedom of the will of each can coexist together with the freedom of everyone in accordance with a universal law."[42] For Kant, the sole, unique right is that of freedom from the compulsory or coercive will of another person or set of persons. Similarly, every person has the right and duty to judge aesthetically upon the basis of his own sensibility and must not be constrained by anyone else.

Kant's aesthetics places the importance of the fine arts in their advancing the goals of humanity at large; the *sensus communis* appears as the aesthetic parallel to Kant's Kingdom of Ends. As such, the *sensus communis* does not place the sensibility of any set of persons over those of another. "There was a time when I despised the masses . . . Rousseau has set me right . . . I learn to honour men," Kant wrote in a copy of the *Observations*.[43] The view of aesthetic judgment that emerges is that each person judges for himself but at the same time risks the verdict of his own taste by making it public and demanding agreement.

The Historical Background of Kant's Aesthetics

The stereotyped picture of Kant as a provincial Pietist with little interest in the fine arts must be dispelled. In the *Observations*, Kant reveals a firsthand acquaintance with the works of Milton, Pope, and Young; of Milton he seems to have been particularly fond. He was not fond of the novelists of the "Sentimental" school, such as Richardson and Klopstock, so unless we assume that he was merely echoing the disapproval of other readers, Kant must have read their works himself. In Part One of the third *Critique*, Kant's knowledge of the Latin classics is evident, as it is throughout all of his writings. He seems always to have an apt quotation from Horace or Sallust at his disposal; he also admits in the third *Critique* to taking a "pure delight" in Latin poetry.[44] Quotations from contemporary poets abound in Kant's writings. From his letters one may fairly conclude that

Kant kept abreast of contemporary developments in painting; his general acquaintance with painting is also evident from certain passages in his *Anthropology*.[45]

However, difficulties present themselves in regard to Kant's acquaintance with British writers on aesthetics. Kant alludes to Hume, Shaftesbury, Hutcheson, and Burke,[46] but it is never clear precisely to which of their works he is referring. It is not known, for example, which of Hume's works on taste or the fine arts Kant actually read. There exists no certain information concerning Kant's knowledge of the English language, and the early history of translations of Hume into German and French is obscure.

Kant's knowledge of French is evident in many of his writings, as is his acquaintance with such writers as Batteux. But because Kant's writings on aesthetics are sparse compared to his writings on ethics, it is impossible to give a history of the development of his views on the fine arts.[47] Moreover, living in the provincial capital of Königsberg, from which he did not travel very far, Kant probably could not have been directly acquainted with many developments in eighteenth-century music, especially opera, or with ballet or architecture.

Whatever Kant's immediate acquaintance with the fine arts and writings on taste during the eighteenth century might have been, it may not be misleading to describe Part One of the *Critique of Judgment* as an attempt to reconcile the conflicting claims of rationalistic and empirical aesthetics. A brief sketch of these two schools is therefore in order.

Unlike the empiricists, the great rationalist philosophers had little to say about aesthetics. Even so, for a century the method and metaphysics of Descartes dominated aesthetics, though he himself wrote almost nothing on the subject. Descartes maintained that concepts must be analyzed to render them "clear" and "distinct." "Clarity" attaches to a concept apparent to the attentive mind; "distinctiveness" attaches to a concept "so precise and different from all other objects that it contains within itself nothing but what is clear."[48] Pain may be a clear perception, though not distinct. It follows that feelings may share an attribute of reason, and it would thus appear that the beautiful is not wholly to be cut off from reason. Aesthetic feelings would belong to a realm of sensuous truth, indistinct and confused, but nonetheless "clear."

Cartesian aesthetics assumed that Nature and reason are identical: the rules that govern science also govern the fine arts.[49] One rule taken as axiomatic in the arts held that poetry and, by extension, all the fine arts imitate Nature. Nature divides itself into genera and species; the artist is to imitate Nature in her most perfect and typical moods and eschew the eccentric, noncharacteristic, or individual. Just as the scientist forms general laws covering all phenomena, so the artist embodies generalities of conduct and character in a sensuous medium.

Given the parallel between art and science, it was only another step to argue for exact rules for judging art. Criticism was described as a science of such rules. Some Cartesians, like Boileau and Roger de Piles, considered the rules to be a priori; other Cartesians, like Corneille and Molière, argued that they were based upon experience.

Cartesian aesthetics had as much sway in England as on the Continent. Dryden, for example, defines a dramatic play as "a just and lively image of human nature." Drawing the conclusion from this "clear idea," Dryden says: "for the direct and immediate consequence is this: if Nature is to be imitated, then there is a rule for imitating Nature rightly; otherwise there may be an end, and no means conducing to it."[50] Dryden wants to be reasonable about a subject which is ordinarily liked because of its unreasonableness —drama. He speaks of "denying minor propositions" and "proving inferences"; he is "fearful of illustrating anything by similitude."[51] Dryden also demands that rules for both creating and judging drama be rigorous, though susceptible of only a high degree of probability.

Aristotle and Horace were sometimes considered the discoverers of the rules of criticism, just as Newton was the discoverer of the laws of physics. Rationalist aesthetics held that rules could be proved without authority. The rules of the fine arts were construed as fundamentally the same; the end of art was to please by teaching. Sir Joshua Reynolds argued that a painting must represent the ideal characteristics of particular species; the painter, like the zoologist or botanist, must illustrate a broad genus by means of perfect examples. Artistic genius must proceed in accordance with rules, however subtle and complicated their formulation.

Rationalist aestheticians did not deny that art is expressive; given that emotions might be strictly defined in the Cartesian manner,[52] physiological changes of emotion could be minutely described. The artist was to school himself in the passions as rigorously as the surgeon in anatomy. Because truthfulness of representation and perfection were taken as the ends of art, the artist would not differ essentially from the scientist.

It awaited A. G. Baumgarten to give the first rigorously Cartesian exposition of aesthetics, which he describes as the sensuous parallel of logic. Using the geometrical method, Baumgarten begins with formal definitions, axioms, propositions, proofs, and corollaries. Sense perception has a formal structure of its own, and the science of aesthetics reveals its perfections. A poem, for example, is a structured discourse composed of sensuous representations. Clarity, the criterion of poetic perfection, gives rise to rules for particular parts of poetry—meter, plot, and diction.

Batteux, a contemporary of Kant's, tried to reduce the arts to a "single principle"; he was the first to distinguish radically between the applied and the fine arts.[53] Lessing also granted a common and definable end to the arts, but he demanded that they be pure and imitate by means of determinate rules of perfection. Thus, aesthetic judgment is made purely cognitive. A passage from the *Critique of Judgment* shows that Kant considered the issue between rationalist and empiricist aesthetics to be sharply divided:

The principle of taste may, to begin with, be placed on either of two footings. For taste may be said invariably to judge on empirical grounds of determination and such, therefore, as are only given *a posteriori* through sense, or else it may be allowed to judge on an *a priori* ground. The former would be the *empiricism* of the Critique of Taste, the latter its *rationalism*. The first would obliterate the distinction that marks off the object of our delight from the *agreeable;* the second, supposing the judgment rested upon determinate concepts, would obliterate its distinction from the *good.* In this way beauty would have its *locus standi* in the world completely denied, and nothing but the dignity of a separate

name, betokening, maybe, a certain blend of both the above-named
kinds of delight, would be left in its stead.[54]

The empiricists were as wary of the imagination, and of metaphor, as the rationalists. Bacon says that poetry is a sort of "feigned
history" which gives a sense of freedom to the mind by improving
upon Nature, whereas reason demands that our ideas of things
conform to nature.[55] Poetry has the same merit as philosophy and
history, though it contributes nothing to knowledge. In the *Leviathan,* Hobbes defines two functions of the imagination: the "simple" holds together the dead impressions left from sensation; the
"compound" joins together particular images in a regular or practical way, or simply by free association. Judgment is the source of
wit or the facility in pointing out differences. Imagination is the
source of fancy, which in genuine art is guided by the structures
provided by judgment.[56]

Hume argues that beauty is not a quality of objects but only
marks a certain pleasure taken in the structured relations between
parts and wholes. Utility sometimes combines with impressions
because human nature, or particular conventions, cause certain
forms to please and others to displease. Moral, as well as aesthetic,
beauty is a contingent relationship, affording no ground of necessity. Though Hume distinguishes unreflective likes and dislikes from
those based on reason and discernment, still he says that the
difference between the agreeable and the aesthetic is one of degree
and not of kind.

Hume allows that it is natural to seek a standard of taste, but
since beauty is not an objective property, there is no more a "real"
beauty than a "real" sweet.[57] Assuming, however, that some tastes
are better than others, just as some works of art are superior to
others, Hume holds that rules must exist, though based solely on
experience. Such rules state causal relationships between particular forms or attributes of objects, and their capacity to please. Some
constitutions, more subtle and fine than others, are pleased by
more intricate forms. Taste can be corrected by sharpening dis-
crimination, by gaining greater experience of a certain kind of art,
and by removing prejudice. Hume concludes that persons who

have removed such sources of error are the final judges. Art that passes the review of qualified observers throughout history is deemed "great art." Taste varies from one generation to another, as well as within a man's lifetime, but since human nature remains fundamentally unaltered, the basis of taste remains unchanged.

In this brief survey of the philosophy of art surrounding Kant's own conception of aesthetics, the term "aesthetic" has shifted and vacillated in numerous ways which will also be reflected in the ensuing study. Shaftesbury, Hume, and other writers of the eighteenth century and afterwards use "aesthetic" to describe a sort of feeling, and sometimes a state of mind. Baumgarten and Kant tend to use "aesthetic" to describe a functionally distinct type of judgment; Baumgarten especially uses the word to describe a certain mode of perception. Many nineteenth-century writers employ "aesthetic" to refer to a class of objects distinct from others— objects of art in particular, and certain natural objects; in Germany this usage is reflected in Adolf Hildebrand, Johann Friedrich Herbart, and Konrad Fiedler; in America, in Josiah Royce, Samuel Alexander, and George Santayana. Sometimes, in such usage, "aesthetic" connotes an evaluation, or approval, as well. And "the aesthetic" is sometimes used to refer to a broadly related set of interests or activities; as such, "the aesthetic" is different from, for example, "the moral," "the cognitive," or "the practical," but not necessarily incompatible with other such "interests."

But to give an inventory of the usages of "aesthetic" from the time that Baumgarten coined the term would require a history of the subject itself. Like "art," the meaning of "aesthetic" might appear both definable and evanescent.

CHAPTER 2

The Analysis of the Beautiful

Substantive and Analytic Aesthetics

Great philosophical questions are sometimes so simple in form that those who ask them risk sounding simple minded. To persons of no philosophical bent, such questions might appear so abstract as to be meaningless; to practical persons they might seem pointless and idle. The question that Kant poses in Part One of the *Critique of Judgment*—How are judgments of the beautiful and the sublime possible?—has an innocent simplicity, but its implications and presuppositions are vast.

To the eighteenth-century European mind the question would have appeared well put, for it was commonly supposed that the beautiful and the sublime exhausted the categories of the aesthetic. For example, the title of Edmund Burke's work, *A Philosophic Enquiry Into the Origin of Our Ideas of the Sublime and Beautiful*,[1] merely incorporated a distinction that was admitted on all hands. The third earl of Shaftesbury, especially in his *Moralists III*,[2] had prepared the eighteenth century to accept a sharp distinction between formal beauties and Nature's irregular sublimities. Hume employed the same two categories, as if the sublime and the beautiful were the only conceivable ways of describing taste. In France the distinction was as widely held and was often explained in a Cartesian spirit by writers such as Montesquieu, La Motte, Fontanelle, Voltaire, and Dubos. In England, however, discussions of the beautiful and the sublime tended to follow the Baconian tradition and were usually psychological or physiological enquiries.

To the twentieth-century mind the first difficulty that Kant's question presents is its seeming irrelevance; much contemporary art is not beautiful, and little of it is sublime. The beautiful, as an

(21)

aesthetic category, is so closely wedded to neoclassical values that it appears to a large degree outmoded. This is especially true for the sublime, which as an aesthetic category presents even greater hurdles for contemporary sensibility. Moreover, even if a place is still reserved for the beautiful and the sublime, they hardly exhaust the spectrum of aesthetic experience. Kant's question might appear too narrow and, to a degree, antiquated.

Yet to the complaint that "the beautiful" is a singularly vacant term, Kant would reply, I believe, that beauty must be the underlying concept of the aesthetic. Beauty is the central term in Kant's aesthetics, just as the concept of cause is central to his theory of our knowledge of the empirical world, though there are other concepts, like substance, change, and event. Beauty is logically prior to all other aesthetic terms, such as totality, harmony, clarity, precision, perfection, and elegance. As I shall attempt to show in chapter three, for Kant the sublime is not ultimately an aesthetic category.

Kant would concede, I believe, that the beautiful can be expressed in markedly different schools and styles. Though his own aesthetic taste was decidedly neoclassical,[3] Kant would maintain that the beautiful is the necessary aesthetic filter, or category, through which any work of art, or aspect of Nature, must pass in order to count as an object of taste. However, until we have examined Kant's conception of aesthetic form, and his distinction between "free" and "dependent" beauty, we shall not fully understand the centrality of the beautiful in Kant's aesthetics or its relation to other aesthetic predicates.

It appears that although Kant does not himself draw the comparison, he would assign the sublime and the beautiful the same logical position in aesthetics that the right and the good occupy in ethics. Just as duties and obligations presuppose the right, and virtues and ideals presuppose the good, so too, Kant might be implying, some aesthetic predicates or values presuppose the beautiful, whereas others presuppose the sublime.

Without too much violence to Kant's philosophical intentions, we might approach his question—How are judgments of the beautiful and the sublime possible?—by asking how aesthetic evaluation in general is to be explained. The scope of language used to reveal attitudes and beliefs about the worth of art is immense and would require a phenomenology of aesthetic language to do it justice. Setting aside this great range of language, we might ask how assertions of aesthetic worth are to be justified. Is it possible to give an analysis of aesthetic sensibility such that judgments of value do not emerge as mere reports of subjective feeling, but lay claim to universal agreement? Are there certain presuppositions of the aesthetic that might support its claim to autonomy? A twofold distinction concerning aesthetic discourse might render Kant's question concerning the possibility of aesthetic judgment more accessible.

1. Many critics and artists attempt to give advice on how to understand and interpret works of art; the goal is to distinguish spurious or academic art from the genuine and original. Philosophers have also given their theories of the beautiful and of genuine art; they have assumed that their task was to set forth systematically the principles or guiding notions of the aesthetic, together with arguments or considerations for their justification. Although writers and artists such as Keats and Liszt have also given their views on art and the aesthetic, they usually content themselves with aphorisms or "preachments."[4] However, a few artists, such as Baudelaire and Wagner, wrote systematic and comprehensive works on a particular branch of the fine arts.[5]

Certain philosophical works on aesthetics might be called reactionary; their authors have argued that much that is called "art" is either decadent or spurious, or both. One thinks naturally of Plato's lacerations of the poet in the *Ion* and *The Republic,* or the Christian primitivism of Tolstoy's *What Is Art?*[6] Other works on aesthetics might be called conservative: they argue that what is generally held to be good art tends to be so. Hume represents such a point of view in his *On the Standard of Taste,* though he also invokes the criteria of the test of time and the impartial connoisseur.[7] The aesthetic liberals argue against elitist definitions of art and try to show how the aesthetic should enter into all phases of man's life. No distinction should be drawn between intrinsic and extrinsic value, or between the fine and applied arts. This sort of aesthetic theory is often called naturalism and is most fully argued for in John Dewey's *Art as Experience*.[8] As the political metaphor implies, there have also been aesthetic radicals, like Nietzsche, who present new and iconoclastic convictions about art.[9] It appears, then, that although philosophers and artists have greatly varied in their aesthetic persuasions, most writers on aesthetics have practical as well as theoretical intentions. Though such writers do not give homilies concerning how to act or what to strive for, as the ethicist sometimes does, still their definitions of art have natural corollaries for action.

2. However, a few writers on aesthetics have eschewed giving advice and have avoided trying to reform taste or sensibility. Their interests are purely theoretical; their purpose is solely philosophical clarification; and their method is the conceptual elucidation of aesthetic concepts. A few aestheticians, such as Kant, have held analysis to be the sole end of their inquiries. Although Kant's kind of analysis is of a special sort that he calls "transcendental" or "critical," his aim is similar to that of many twentieth-century writers on aesthetics, especially in Anglo-Saxon countries.

It might be useful to call practical or applied aesthetics "substantive," as opposed to "analytic" aesthetics, which would include Kant's transcendental conceptual analysis as well as more current linguistic aesthetics. Substantive aesthetic statements, or theories, are actual or "living" aesthetic statements, concerning either particular or general states of affairs. For example, the assertion "The aria 'Vissi d'arte, vissi d'amore' in *Tosca* should have been omitted because it retards the pace of the opera and is too much of a set-piece to fit in with the action of the music" is, despite its cumbersomeness, an example of an actual, particular, aesthetic judgment. Interesting aesthetic judgments are not simple outbursts like "*Don Giovanni* is a great opera," though some contemporary philosophers have taken such statements as paradigms of substantive aesthetic judgments.[10] A substantive aesthetic judgment may also be general; the following are crude examples, given only as illustrations:

Genuine art spontaneously communicates a common feeling of brotherhood to all mankind.[11]

Art must transmit the great traditional values of civilization.[12]

Analytic aesthetic statements, or theories, purport to explicate the meanings of substantive aesthetic statements and to show the rationale behind criticism as well as informal discourse about aesthetic objects. The aim is to throw into relief the presuppositions of the aesthetic life of man. As examples drawn from twentieth-century analytic aesthetic theories, no matter how stilted they might appear in such truncated form, the following might illustrate what I have called analytic aesthetics:

Criticism of the fine arts is neither syllogistic nor based only upon experience: it is a form of directive, nonfactual discourse.[13]

Aesthetic judgments are only expressions of pro-or-con attitudes, sometimes coupled with the intent that they invoke similar attitudes in other persons.[14]

Taste is like fashion: both are only matters of convention.[15]

The distinction between substantive and analytic aesthetics is tenable despite the validity of particular theories or statements advanced under either head. Moreover, analytic aesthetics does not arise until and unless considerable data are provided by substantive aesthetics.

To return now to Kant: in asking how judgments of the beautiful and the sublime are possible, Kant is also asking how aesthetic judgment fits into the requirements of experience in general. One might say that Kant had provided a formal and highly general map of the mind in his first *Critique;* in the third *Critique* he is asking how aesthetic judgment relates to the other faculties of knowledge, as well as to reason and sensibility. He states in the *Critique of Pure Reason:* "The postulate of the *possibility* of things requires that the concept of the things should agree with the formal conditions of an experience in general. But this, the objective form of experience in general contains all synthesis that is required for knowledge of objects."[16] Though Kant's chief interest is in revealing how aesthetic judgment coheres with his entire system of philosophy, the reader's interest in his analysis must ultimately rest upon the insight that Kant's analysis gives to art and the aesthetic.

Kant's question concerning the possibility of aesthetic judgment has overtones in regard to the distinction that I have drawn between substantive and analytic aesthetics: (1) Are any particular substantive aesthetic statements or theories sound enough that any person should be expected to see their validity, even though this validity cannot be defined in a purely scientific or purely practical manner? (2) Given the evident facts that the fine arts exist and that persons sometimes regard Nature in an aesthetic way, must there be certain presuppositions of the aesthetic sensibility of man? (3) In what ways is aesthetic perception to be distinguished from nonaesthetic perception? Or is this distinction even tenable? I shall attempt to expound these further questions in the chapters that follow.

As I have described substantive as opposed to analytic aesthetics, given that the former tends to be prescriptive and reformative in tone, and the latter couched in cool descriptive language, a particular substantive point of view cannot be strictly inferred from a particular breed of analytic aesthetics. The converse would also seem to hold. Though it would carry us far afield to enter into the somewhat tired controversy between facts and values, or between normative and descriptive discourse, it seems that inarticulate or neutral facts cannot of themselves give a basis for aesthetic value. In general, however, substantive aesthetic judgments presuppose analytic aesthetic theories, or at least types of theories. For a crude example, if a substantive aesthetic judgment claimed that all tastes ought to be considered on a par, and that only "conditioning" or "culturalization" explains why one taste differs from another, then a certain type of analytic aesthetics is proposed, which we might characterize as aesthetic relativism.

In his preface to the third *Critique*, Kant clearly states that his object is the analysis of the "transcendental aspects" of taste, or, if the term be allowed, "meta-aesthetics": "The present investigation of taste, as a faculty of aesthetic judgments, not being undertaken with a view to the formation or culture of taste, (which will pursue its course in the future, as in the past, independently of such inquiries,) but being merely directed to its transcendental aspects."[17] Kant appears to be claiming, then, that criticism presupposes aesthetics, even though the critic might have no acquaintance with its "transcendental aspects." Still, it should be added to Kant's claims that the soundness of any given type of analytic aesthetics—such as relativism, expressionism, or what might be called Kant's transcendental formalism—does not guarantee the validity of any substantive aesthetic view.

Judgment and the Origins of the Four "Moments"

As a preliminary to Kant's analysis of the beautiful, we must examine his various meanings of "judgment." It might be best to begin with the title of the book itself. Although both Meredith and Bernard translate the title as *Critique of Judgment,* the novelist W. Somerset Maugham gives a more apt translation, and one which is truer to the German *Urteilskraft.* In his "Reflections on a Certain Book," Maugham writes:

I have given this brief account of what sort of man Kant was, and what sort of life he led, in the hope of sufficiently whetting the reader's interest in this great philosopher to induce him to have patience with me while I submit to him the reflections that have occurred to me during the reading of a book of his with the somewhat forbidding title of the *Critique of the Power of Judgment.*[18]

By "judgment," or *Urteilskraft,* Kant sometimes means the power or capacity to judge and sometimes particular acts of judging (*Urteil*). He occasionally speaks of what might be called the "product" of judging; this third sense of "judgment" would be a statement, or proposition, or what is sometimes called an aesthetic judgment. Given the strong parallels between Kant's legal philosophy and his aesthetics—parallels that I attempted to point out in the first chapter of this book—the third sense of judgment also has connotations of "verdict" and "decision." On the whole, however, Kant is chiefly concerned with explicating the power of discernment, or the capacity of judging, and its particular aesthetic functioning. For Kant, "experience" is always used as "experience of objects," which is constituted by judgments: judgments are not founded upon experience but constitutive of it. It is only in the third sense of "judgment" just mentioned that it makes sense to speak of judgments founded upon experience, for it is only in such cases that judgment is verbalized, or propositional in character.

What must further be borne in mind is that Kant, from the outset of his analysis, is concerned with what he calls "pure" aesthetic judgment. For the moment it will suffice to describe such judgments as those which contain nothing empirical or material as their object, but concern only the form or structure of what is presented to the mind. Again, I must defer the reader's attention from the "purity" of aesthetic judgments to my later discussion of form and the distinction that Kant draws between "free" and "dependent" beauty.[19]

It would not be misleading, and perhaps may actually be helpful to readers more acquainted with Humean philosophy, to substitute "belief" for Kant's "judgment" or *Urteil*. Kant is enquiring into the function of the mind whereby it arrives at the notion or belief of anything, and in a more restricted sense, the power or faculty of arriving at aesthetic beliefs. Although Kant sometimes uses the now outmoded language of "faculty" and "power," and though he sometimes slips into what appears to be a psychological description of the "faculty of estimating the beautiful," his avowed enterprise in the "Analytic of the Beautiful" is not psychological.

As I mentioned in chapter one, it is not certain which of Hume's writings were directly known to Kant; still, as is well known, Kant strongly disagreed with Hume in regard to the nature of belief. In a famous passage following his description of the varieties of scepticism, Hume writes:

My intention then in displaying so carefully the arguments of that fantastic sect, is only to make the reader sensible of the truth of my hypothesis, *that all our reasonings concerning causes and effects are deriv'd from nothing but custom; and that belief is more properly an act of the sensitive, than of the cogitative part of our natures.*[20]

What struck Kant as particularly invidious about Hume's view of judgment as applied to the aesthetic is that it founds judgment on subjective and private conviction. Kant argues that what is essential to belief, or to judgment that something is or is not the case, is intersubjective validity. One does not commit only oneself in judgment; one commits all rational, sensuous beings as well. Only if judgment is construed as interpersonally binding can it be called "objective." To describe thinking in terms of association of ideas, as Hume does, is to reduce the formal structure of reality, and of laws, to purely private reveries. One of Kant's main endeavors in the third *Critique* is to elucidate and justify the intersubjective validity of aesthetic judgment or belief, a validity which is not founded upon mere psychological homogeneity.

To understand the role of what Kant calls the four "moments" of the aesthetic, a necessarily rough recapitulation is required. In the first *Critique*, Kant argues that if appearances are to be brought together in accordance with necessary laws (which is mandatory, he argues, given the apodictic quality of knowledge), then the mind must be in possession of certain a priori concepts. Such concepts must be knowable apart from any empirical experience and dictate the forms of all possible experience, though they are themselves barren unless supplied with empirical data. For example, the form of causation is dictated or imposed a priori to experience of the world; for rational and sensuous beings such as ourselves, no experience can comprise an uncaused event, though the actual cause is determined solely by experience.

Kant assumes that judging and using a priori concepts are parallel, if not the same activities described in different terms. In the first *Critique*, Kant attempts to give an exhaustive list of such concepts by analyzing the properties of judgment as described by Aristotelian logic. Given that human understanding is discursive, understanding must be by means of concepts:

Concepts are based on the spontaneity of thought, sensible intuitions on the receptivity of impressions. Now the only use which the understanding can make of these concepts is to judge by means of them. . . . Now we can reduce all acts of the understanding to judgments, and the *understanding* may therefore be represented as a *faculty of judgment*.[21]

The problems involved in Kant's attempt to readapt the table of judgments to fit his a priori concepts have been dealt with in the standard commentaries. I am here concerned only with Kant's attempts to make use of distinctions that he obviously believed he had sufficiently established in the first *Critique*. Kant there argued that if one abstracts all empirical data from a given judgment, thereby isolating the pure forms of understanding, it will be seen that judgment must always function under four "heads," each of which has three "moments."[22] Judgments must have a quantity: universal, particular, or singular; they must have a quality: affirmative, negative, or infinite; a relation: categorical, hypothetical, or disjunctive; and a modality: problematic, assertoric, or apodictic. In the third *Critique,* Kant alters his terminology, calling the four "heads" the four "moments." Thus Kant approaches his analysis of aesthetic judgment by trying to ascertain the quantity, quality, relation, and modality of the powers of aesthetic judging. He begins, however, with the "moment" of quality, simply because "this is what the aesthetic judgment on the beautiful looks to in the first instance."[23]

Before proceeding to the four "moments," we might ask whether Kant has prejudiced his argument for the intersubjective validity of the aesthetic simply by using the word "judgment." For judgments are ordinarily true or false, good or bad, or well or ill warranted. The question whether aesthetic judgments, or substantive aesthetic statements, are such that any person should assent to them can only be answered in the affirmative by the meaning of "judgment." It might be argued that aesthetic "judgment" ought not strictly to be called "true" or "false," for these predicates should be restricted to purely descriptive judgments like "All swans are white," or definitional statements like "All bachelors are unmarried males." Because aesthetic judgment is not verified by a simple appeal to the sensuously given, nor inferred necessarily from other judgments, the product of aesthetic judgment should best be treated as a disguised imperative, or as a hybrid form of interjection. Such forms of speech are neither "true" nor "false," and a fortiori cannot be "intersubjectively valid."[24]

Against this objection one could reply that in ordinary language we do speak of aesthetic judgment as "true" and "false." Kant would agree that aesthetic judgment is not merely experience of the sensuously given; for, as he will argue later, aesthetic judgment is "exemplary"—it commands the assent of everyone and partakes of a kind of necessity which is neither logical nor empirical.

It might further be objected against Kant that persons might readily agree about the factual or descriptive aspects of a work of art but draw different aesthetic conclusions, or come to different judgments. It might be urged that Kant is mistaken to begin his analysis with the assumption that aesthetic judgment is somehow intersubjectively valid. Aesthetic judgment expresses either the attitude of an individual person, or the artistic bent or ideology of a certain coterie. It might further be argued that dominant substantive aesthetic theories are simply reflections of class interest or economic status. Even supposedly "pure" aesthetic theories, like the art-for-art's-sake movement headed in France by Gautier and Flaubert, and in England by Whistler and Wilde, are merely expressions of aesthetic attitudes codified into manifestoes. It would be less misleading to compare aesthetic judgment to expressions of policy or commitment.

However, even though the arts obviously have economic underpinnings, art is as often retrograde as futuristic; a nice parallel between economic conditions and art does not always obtain. But since the entire question of art as related to politics and economic structure falls outside the main concerns of the third *Critique*, I shall skirt Marxist criticisms of Kant's aesthetics.[25]

It is undeniable that many substantive aesthetic theories do have the ring of manifestoes and are often highly persuasive and prescriptive in tone; they reveal more the heat of the reformer than the cool dispassion of the analyst. Many eighteenth-century writings on aesthetics with which Kant may have been acquainted disclose important class commitments, for example, Lord Kames's *Elements of Criticism*,[26] Gerard's *Essay on Taste*,[27] and Reid's essay on taste in his *Essays on the Intellectual Powers of Man*.[28] Examples drawn from more modern writings appear even more like aesthetic manifestoes, such as parts of Nietzsche's *Birth of Tragedy* or Zola's "Experimental Novel."

Kant would not deny that the aesthetic and the affective are closely linked, or that aesthetic judgment is often charged with feeling and passion. It is perhaps natural to distrust those who deliver themselves of their aesthetic beliefs in clinical tones; one demands a certain fervor and commitment, not a mere recital of what other people call "great art." As Kant's theory develops, however, he attempts to exclude rigorously "mere emotions" from "pure" aesthetic judgment.

In general, one would hesitate to claim that aesthetic judgment expresses attitudes, for strong feelings of approval towards a certain work of art might occur without the belief or judgment that the work is good. Emotional attitudes might attach one to a certain artist, but aesthetic judgment might make one keep his distance. Moreover, attitudes often lead persons to behave in certain ways but do not necesarily justify their behavior. Though Kant does not state the parallel explicitly, conflicts arise between emotional attitudes and aesthetic beliefs just as they do between inclinations and moral duty. Such conflicts would be inexplicable if aesthetic judgment consisted in mere emotional attitudes.

Sensation, the "Moments," and Form

Kant begins the "Analytic of the Beautiful"[29] by isolating what he believes to be both common and unique to judgments of taste. As I have already indicated, because Kant draws the four "moments" from the logical table of judgments, he assumes them to be exhaustive. Though I have perhaps already belabored the paradoxicality of many of Kant's starting points in my first chapter, each of the four "moments" involves a kind of paradox, or "logical oddity," that Kant attempts to resolve. As a prelude to Kant's analysis of the four "moments," it might be helpful to point out each of the four conundrums involved, but with the important proviso that Kant himself does not describe the four "moments" as actually involving paradoxes. Even so, the burden of Kant's analysis, as I hope to make clear in this section, can be fruitfully seen as a thesis-antithesis-synthesis development. At this point in my exposition, I shall only indicate the theses and antitheses that underly each of the "moments." It must also be borne in mind that my way of describing the four "moments" in such dialectical terms is not Kant's; he reserves the language of "thesis-antithesis-synthesis" in Part

One of the third *Critique* for his exposition of what he calls the antinomy of taste.[30]

1. Quality: The thesis indicates what is admitted on all sides, that the aesthetic is intimately connected with pleasure in some sense or another of that vast term.[31] The antithesis indicates that such pleasures are nonetheless "disinterested," "detached," or "nonpersonal."

2. Quantity: The thesis states that aesthetic judgment is singular in form, that is, it judges particular representations related to the feelings of pleasure and displeasure. The antithesis claims, however, that such judgment entails universal assent, or intersubjective validity.

3. Relation: The thesis argues that aesthetic judgment is not based upon a precise notion of what the object ought to be, which is the case in cognitive and moral judgment. The antithesis sets out the claim that aesthetic judgment is based upon the purposefulness of the object, or upon an unstatable notion of completeness or preadaption to the cognitive faculties.

4. Modality: The thesis holds that aesthetic judgment must be one's own judgment, that is, autonomous and based upon one's own feelings, as opposed to being borrowed from other persons' aesthetic verdicts. The antithesis holds that like all judgments or beliefs, aesthetic judgment logically lays claim to the assent of all persons.

This skeleton of Kant's "Analytic of the Beautiful" must be filled in with many details, and this is the aim of this section. Despite a certain pedantry in Kant's analysis under these logical modes, there is sufficient compensation in the definition that results. One of the common complaints made by Wittgensteinian philosophers against definition in general and aesthetic definitions in particular, is that definitions should not try to state one characteristic supposedly common and peculiar to a wide range of phenomena. Against such "essentialist" definitions, many philosophers in the "ordinary language" and Wittgensteinian schools argue for "family resemblance" or "open concept" definitions.[32] Because it would carry us far afield to enter into the details of this view of definition, and because the general stance is too well known to need footnoting, I mean simply to point out that Kant is not proposing an "essentialist" definition or one that involves a sole and unique ground of aesthetic judgment. Indeed, given the vast realm of the aesthetic, it would seem improbable that an essentialist definition could be given. Throughout the history of philosophy, such attempts in both ethics and metaphysics have notably failed. The varieties of aesthetic experience are of much greater richness than the varieties of moral goodness, and the search for one exclusive ground seems all the more idle.

As I interpret Kant, each of the four "moments" concerns what not only might, but actually does, exist in nonaesthetic contexts. In regard to quality, for example, no one would balk at the statement that much pleasure is decidedly nonaesthetic: for example, the pleasures of gluttony, of mere entertainment, of sexual sensation. In regard to quantity: many nonaesthetic judgments both are singular in form and lay claim to common support or acquiescence, for example, reports on seeing a certain color, or hearing middle C. As for Kant's "moment" of relation, nonaesthetic judgments sometimes make reference to a general sense of purposefulness without stating a definite purpose, for example, archaeological judgments about traces left by vanished tribes, or biological judgments.[33] For an example of nonaesthetic judgments evincing the fourth "moment," modality, it might be to the purpose to instance Kant's way of limiting speculative reason in religious matters in *Religion Within the Limits of Reason Alone*. Kant does not rule out the existence of religious mysteries, or "holy mysteries," which he defines as something that is "known by each single individual but cannot be made known publicly."[34] Though other illustrations of such nonaesthetic judgment under modality could be given, the religious example seems closest to the aesthetic. According to Kant, both aesthetic judgment and religious belief involve a peculiarly private judgment that cannot be based upon either empirical or logical justification; yet both also lay claim to the assent of all persons.[35]

My point in this digression, before turning to the details of the "moments," is that Kant's definition is, from the methodological point of view, quite sophisticated: only insofar as the four characteristics overlap is it a question of "pure" aesthetic judgment. Kant's analysis could therefore readily explain borderline cases. His procedure is to begin with the most clear-cut or paradigmatic cases of aesthetic judgment.

Kant's first "moment" implies that to discern whether anything is beautiful one must attend to the feelings caused in us rather than to the properties of the object. Aesthetic judgments are referred either to actual feelings of pleasure or displeasure, or to our capacities to have such feelings. Kant implies that taste is the regulation and formation of the capacities to feel pleasure and displeasure. He is also making use of a familiar distinction between the knowing person (the subject), and the thing or event to be known (the object). A second familiar distinction is also present: the subject does not know or discern the object directly, but rather a representation of it. And a third distinction is made which might be called Kant's Copernican revolution in taste: rather than to suppose that the knowing subject must adapt itself to the representation of the object, we must suppose that an object is called beautiful because of its capacity to accommodate itself to our aesthetic sensibilities. In other words, as far as aesthetics is concerned, Kant is not interested in the objects of experience but rather in the cognitive dispositions and effects of objects upon the person.[36]

It is not strictly relevant here to assess the legitimacy of the first two of these distinctions. The first would carry us into metaphysics; and except in the sense that aesthetic experience has sometimes been described as a mystical union of subject and object (for example, by Plotinus and sometimes by Schopenhauer), discussion of the subject-object distinction would not lead to any insight into Kant's aesthetics.[37] The subject-object distinction is in itself so banausic, and of such harmless consequence to Kant's aesthetics, that it is on a par with his second assumption involving a representationalist theory of knowledge. I mean to imply not that Kant's version of representationalism is tenable, but that its truth or falsity does not directly bear upon Kant's aesthetic theory.

The third distinction, however, which involves a radical distinction between objective and subjective judgment, takes us into the heart of Kant's aesthetics. Though Kant describes the beautiful as nonconceptual, his aesthetics presents a decidedly cognitive theory; it would be a major misunderstanding to describe his aesthetic as noncognitive. Yet, paradoxically, Kant says that the beautiful is "subjective." The paradox might vanish if it is recalled that for Kant, conceptual or logical judgment purports to describe or refer to the objective world; aesthetic judgment, though it might seem to refer to objective properties of things, is actually related to the subjective feelings of pleasure or displeasure. On first glance, Kant's statement that "the judgment of taste . . . is one whose determining ground *cannot be other than subjective*"[38] seems like a truism; for part of the accepted meaning of "aesthetic" is "pertaining to the senses or the feelings." But the word "subjective" often implies "prejudiced," "partial," or "relativistic," which are connotations against which Kant vigorously argues. Neither does Kant mean that aesthetic judgments are mere reports upon psychological states, or expressions of certain sorts of attitudes.

To clarify further what Kant means by calling aesthetic judgment "subjective," in his restricted sense, a brief recapitulation of his mature view on the relation between concepts and the objective is in order. In a letter written to a friend in 1772, Kant distinguishes what he calls "*intellectus ectypus*" from "*intellectus archetypus*." The former he describes as a type of intelligence that draws "the data of its logical procedure from the sensuous intuition of things." It would seem, therefore, that concepts employed by such an intelligence would be guaranteed to relate to objects: concepts would inevitably picture the objective world. The latter kind of intelligence, Kant writes, is akin to God's, or that of the Universal Mind: the concepts of this intelligence are the very grounds of objective things themselves and determine their being. Objective knowledge presents no problem in Divine Intelligence because it creates the objects of its knowledge.[39]

What is peculiar to the concepts of rational and sensuous beings like ourselves, Kant argues, is that some of our concepts are not arrived at empirically, but are in fact imposed by us upon the objective world. Moreover, our concepts are never creative in the same way that we can at least imagine the concepts of a Divine Mind to be.[40] In the first *Critique,* Kant attempts to reason his way out of the apparent paradox of having objective knowledge based on concepts imposed by the mind by what might be called, with a degree of facetiousness on my part, a typographical maneuver. Kant says that the concepts imposed by the mind do refer to the "objective" world, that is, the phenomenal world. Pure concepts determine what is "objective" for the world of appearances or the phenomenal, but cannot legitimately be used to describe what is *really* objective—"things-in-themselves" or the noumenal.

For Kant, an objective judgment always entails dependence upon the human mind. More precisely, knowledge of the phenomenal world is only possible because the pure concepts are imposed upon experience. Kant calls an objective judgment "logical" because it predicates something of an object. A subjective judgment is "nonlogical" because it predicates nothing of an object but only registers feelings of pleasure or displeasure. For example, a judgment about the atomic weight of a chemical or the distance between two planets would be objective, in Kant's sense, as well as logical; such judgment predicates attributes to objects. A judgment about the distastefulness, the tediousness, or the pleasantness of something would be "subjective" or "nonlogical," though not therefore necessarily aesthetic.[41] Obviously many judgments concern feelings and reactions to things which are not judged aesthetically.

Moreover, "objective" judgments involve both knowing and bringing concepts to bear on the object of knowledge. It is part of Kant's theory that aesthetic judgment is nonconceptual, though cognition plays a significant role. Before proceeding to this last point, we should observe that by calling aesthetic judgment "subjective," Kant also means that feelings of pleasure or displeasure are a necessary but not a sufficient condition for aesthetic judging; however, it is necessary and sufficient for judging that something is sweet that it taste so. For something to be judged beautiful, so Kant holds, the capacity of feeling pleasure must be, as it were, set in motion; Kant never identifies the beautiful with feelings.[42]

In the "First Moment," Kant mentions two different kinds

of interest, which he opposes to the pure disinterestedness of the beautiful. First, he points out that persons are obviously interested in maintaining or cultivating agreeable sensations; these are sensuous or fleshly interests leading to desires for certain kinds of things or experiences for their own sakes. Such interests might vary from one person to another, but it makes no sense to demand that other persons share them. Kant calls such kinds of pleasure the "agreeable"; and no one needs to be told that people in general have an interest in what gratifies the senses. Second, Kant mentions utilitarian or ethical interests, which he calls in general "interest" or "delight" in the good. "We call that *good for something* (useful) which only pleases as a means; but that which pleases on its own account we call *good in itself*."[43] As he states in the *Fundamental Principles*, hypothetical imperatives correspond to the former. They prescribe rules for making something (technical imperatives) or for conforming one's behavior to the externals of the law (prudential imperatives). The Categorical Imperative prescribes ethical action, or action for the "good in itself." But all rational human beings must logically be interested in maintaining the moral order, not, however, because of any pleasure which might ensue, but because "the good is the Object of will, i.e., of a rationally determined faculty of desire."[44] "Morality, therefore, consists in the relation of every action to that legislation through which alone a realm of ends is possible."[45]

Kant gives aesthetic judgment, and its peculiar kind of pleasure, the technical designation of "disinterestedness," which he first defines negatively as involving neither the agreeable nor the good. Although the aesthetic might overlap the agreeable, the utilitarian, or the moral, these categories can supposedly be distinguished. A building, for example, might be purely utilitarian, or both utilitarian and the object of disinterested pleasure. Again, a poem such as Milton's *Paradise Lost* (of which Kant was evidently very fond) might be the object of "disinterest" and of moral interest. What Kant calls "free beauties of nature," such as "flowers . . . the parrot, the hummingbird, the bird of paradise, and a number of crustacea,"[46] can be objects of intellectual interest for the naturalist but are especially apt for "disinterested" pleasure.

Describing the aesthetic as "disinterested" at first seems incompatible with the great compelling power the beautiful exerts upon the attention, especially upon the very spirit and fiber of the creative artist. Even if the obvious distinction is made between being uninterested as opposed to being disinterested in something, still "disinterest" seems too frail to characterize what is one of the great and perennial interests of mankind. Moreover, Kant asserts much later in the third *Critique*, in a section entitled "The Empirical Interest in the Beautiful":

A man abandoned on a desert island would not adorn either himself or his hut, nor would he look for flowers, and still less plant them, with the object of providing himself with personal adornments. Only in society does it occur to him to be not merely a man, but a man refined after the manner of his kind.[47]

The same observation would hold for all of man's interests, both intellectual and moral, as well as aesthetic endeavors; what would be excluded are Robinson Crusoe–style practical and sensuous concerns. There also exists a tension to be resolved between aesthetic interests and Kant's demand that they be "disinterested." Kant's analysis of the first "moment" is so far chiefly negative: we are shown what the aesthetic is not, but the term "disinterest" does not show us what it is.

I do not believe, however, that what Kant means by "disinterestedness" is so elusive; it is actually a striking feature of the aesthetic. In the following section on the affective underpinnings of Kant's aesthetics, such pleasures may become more clear. For the moment, "disinterested pleasure" might best be illustrated by an example: when somebody makes a good joke at our expense, or a witticism that we know is pointed at ourselves, we can disengage ourselves from the situation and take pleasure in it. The joke must be fairly intricate, and keep one in suspense:

Something absurd (something in which, therefore, the understanding can of itself find no delight) must be present in whatever is to raise a hearty convulsive laugh. Laughter is an affection arising from a strained expectation being suddenly reduced to nothing. This very reduction, at which certainly understanding cannot rejoice, is still indirectly a source of very lively enjoyment for a moment.[48]

Before turning to the second "moment," we might consider a few minor difficulties still involved in the first. Kant says that "to apprehend a regular and appropriate building with one's cognitive faculties, be the mode of presentation clear or confused, is quite a different thing from being conscious of this representation with an accompanying sensation of delight."[49] Although Kant's beginning point is that aesthetic judgment must be referred to the feelings of pleasure or displeasure, he might have asked whether "apprehending a regular and appropriate building" were not untouched by feeling or affective response. For the terms "regular" and "appropriate" in this context seem to reveal an affective overtone, which implies that such judgment is not purely cognitive, as Kant maintains. It is also unclear how Kant would describe aesthetic judgments of indifference, that is, judgments of aesthetic but mediocre objects. Anyone walking down the corridors of most museums could not but observe that much is aesthetic, but indifferent; what gives aesthetic pleasure is often as rare as what actually displeases. It would be idle to argue that what is aesthetically mediocre or indifferent gives rise to only a minimal amount of pleasure, for pleasure that becomes so minimal might cease to be experienced, even subliminally. At this point, either of two conclusions would seem to be in order: either Kant's use of "pleasure" is extremely broad and therefore requires an analysis of the entire hedonic spectrum; or pleasure and displeasure are not necessarily linked with the aesthetic, though they often accompany it. If Kant means that the aesthetic is necessarily linked with human sensibility or with human feelings, I think no one would quarrel. I have already suggested that Kant's form of subjectivism is very special indeed: he speaks loosely of pleasure and pain, but all his theory requires is that the aesthetic be necessarily connected with the capacity of feeling pleasure and displeasure.

Kant sometimes describes man's sensuous or phenomenal side as animality; and his noumenal side as "rationality." Kant's account of both ethical obligation and aesthetic judgment clearly places man in the spheres of rationality and of animality, thereby revealing yet a further parallel in his thought on these two branches of philosophy. For Kant, the purely rational will is the holy will, which cannot be called "good," because by definition it cannot err. On the other hand, a purely sensuous "will" should rather be called a "voluntary" will, but not a "choosing" will. Animals, for example, act sometimes voluntarily, sometimes involuntarily, but never, Kant would claim, from choice. But man is described as capable of having a "good will": he has sensuous inclinations, but also reason; the aesthetic, similarly, points to man's dual nature. Sensuous passivity gratifies or stimulates, whereas aesthetic judgment brings about the play of the mental faculties, which results in a peculiarly human or intellectual pleasure. Two further parallels between Kant's ethics and aesthetics might throw the first "moment" into sharper relief.

First, both ethical and aesthetic judgment supposedly recall one's superiority to sensibility and the phenomenal world. Just as moral duty recalls the individual to his citizenship as a free agent in the supersensible world, so contemplating aesthetic objects unites the world of Nature with the world of reason. It is as if disinterested pleasure quieted man's phenomenal will.[50] Judging aesthetically places one outside the phenomenal world of cause and effect, the habitat of ordinary perceptual judgments.

Second, Kant's interest in both the third *Critique* and in the *Foundations of the Metaphysics of Morals* is in the nonempirical or the "pure." A "pure" moral action is one committed exclusively out of the pure sense of duty. Kant warns that because the powers of self-deception are so wily and insidious, we can never be sure whether our sole or actual motive was duty. Self-examination often reveals prudential or sensuous grounds:

It is in fact absolutely impossible by experience to discern with complete certainty a single case in which the maxim of an action, however much it may conform to duty, rested solely on moral grounds and on the conception of one's duty. It sometimes happens that in the most searching self-examination we can find nothing except the moral ground of duty which could have been powerful enough to move us to this or that good action and to such great sacrifice. But from this we cannot by any means conclude with certainty that a secret impulse of self-love, falsely appearing as the idea of duty, was not actually the true determining cause of the will.[51]

A similar parallel holds in aesthetic judgment: many nonaesthetic or adventitious interests often overlay or belie our perception. For Kant, purity is evidently an ideal; though there are clear cases, however rare they might be, of action done from a "pure" sense of duty, or of "pure" aesthetic judgment, even these should not be called indubitable. Such cases can nonetheless be contrasted with mixed actions in morals, such as those in accordance with the moral law but committed for prudential reasons; and cases that involve enjoying some masterpiece of art, such as Manet's *Déjeuner sur l'herbe*, for prurient reasons.

But though the parallel between Kant's concern for "pure" judgment in ethics and aesthetics seems obvious, and though it is plausible to call such judgments "ideal," still difficulties concerning the sources of error in both kinds of judgment arise. For example, self-deception and self-love, which Kant implies are the chief courses of spuriously "pure" moral action, do not have an apparent corollary in aesthetic judgment. Moreover, given that Kant could hardly propose a formal criterion for aesthetic judgment comparable to the Categorical Imperative in his ethics, the sources of error in aesthetic judgment could not be attributed to self-contradictoriness, unless that criterion were construed far more broadly than Kant applies it in his ethics. But analogies naturally give rise to discrepancies. Kant's explanation of erroneous aesthetic judgment is an integral part of showing how aesthetic judgments can be veracious. I shall return to such problems at the end of this chapter.[52]

From the independence of particular interests described by the first "moment," Kant can readily argue for the universality of aesthetic pleasure, which is the thrust of the second "moment." To show Kant's logic in an alternative way: Kant can infer the second "moment" from the first because, given that "disinterested" pleasure has no particular ground (such as sensuous penchants or inclinations, or utilitarian or moral ends), the capacity to feel aesthetic pleasure is, in an important sense, universalizable.

Using the word "aesthetic" in the broad sense, that is, "referring an object to our feelings," Kant distinguishes "judgments of sense" from "judgments of taste." The former are private and express only the agreeableness of sensation. Kant's examples are Canary wine and the color of violet, which might be agreeable to some persons but not to others; it is nonsensical to require persons to share such reactions. For judgments of sense, the hackneyed phrase of Horace's, "There is no disputing about taste," is true. Aesthetic judgments, however, are public and lay claim to universal though subjective validity. Though we often anticipate disagreement in taste, and though we might be mistaken in our own judgment, we demand everyone's agreement, for we must assume that everyone has the same fundamental capacity of aesthetic judgment. Even though artistic training or acquaintance is sometimes necessary, together with uprooting prejudices and biases, we impute agreement to everyone. Kant argues that in regard to sensation we tend to expect agreement but not to demand it; as for taste, even when we do not expect agreement, we demand it.

Kant presents a number of considerations for the claim that taste must be universalizable. The first seems to be either a simple logical mistake or incomplete:

This definition of the beautiful is deducible from the foregoing definition of it as an object of delight apart from any interest. For where any one is conscious that his delight in an object is with him independent of interest, it is inevitable that he should look on the object as one containing a ground of delight for all men.[53]

What is true of the individual is of course not necessarily true of the class. To say that one's delight in something is neither sensuous, nor practical, nor moral does not entail that it must be an object of delight for everyone. Kant would reply, however, that such delight must be taken in the form; for if not, the delight or pleasure could only be a reaction to the content or "material" of judgment, that is, its sensational presentation—like color or sound. The pleasure, then, would be sensuous and nonuniversalizable. If the delight or pleasure is taken in the form, the second "moment" must follow. If the delight is in the social agreeableness of something, then we impute only a general—as opposed to a universal—agreement. What becomes fundamental to Kant's entire aesthetics is that sensation can and must be sharply distinguished from form. I shall return to this assumption in a moment.

Kant's attempt to deduce the second "moment" from the first becomes more compelling once he adds the assumption that in aesthetic judgment we mean to speak with a universal voice. There might be wide empirical agreement on the sensuously agreeable, but we do not demand it. As for the agreeableness of social conventions, we might both expect and demand agreement, but only from persons in our culture. In ethics, Kant holds, we demand universal agreement, but by means of rules or concepts. Kant points out that we can no more be reasoned into liking something than into receiving aesthetic pleasure from it.

Kant's claim that aesthetic judgment must be universalizable seems important, for only if aesthetic judgment is public and demands agreement does it represent a risk. Purely private signs of approval and disapproval are by definition incorrigible; judgment that makes itself known and is a "commanding thing," as Plato describes the good, is a major aid to the improvement of taste. For aesthetic judgment that lays claim to other persons' tastes and sensibility, even if it be proved false or unfounded, requires reason and explanation. Such judgment is therefore corrigible and enters into the realm of cognition. The universality of taste is essential to the formation—literally the "giving form to"—and regulation of the feelings. Taste, as regulative, demands first that feelings be self-consistent, and second that they be harmonious with those of other persons: such are the ideals of "pure" aesthetic judgment. The second "moment" also seems to imply that taste, or the capacity of aesthetic discernment, is impersonal as well as interpersonal, and that it expresses itself impartially as well as unwaveringly. From the second "moment," taste emerges as a cognitive discipline, albeit in accordance with "indeterminate" concepts. I shall deal with such concepts in my exposition of the third "moment."

Kant mentions a linguistic consideration for the second "moment" which supplies further force. We do not object if someone adds "to you" when we assert "This is pleasant." We would so object when we say, "This is beautiful." We might say, "It was beautiful *to him*, but *I* don't share his opinion." In effect, liking something is not sufficient ground for calling it beautiful. It makes no sense to say "It is beautiful, *and* I don't like it"; but, happily, it is always in our power to say, "It is beautiful, *but* I don't like it." The concessive "but" might simply indicate that other persons call it beautiful, but that I do not like it. Or again, I might concede that it is in a certain way beautiful, but that I have considerable reservations about it. And again, we might recognize that the object is beautiful as an example of a certain style which we do not like. Aesthetic judgment has a far wider scope than likes and dislikes.

In the same regard Kant compares and contrasts a number of assertions. "This rose is agreeable to smell" is a judgment of sense which does not lay claim to universality. "Roses are beautiful" is a logical judgment based upon aesthetic judgment, resulting from comparing many experiences with one another. Such a judgment is equivalent to: "Anbody would very likely take aesthetic pleasure in roses." The aesthetic judgment of taste, however, is always singular in form: for example, "This rose is beautiful." Unlike mere reports upon the agreeableness of sensation, or general claims imputing an attribute to a range of phenomena, a judgment of taste lays claims to universal assent.

As I have already mentioned, one of Kant's fundamental assumptions is that sensation can be radically distinguished from form. Sensation might be pleasant but never purely aesthetic, and it must necessarily be private. To say that sensations are private—like the tone of a musical instrument or the color of violet—might mean that sensations vary for different persons or that persons enjoy them differently. Kant suggests that though sensations are the same for everyone, enjoyment might vary: "A violet color is to one soft and lovely; to another dull and faded. One man likes the tone of wind instruments, another prefers that of string instruments."[54]

A sensation may add to what Kant calls the "charm" of art, but never to its aesthetic merit. One wonders, however, at the risk of putting too Humean a question to Kant, what would count as "*a* sensation." If we must stop to hunt for one, it might be that single sensations are never found in the real world but only in books on philosophy. Would a single sensation be like a small square of violet color on a color chart? Such a sensation, however, would not be single, for the color would be presented under three aspects —saturation, intensity, and hue. Although the philosophical abstraction of "a sensation" can be formed, given that it does not obtain in actual aesthetic judgment, it seems fruitless to ask whether it is beautiful. The same tone might be beautiful sounded on one violin, but not on another instrument; though the pitch is the same, or "single," it need not have the same volume or timbre. It seems that sensations in aesthetic experience cannot be considered in isolation but are linked to and saturated with other sensations. Colors play off other colors, sounds enrich and anticipate one another, and poetic meanings enjoy one another's connotational overtones. The sensuousness of sounds and colors cannot be experienced in the pristine and simple way that Kant seems to require for drawing a radical distinction between sensation and form. Though we might concede that a single color is not beautiful, the reason would be that it is single, not that it is a sensation.

This criticism, however, might give too much weight to a Humean or atomic theory of perception, which is certainly not Kant's view of sensation; it might also assume that because our actual aesthetic experience does involve a blending or fusing of sensations, we cannot therefore primarily or solely judge aesthetic form. If Kant's meaning is that "pure" aesthetic judgment is exclusively concerned with form, which can ideally be judged independently of sensuous content or sensation, then what he calls "the play of sensations"[55] must be an instance of the larger class "aesthetic form." Further, if "individual sensations" be construed as "isolated sensations" instead of "single" or "atomic" sensations, then Kant's claim that "isolated" colors or sounds can be merely agreeable seems more plausible. What complicates this interpretation, however, is Kant's notion of "pure" sensations, which he says have aesthetic form, and therefore beauty:

A mere colour, such as the green of a plot of grass, or a mere tone . . . like that of a violin, is described by most people as in itself beautiful, notwithstanding the fact that both seem to depend merely on the matter of the representation—in other words, simply on sensation, which only entitles them to be called agreeable. . . . sensations of colour as well as of tone are only entitled to be immediately regarded as beautiful where, in either case, they are *pure*. This is a determination which at once goes to their form. . . . For this reason all simple colors are regarded as beautiful so far as pure. Composite colors have not this advantage, because, not being simple, there is no standard for estimating whether they should be called pure or impure.[56]

From the tone of this passage no one could doubt whether Kant would prefer to exclude all colors and sounds from the beautiful, in spite of what "most people" might say. It is by no means clear that Kant adopted Euler's notion that "colors are isochronous vibrations (pulses) of the ether, as sounds are of the air in a state of disturbance,"[57] to which Kant refers in his exposition of the third "moment."[58] The suggestion is that we might attend to the regularity of stimuli impinging our senses, and thus become aware of the structures or "play" of sensations. Our experience of sounds and colors is of course not an experience of vibrations or sound waves; Kant implies that aesthetic judgment is of the phenomenally given and is not related to physical theories that might explain the causes or nature of sensation.

What Kant appears to mean by the aesthetic form of sensations is that insofar as their interplay and composition are attended to, they count as beautiful. The play of tones and the play of colors are to be construed as their form. Although aesthetic judgment naturally includes being sensible to the "parts" played upon, the tonal or visual "parts" are the sensible "data" which are incorporated into form. In music, for example, the relationships of counterpoint, syncopation, inversion, harmonization, dissonance, development—among others—comprise the form. Kant would call such relationships the "play" or "form" of sensations.

To support this interpretation further, and to relate it to a previous point concerning the noumenal parallel in Kant's aesthetics and ethics, it might be mentioned that Kant often describes aesthetic form as promoting subjective freedom. With the aesthetic, we are interested not so much in the "data," or the sensible content of judgment, as in how such content is arranged, structured, and played upon. Our sense of freedom as noumenal beings is thereby subjectively awakened; it is as if we were dictating aesthetic form from our own nature and recomposing the sensible manifold in accordance with our own will. It must be borne in mind, however, that for Kant, even aesthetic spontaneity is in accordance with the fundamental lawfulness of understanding.

Just as Aristotle argues in the *Poetics* that mimesis is a natural activity to man, so Kant appears to argue that the delight in ordering as such, or of imposing form, is natural to humankind. Aesthetic pleasure is taken either in forming constructs out of sensation —the role of the artist; or in apperceiving the formal interplay of sensation—the role of the listener, spectator, or reader. In both cases, the pleasure is intersubjectively communicable. Though we cannot psychologically be aware of form without sensation, "pure" aesthetic judgment centers upon formal interplay.

Kant's theory of "pure" sensation, then, appears broad enough to explain the delight in kinds of painting that he naturally could not have known, for example, highly abstract painting in which only two colors might be opposed to each other, as in certain of Rothko's paintings. It is not the colors as such, but their interplay (the varieties of which seem infinite) that forms the ground of aesthetic judgment. The implication is that though colors and sounds considered in isolation can never be more than agreeable, it does not follow that their inclusion in an aesthetic whole is irrelevant. Sensations in their interplay might form a whole which not only exceeds the total value of the individual sensation, but is categorically different: an object of aesthetic judgment.

It should be noted that Kant does not exclude color and tone from "pure" aesthetic judgment because they are subjective properties. On the contrary, he asserts that "*Sensation* (here external) also agrees in expressing a merely subjective side of our representations of external things, but one which is properly their matter (through which we are given something with real existence)."[59]

For Kant, colors are not Lockean "secondary properties" which depend for their existence upon the human mind. Color and tone are objective: "the green color of the meadows belongs to *objective* sensation, as the perception of an object of sense."[60] It is only because color and tone can at most be agreeable that Kant excludes them from "pure" aesthetic judgment. Though their agreeableness is of course subjective, the sensations are objective.

To ensure that the Lockean distinction between primary and secondary properties is kept apart from Kant's account of aesthetic sensation, the following scheme might be of help:

1. "Properties" of "things-in-themselves." Such properties are by definition unknowable by us; it might even be a presumption to call them properties.
2. Properties of the world of appearances. Such properties are objective for all rational-sensuous beings like ourselves and include color and tone.
3. Aesthetic properties, or properties dependent upon our individual organs of sense and of feeling. Such properties are either "of sense" (for example, the agreeableness of a certain tactile sensation) or "of taste" (that is, the disinterested pleasure of the play of sensations).

Kant does not trouble himself to argue that material from the "lower senses"—smell, taste, touch, and what might be called the kinesthetic sense—is excluded from judgments of taste. It is aesthetic merely in the sense of being passively enjoyed. Reasons for Kant's exclusion of such material are not difficult to find: data from the "lower" senses do not admit of a complexity comparable to that of visual and auditory data. Sound admits of pitch, timbre, and volume; color admits of hue, saturation, and brightness. One does not dwell or linger over data from the "lower" senses, for their simplicity fails to hold the attention and they are not susceptible to formal arrangement. Nevertheless, though such data are only "of sense," they might enter into judgment "of taste." In music, and in romantic music especially, sound and timbre invariably give rise to associations derived from the so-called lower senses. Although it detracts from listening to music to imagine particular things or events (which was the intention of program music), the timbre, rhythm, and modulations are redolent with nuances derived from nonauditory and nonvisual experience. We speak of "warm" sounds, of "moist" or "dry" colors, of "lush" musical transitions, of "velvety" phrasing. The language used to characterize aesthetic experience is drawn from all the senses, though Kant is certainly right in implying that sensations from the lower senses do not admit of much formal interplay.

Although further aspects of Kant's conception of form await discussion, his views will be thrown into greater relief if the third "moment," which presents fewer difficulties than the preceding two, is now examined. The "moment" of relation begins with the unobjectionable postulate that it is an inherent feature of the mind to approach anything whatsoever under the rubric of purposefulness.[61]

Kant describes "reflective judgment," which includes the aesthetic as a species, as judgment of a particular in search of a universal concept or rule; he describes "determinate judgment" as that in which the universal is given and under which a particular is subsumed. Practical judgment, comprising utilitarian, prudential, and ethical judgment, is determinate; that is, we are in possession of a determinate concept concerning what is useful, prudential, or utilitarian, and we bring the concept to bear upon the particular situation. Even ethical choice presupposes a determinate rule: the Categorical Imperative. Briefly, the determinate rule of ethics requires each person to legislate his own moral maxims for all members of the moral community.

Cognitive judgment also presupposes determinate purposes, discoverable by empirical inspection in subjects such as chemistry or physiology, or by rational analysis, as in mathematics. The description of an event or object in the external world as purposeless is a euphemism for human ignorance. Kant also claims that psychological faculties, as well as man's physiological constitution, are intrinsically purposive and that such purposes can be described in determinate concepts. The following argument from the *Foundations* illustrates Kant's claim:

In the natural constitution of an organized being, i.e., one suitably adapted to life, we assume as an axiom that no organ will be found for any purpose which is not the fittest and best adapted to that purpose. Now if its preservation, its welfare, in a word, its happiness—were the real end of nature in a being having reason and will, then nature would have hit upon a very poor arrangement in appointing the reason of the creature to be the executor of this purpose. For all the actions which the creature has to perform with this intention, and the entire rule of its conduct, would be dictated much more exactly by instinct.[62]

Kant's point of view is clearly teleological: Nature does nothing without a purpose. Even though he greatly restricts his notion of teleology in Part Two of the third *Critique* by describing it as a heuristic demand of our understanding, he gives no convincing ground for assuming that whatever Nature brings into existence is "the fittest and best adapted to that purpose." One might object that though the liver does a fair job as a filter, it could have been more efficiently designed; the same observation holds for most, if not all, the physical organs impressed into man's service. We might grant, then, the general plausibility of Kant's heuristic notion of purposefulness without adopting the conclusion that happiness could not be the end of the erring and bungling reason.

Aesthetic judgment, so Kant says, does not require a determinate concept. That is, we do not need a notion of what the object must be, or of its perfection, to feel disinterested pleasure. Although the notion that the aesthetic presupposes what Kant calls "indeterminate concepts" appears at this point rather vague and romantic, at least superficially his meaning is clear: one can take aesthetic delight in some objects without knowing purely scientific things about them. "Hardly any one but a botanist knows the true nature of a flower, and even he, while recognizing in the flower the reproductive organ of the plant, pays no attention to this natural end when using his taste to judge of its beauty."[63] Whether Kant can so radically distinguish between "pure" aesthetic judgment (which he describes as involving indeterminate concepts) and judgment mixed with ideas of perfection (which he says involves determinate concepts) is a difficulty that I shall put off until the discussion of the antimony of taste in chapter four. It appears quite false to say that aesthetic pleasure can be derived from something about which one has no clear or determinate idea; for example, pleasure taken in the nuances of styles of Greek pottery, or in the development of mannerist painting in France, presupposes knowledge and definite acquaintance. Moreover, when no definite concept or knowledge of the object is required for "disinterested pleasure," the difficulty of knowing that one's judgment is "pure" seems all the more insuperable. I shall deal with such problems in the next section. We may simply grant Kant's point, by way of preface to the third "moment," that no "determinate concept" is required to take pleasure in wildflowers; whether this is true of taking pleasure in Monteverdi or Titian remains to be seen.

To say that art is without a purpose would seem to be a surprising exception to the general assumption that artifacts have purposes; for a work of art is at least an artifact or something manmade.[64] It would be paradoxical to describe artistic activity—creating or performing works of art—as having no purpose or end; for "a purposeless activity" bears connotations of futility or frivolity. Kant also deems it unacceptable to describe aesthetic judgment of Nature as a purposeless activity or as one for which the object is purposeless. Kant tries to resolve the paradox between the general assumption of purposefulness for all human experience and the lack of definite or determinate purpose in aesthetic judgment in this passage:

> But an Object, or state of mind, or even an action may, although its possibility does not necessarily presuppose the representation of an end, be called final simply on the account of its possibility being only explicable and intelligible for us by virtue of an assumption on our part of a fundamental causality according to ends, i.e., a will that would have so ordained it according to a certain represented rule. Finality, therefore, may exist apart from an end, insofar as we do not locate the causes of this form in a will. . . . So we may at least observe a finality of form, and trace it in objects.[65]

Kant's curious phrase, "purposiveness without purpose" ("*Zweckmässigkeit ohne Zweck*") indicates two rather uncurious observations: (1) Many activities and objects have implicit purposes obvious to everyone. Often, however, the particular purpose of an object or form of behavior—such as an artifact from a vanished civilization, a taboo, or a neurotic symptom—is not clear. Nevertheless, it is assumed that a definite purpose is theoretically discoverable. (2) Certain objects, because of their formal composition or their unity amidst variety, appear aesthetically purposive, as if they were preadapted to be objects of judgments of taste; for example, snowflakes, crystals, wildflowers, and galaxies evince gratuitous beauties which nonetheless resonate to man's aesthetic sensibilities.

Aesthetic objects, Kant therefore maintains, belong to the general family of purposive objects. What distinguishes the beautiful from other objects is that no extrinsic or determinate end is assigned to it:

We are thus left with the subjective finality in the representation of an object, exclusive of any end (objective or subjective)—consequently the bare form of finality in the representation whereby an object is *given* to us, so far as we are conscious of it—delight which, apart from any concept, we estimate as universally communicable.[66]

In a trivial sense a work of art might have a definite purpose: it was made to earn one's living, to satisfy one's patron, to develop some new technique. Novels are sometimes written to ease the tensions of their authors; music is sometimes composed to celebrate military victories. Some poems are written to justify the ways of God to men; other poems, like Voltaire's verses on the great earthquake of Lisbon, are written to show that God's ways cannot be justified. But such purposes, though interesting in their own right, are not specifically aesthetic, for a work does not become art because of the artist's intentions. If his intentions are not implicit in his work, historical or extrinsic information cannot incorporate them. If intentions are implicit, they must speak for themselves. A musical passage, for example, fits into place not simply because of a composer's intent, but because the passage intrinsically fits into the aesthetic structure. Although historical or biographical information might reveal the purpose or meaning of certain parts in a composition, such information only accentuates what is present. It appears that for Kant an aesthetic object is purposive because of its inherent form and its adaptability to the demands of "pure" taste.

Imagination in aesthetic judgment looks to the understanding for discipline and guidance, but without a particular law's being placed upon it, just as Caliban must look to Prospero. Without a master, Caliban is wayward and purposeless; the imagination without a general rule of lawfulness remains in the shackles of its own freedom. Kant states in the General Remark:

But that the *imagination* should be both free and *of itself comfortable to law*, i.e., carry autonomy with it, is a contradiction. The understanding alone gives the law. Where, however, the imagination is compelled to follow a course laid down by a definite law, then what the form of the product is to be is determined by concepts; but, in that case, as already shown, the delight is not delight in the beautiful, but in the good (in perfection, though it be no more than formal perfection).[67]

The pleasure that arises from purposiveness without a definite purpose is therefore different from mere agreeableness. When Kant remarks that aesthetic judgment is not concerned in or dependent upon the existence of the beautiful, he means that, unlike our interest in the agreeable, our aesthetic experience does not require our owning, monopolizing, or craving the object of such judgment. Kant does not mean that one does not want the beautiful to persevere in its existence as a permanent occasion of aesthetic pleasure, but that one's taste dwells "on the contemplation of the beautiful because this contemplation strengthens and reproduces itself. . . . Taste that requires an added element of *charm* and *emotion* for its delight, not to speak of adopting this as the measure of its approval, has not yet emerged from barbarism."[68]

The fourth "moment," that of modality, is also based upon distinctions drawn in the table of judgments in the first *Critique*.[69] A judgment in general must either affirm or deny, but it might do so in one of three, and only three, modes: (1) problematically: the judgment expresses only logical possibility; (2) assertorically: the judgment affirms or denies what is viewed as real or true; (3) apodictically: the judgment expresses what is logically or necessarily true. Aesthetic judgment, therefore, must exhibit a particular modality. The subject of such judgment must make reference solely to form, and the predicate refers to the disinterested and therefore universal pleasure following from the free play of the imagination and the understanding. The copula "must be" or "ought" serves notice that such judgment is put forth with a claim upon everyone's assent, *as if* beauty were an objective or logical predicate. The peculiarity of aesthetic judgment is its claim to universal assent even though it is based on the subjective feelings of pleasure and displeasure.

Kant is careful to distinguish the various kinds of necessity that might attach to judgment. The necessity of aesthetic judgment is neither logical nor theoretical, for one cannot infer a priori that everyone will feel disinterested delight in aesthetic form. Neither is the necessity of a practical sort, as in ethical judgment, for which there exists a supreme formal rule prescribing unconditional adherence to duty as the sole ethical motive. "Everyone must admit that a law, if it is to hold morally, i.e., as a ground of obligation, must imply absolute necessity."[70] Both theoretical and practical necessity rest upon determinate concepts or definite rules; their force is consequently apodictic. Aesthetic judgment has what Kant calls "exemplary validity"; anyone calmly and critically experiencing the form of the object must be sensible to the same disinterested pleasure: "Here I put forward my judgment of taste as an example of the judgment of common sense, and attribute to it on that account exemplary validity."[71]

The special necessity of aesthetic judgment rests upon a peculiar foundation. Just as the possibility of theoretical communication presupposes homogeneity of the faculties of human knowledge, so the possibility of sharing aesthetic beliefs and feelings presupposes homogeneity of disinterested pleasure when the faculties are simply idling, or engaged in free play:

But if cognitions are to admit of communication, then our mental state, i.e., the way the cognitive powers are attuned for cognition generally, and, in fact, the relative proportion suitable for a representation . . . from which cognition is to result, must also admit of being universally communicated. . . . And this is always what actually happens where a given object, through the intervention of sense, sets the imagination at work in arranging the manifold, and the imagination, in turn, the understanding in giving to this arrangement the unity of concepts.[72]

At the foot of aesthetic judgment is what Kant calls "a common sense," which must not be confused with "common sense." In the "Analytic of the Beautiful," Kant describes the "common sense" as a disposition that provides the interpersonal basis for aesthetic judgment. Unlike moral "common sense," which works confusedly, but which is nonetheless based upon secure and determinate principles, the aesthetic "common sense" cannot be articulated in a determinate way. This is not because a Newton of aesthetics has not yet appeared upon the scene, but rather because to formulate the aesthetic into laws or determinate concepts would reduce it to either psychology or physiology. Kant argues that there is an important difference between (1) the professional critic and the ordinary amateur of art and (2) the ethicist and the ordinary man. For both the ethicist and the ordinary man appeal to the same ethical principles, which can be stated in precise and perspicuous form; whereas neither the professional critic nor the mere amateur of art has any comparably precise principles to which he can appeal.

The man in the street, when he says that deceit is wrong, bases his judgment on confused, but the philosopher on clear grounds, while both appeal in reality to identical principles of reason. But I have already stated that an aesthetic judgment is quite unique, and affords no, (not even confused), knowledge of the Object.[73]

Kant appears to base "exemplary validity" upon considerations such as these: given that the imagination belongs to both sensibility and understanding, aesthetic form arises out of the general harmony or "cooperativeness" of the cognitive faculties, resulting in a unique kind of pleasure. In cognition the imagination is directed by rules of thought; in aesthetic judgment the imagination is in free conformity to understanding; thus, imagination conforms to the basic lawfulness of understanding, but not to the dictates of any particular law. In aesthetic judgment it is as if imagination itself dictated form to the perceived object.

If imagination and understanding were not fundamentally in harmonious league, no knowledge whatsoever would be possible; in the beautiful the imagination exhibits its basic lawfulness, and reflection upon such a "state" is pleasurable.

A few illustrations from E. H. Gombrich's *Art and Illusion* might help to make this admittedly difficult doctrine more intelligible. Describing the ways in which the imagination "sees" what is not there, Gombrich argues that such forms of highly interpretive perception are not unique to aesthetic judgment, but nonetheless a very pronounced feature of it:

The connoisseur, therefore, is no longer advised simply to stand back. He should look at the painter's handiwork closely. . . . There is an increasing awareness of the fact that what we enjoy is not so much seeing these works from a distance as the very act of stepping back, as it were, and watching our imagination come into play, transforming the medley of color into a finished image. The growing psychological interest of eighteenth-century critics made this idea more explicit. At the turn of the century we find Roger de Piles discussing the source of enjoyment in projection: "As there are styles of thought, so there are also styles of execution . . . the firm style gives life to work, and excuses for bad choice; and the polished finishes and brightens everything; it leaves no employment for the spectator's imagination, which pleases itself in discovering and finishing things which it ascribes to the artist *though in fact they proceed only from itself.*"[74]

The indeterminateness which Kant describes as essential to aesthetic judgment might also be illustrated from Gombrich, who argues that to understand the ideals of beauty one should find out how they were taught to apprentices. For a long while in "workshops all over Europe" the apprentice was instructed to copy endless patterns and forms contained in manuals of anatomy, perspective, architecture, and even human expression. The apprentice had to work for years copying what Kant would call "determinate concepts." Gombrich quotes from a seventeenth-century treatise by a German painter named Joachim von Sandrart: "When our Understanding issues its well-conceived concepts, and the hand, practised by many years of industrious drawing, puts them to paper according to reason, the perfect excellence of both the master and his art becomes manifest."[75]

The link between the Kantian indeterminate and disinterested pleasure was clearly perceived by Reynolds's description of Gainsborough's portraiture, quoted by Gombrich:

I have often imagined that this unfinished manner contributed even to that striking resemblance for which his portraits are so remarkable. Though this opinion may be considered as fanciful, yet I think a plausible reason may be given, why such a mode of painting should have such an effect. It is presupposed that in this undetermined manner there is the general effect; enough to remind the spectator of the original; the imagination supplies the rest, and perhaps more satisfactorily to himself, if not more exactly, than the artist, with all his care, could possibly have done.[76]

For Kant, indeterminateness is a necessary feature of aesthetic judgment. Though he never speaks of degrees of conceptual control, he makes it clear that some concept, however indeterminate, must be present in aesthetic judgment. Byzantine icons, to take an example that is not Kant's, supply the imagination with a form or controlling concept that is rigid but nevertheless highly stylized. Gombrich's contention that "it remains true that all representations can be somehow arranged along a scale which extends from the schematic to the impressionist"[77] is not only compatible with Kant's claim that aesthetic judgment involves indeterminate concepts but complements this claim. Comparing two paintings of horse races (one by Manet—*At the Races*, ca. 1875, and the other by Frith—*Derby Day*, ca. 1858), Gombrich gives a good illustration of Kantian free play of the imagination: "Manet's spirited sketch of a race certainly will tell the historian less about those bygone days than will that famous showpiece of Victorian realism, 'Derby Day' by Frith. One is tempted to say that in contrast to Manet, Frith leaves nothing to the imagination, but in fact, as we have seen, there is no representation of which this can ever be true."[78]

The painter's technique of the indeterminate ranges from simple optical illusions and *trompe l'oeil* to *sfumato*: "No wonder, therefore, that the greatest protagonist of naturalistic illusion in painting, Leonardo da Vinci, is also the inventor of the deliberately blurred image, the 'sfumato,' or veiled form, that cuts down the information on the canvas and thereby stimulates the mechanism of projection."[79] Similar techniques exist in poetry: metaphor, ambiguity, irony, and the pun are all ways of enriching meaning indeterminately. In reference to a passage from Calderón, Gombrich says that "the poet succeeds where many psychologists have failed in describing the panorama of illusions that may be evoked by the indeterminate. It is the power of expectation rather than the power of conceptual knowledge that molds what we see in life no less than in art."[80]

I do not believe that Kant must hold indeterminateness to be unique to aesthetic judgment, for the indeterminate characterizes reveries, hallucinations, drugged states, and dreams, which for Kant are not objects of taste. What distinguishes the indeterminate of art is its ultimate subordination to form. Kant seems to be describing romantic excess when he says: "If enthusiasm is comparable to *delirium*, fanaticism may be compared to *mania*. Of these the latter is least of all compatible with the sublime, for it is *profoundly* ridiculous. In enthusiasm, as an affection, the imagination is unbridled."[81]

The illusions and perceptual ambiguities of life must be solved to satisfy practical needs and intellectual problems. In art, indeterminateness is a positive value whereby the understanding lingers over the schemata of illusion. The Kantian indeterminate readily comprehends the kind of verisimilitude which art may provide. John Constable's notion of painting as performing experiments in "natural philosophy" is what Kant might have called sensuous representations of indeterminate concepts.[82]

I shall conclude this section with a few final observations on Kant's doctrine of aesthetic form. It might be helpful to begin at the most obvious level—Kant's general way of giving the topography of form. I shall then suggest that the most fruitful way of looking at Kant's doctrine of form is to be extrapolated from the very difficult section in the first *Critique*, on "Schematism."[83] In this regard I shall again call in Gombrich's help, and what he calls "schemata" in the pictorial arts, to illustrate my interpretation of Kant's meaning of artistic form.

Kant divides form into nontemporal and temporal. The former comprises spatial composition and delineation; the latter comprises time structure and poetic or literary composition. Kant speaks of nontemporal forms as those of *Gestalt*, or "figure," and temporal forms as those of *Spiel*, or "play." The form of nontemporal aesthetic objects is perceived intuitively, or at once, but it can be analyzed into further parts. Temporal forms are perceived or understood in judgment discursively, and imagination brings the parts into synthesis. Judging both temporal and nontemporal form requires imagination, as Kant explains in the first *Critique:* "Synthesis in general . . . is the mere result of the power of imagination, a blind but indispensable function in the soul, without which we should have no knowledge whatsoever, but of which we are scarcely ever conscious."[84] The two broad distinctions between the temporal and the spatial arts seem so innocent that no one would take exception to them except, perhaps, because of their emptiness. Let us sort through the various aesthetic usages of "form" to see whether they relate to "figure" and "play."

"Form" sometimes means "shape," of either a mathematically describable surface or a three-dimensional object. Kant makes it clear that shape is not the same thing as aesthetic form, though it may be one of its elements. "One would scarce think it necessary for a man to have taste to take more delight in a circle than in a scrawled outline, in an equilateral and equiangular quadrilateral than in one that is all lob-sided."[85]

"Form" often refers to "fixed form," or a set of rules defining a pattern or structure. In prosody, rules exist for the fixed forms of the villanelle, the Petrarchan sonnet, the ballade; in music there are rules for the sonata, the fugue, the canon. By definition such forms are repeatable; nothing is guaranteed as aesthetic simply because it adheres to one of the "fixed forms." Adhering to the form is a necessary condition of being a good instance of the type but not a sufficient condition for having aesthetic form.

Because Kant has already argued that aesthetic judgment

must be singular, it seems that whatever else "form" entails, it must entail what is peculiar to or individual about the object. If one painting were an exact reproduction of another, then the form of the first would necessarily be identical to that of the second. But even if only minor differences occurred in a set of paintings—like Monet's water lilies—what is true of the form of one does not strictly imply anything about the form of the other paintings in the same set. Though it is often fruitful to compare paintings to discern the different complexities of their structure and organization, what compels perception to linger, in "pure" judgment of taste, is the individuality of the form.

As I pointed out in my discussion of sensation, Kant is not implying that "form" is to be arrived at in the same way that Locke tries to describe an "abstract idea." Kant does not hold that one must set aside sensuous and emotional content of aesthetic judgment and put moral, utilitarian, and theoretical interests into check. If form were arrived at in this way, judgment would be barren, without content. For example, if one abstracted the colors and atmosphere from, say, Watteau's *The Embarkation from the Isle of Cythera*, not even "delineation" would remain. If "delineation"—or "form"—were a tracing or stencil of the Venus mount in the foreground supporting the figures, and the icy peaks in the distance, such a delineation would give a visibility of line alien to Watteau. The "form" would be a falsification of the painting. Though line is graphically visible in the work of a mannerist painter, such as Bronzino's *St. John the Baptist*,[86] painting is obviously not a matter of filling in the delineated "forms" with expendable colors. Rather, it involves grouping color masses, opposing surfaces to other surfaces, and modeling through shade and overtone. Kant implies that form arises out of the interplay of such modes of organization.

A melody in music can survive being changed into another key, but it is not the same melody when any single note is changed. *The Embarkation* obviously cannot survive being repainted monochromatically, nor Mozart's piano sonatas being played by violins, nor the Cathedral of Chartres redone in precast concrete.

It is mistaken to interpret Kant as taking over the hackneyed distinction between form and content, equating the former with structure or delineation, and the latter with sensuous matter. In symbolic logic the forms of propositions and arguments can be abstracted from subject matter, and their various permutations and entailments can be shown. Just as logical relationships, or forms, must hold for any rational being, so aesthetic judgment has an "exemplary validity" based solely on the interplay and structuring of "constants": colors, sounds, or poetic "ideas." This analogy (which is of course mine and not Kant's) must be a guarded one. "Constants" in aesthetic judgment represent both a simplification and a falsification; for though any number of musical compositions may contain the same note (which might be called a "constant"), its musical role depends upon the interplay with its structural positioning with other notes. Again, logical forms are by definition repeatable; however, the peculiarity of interplay in a work of art can be imitated, or redeveloped, but not instantiated, except in the sense of being forged, reproduced, or mass produced.

Kant sometimes prefixes "mere" to "form" to clarify this central term in his aesthetics. "Free beauty" (*pulchritudo vaga*) is free of a concept of what the object must be, or its perfection. "In the estimate of a free beauty (according to mere form) we have the pure judgment of taste."[87] "Dependent beauty" (*pulchritudo adhaerens*) rests upon a notion of what the object ought to be; Kant gives as examples: "the beauty of man (including under this head that of a man, woman, or child), the beauty of a horse . . . presupposes the concept of the end . . . and consequently a concept of its perfection."[88] Kant does not deny that such intellectual or moral ideas may be combined in aesthetic judgment; they must, however, not intrude or subvert the "free beauty." (One remembers Proust's comment that a work of art with a "theme" is like an article with a price tag.) Kant implies, then, that "mere" or "pure" aesthetic form is either what the artist imparts by the workings of his own subjective schematism, or what the perceiver, in aesthetic judgment, recognizes as what would be an expression of his own subjective schematism.

To disentangle the admittedly abstruse claim in the last paragraph, I shall first give a brief account of what I take to be "objective schematism" in the first *Critique*. Although this is generally admitted to be one of Kant's most difficult doctrines, I mean here to develop only the claim that Kant's conception of aesthetic form might be described as "subjective schematism." In the first *Critique*, "schematism" is said to be required both for mathematical concepts that originate in experience, like triangularity, and for "pure" concepts that do not so originate, like causality.[89] Schematism is thus a process or a capacity to spell out categories and concepts into temporal form. A schema is not imagistic, but rather the expression of an ability or capacity to embody formal concepts into constructs or models. Although a pure concept of the understanding cannot, by definition, be pictured or formed into an image, there must be a "bridge" between the entirely empty but meaningful concepts and their application to the phenomenal world. The "transcendental determination of time" provides the link, or scheme, between wholly abstract ideas and the world of experience. Objective knowledge is possible because the pure categories can be translated or schematized by the imagination into the phenomenal:

Although the schemata of sensibility first realize the categories, they at the same time restrict them, that is, limit them to conditions which lie outside the understanding, and are due to sensibility. The schema is, properly, only the phenomenon, or sensible concept, of an object in agreement with the category.[90]

Kant has almost nothing to say of schematism in the third *Critique*, except to repeat that judgments of taste do not unite "understanding and imagination in the estimate of the object so as to give a cognition of the Object, . . . (as in the objective schematism of judgment dealt with in the Critique)."[91] Much later, in the "Analytic of the Sublime," Kant refers again to schematism, as if implying that there is a subjective corollary to the same capacity of schematism discussed in the first *Critique*:

For the imagination, in accordance with laws of association, makes our state of contentment dependent upon physical conditions. But acting in accordance with principles of the schematism of judgment, (consequently so far as it is subordinated to freedom,) it is at the same time an instrument of reason and its ideas."[92]

Kant's "free play" of the imagination appears to involve an image-making or "form-imposing" spontaneity on the part of imagination, not in accordance with determinate concepts, but solely in relation to the subjective feelings of pleasure and displeasure.

To develop this interpretation, I shall again turn to Gombrich's discussion of "schemata," though with the important proviso that I understand Gombrich to be engaged in psychology of perception, or what might be called "phenomenology of perception." I do not intend to strain here to maintain a radical difference between such forms of enquiry and Kant's "critical" or "transcendental" methods.

Because most of my discussion in this section has been from the beholder's point of view, it is only fair to begin with Gombrich's description of the artist's use of schemata. "Every artist has to know and construct a schema before he can adjust it to the needs of portrayal,"[93] though an artist need not be enslaved by the schemata developed by other artists. But the "artist who copies will always tend to build up the image from the schemata he has learned to handle."[94] Gombrich maintains that artists owe much more to one another's styles and schemata than they do to what might be hypostatized as "Nature." (A similar description of the history of philosophy was implied by G. E. Moore, when he commented that he had received most of the impetus of his own philosophy from the errors of other philosophers rather than from reality.) Even the most creative artist, so Gombrich maintains, "must have a starting point, a standard of comparison, in order to begin that process of making and matching which finally becomes embodied in the finished image. The artist cannot start from scratch but he can criticize his forerunners."[95]

The artist begins with his idea or concept of what a thing or expression is like, in a "pure" but barren way, and then proceeds to embody it, as if the capacity of "in-forming" or "schematizing" gave vent to artistic activity. Describing the artist, Gombrich says: "He begins not with his visual impression but with his idea or concept: the German artist with his concept of a castle that he applies as well as he can to that individual castle."[96] The artist, like the lawyer or the statistician, must look at the individual case "within the network of a schematic form."[97] The individual is thus assimilated into one's own schemata.

As for mistakes in judgmental perception, Gombrich attributes some of them to lack of schemata: "What I called the pathology of portrayal, the curious mistakes made by copyists and topographic artists, often turned out to be due to the lack of a schema."[98] Connecting his own conception of "schematism" with Sir Karl Popper's philosophical methods, Gombrich describes the self-correctiveness of artistic schemata: "Now in looking for regularities, for a framework or *schema* on which we can at least provisionally rely (though we may have to modify it for ever), the only possible strategy is to proceed from simple assumptions."[99]

Gombrich's central thesis is not only that the artist must be in possession of schemata, but that the beholder must also possess them even for "ordinary" or day-to-day perception. "The child—it is argued—does not look at trees; he is satisfied with the conceptual schema of a tree that fails to correspond to any reality since it does not embody the characteristics of, say, birch or beech, let alone those of individual trees." He adds: "All art originates in the human mind in our reactions to the world rather than in the visible world itself, and it is precisely because all art is 'conceptual' that all representations are recognizable by their style."[100]

If, however, schemata are required by both "ordinary" and aesthetic judgment, it might appear that only a matter of degree distinguishes the two: aesthetic judgment requires more of the beholder and gives him a greater or more complex visual field for what Kant calls "free play of the imagination." Gombrich implies that part of the difference between "ordinary" and aesthetic judgment does rest upon what is required of the beholder:

The limits of likeness imposed by the medium and the schema, the links in image making between form and function, most of all, the analysis of the beholder's share in the resolution of ambiguities will alone make plausible the bald statement that art has a history because the illusions of art are not only the fruit but the indispensable tools for the artist's analysis of appearances.[101]

Gombrich distinguishes between diagrammatic or scientific illustrations and schemata. Instancing a diagram of the muscles of the neck from Gray's *Anatomy*, Gombrich makes the observation that scientific illustration succeeds "in packing more correct visual information into the image than even a photograph contains."[102] The suggestion might be that scientific diagrams give highly condensed objective knowledge, whereas the aesthetic use of schemata rests upon the intersubjective feelings of pleasure and displeasure. What Kant calls "pure" beauty or *pulchritudo vaga* seems to be a conscious attempt, at least in the fine arts, to exclude "determinate concepts." Gombrich writes that "the very laws of proportion and style that held the schemata of beauty together in past centuries may have served this additional aim of preventing too much life from entering the artist's creations."[103]

It is perhaps not implausible to construe Kant's doctrine of aesthetic form as the subjective employment of schemata, or schematism as related to the feelings of pleasure and displeasure. But because such feelings form the basis of Kant's entire aesthetic, I shall now turn to Kant's doctrine of pleasure.

The Hedonic Assumptions of the Kantian Aesthetic

The difficulty of examining one of Kant's central theses—that aesthetic judgment and the feeling of pleasure and displeasure are conceptually linked—arises from the general difficulty of asserting anything whatsoever of philosophical interest about pleasure. Kant is hardly the first philosopher to found his aesthetics upon hedonic considerations. Aristotle, for example, assigns the pleasures of mimesis and catharsis a major role in the *Poetics*. Both St. Augustine and St. Thomas refer to the peculiarly aesthetic delight in harmony and clarity, fullness and expression. The Thomistic definition of beauty as what pleases upon being seen (*"Pulchra enim dicuntur quae visa placent"*)[104] is both too well known and too frequently restated, though with modifications, to require elaboration here. A history of aesthetics could be written on the sole leitmotif of pleasure, though such is not my intention here.

Kant nowhere attempts an explication of his conception of

pleasure. In *The Metaphysical Elements of Justice,* he implies that little can be said about the feeling of pleasure, because it reveals nothing in the object, but only marks out a relation between subject and object.[105] After mentioning that pleasure sometimes follows as the effect of an activity and is sometimes dependent upon an antecedent desire, Kant defines "feeling" as the capacity of experiencing pleasure or pain when a mental representation is present. Kant holds that to say anything further about pleasure or pain leads to empirical descriptions of the consequences of pleasure and pain in certain relations. In his *Anthropology from a Pragmatic Point of View,* Kant describes such effects and aspects of pleasure, as well as the "feeling of the beautiful," which he discusses in the Second Book, entitled *The Feeling of Pleasure and Displeasure.* The subtitle of the section concerned with the aesthetic bears the revealing title "Concerning the Feeling for the Beautiful, that is, the Partly Sensuous, Partly Intellectual Pleasure in the Reflective Judgment, of Taste." [106] Beyond reaffirming his contention, already propounded in the third *Critique,* that aesthetic judgment possesses exemplary validity good for all persons, and that taste is the capacity so to judge, Kant makes no further attempt to explicate pleasure. In Part One of the third *Critique,* he invokes pleasure and displeasure at every turn of his exposition. His claims are both so various and so central to his philosophical account of the aesthetic that I shall proceed through them, step by step.

1. Sensations, Kant clearly states, may give rise to pleasurable feelings; however, they must be called not "disinterested" feelings of pleasure, but merely "agreeable." Though Kant says little about "agreeable" sensations in the third *Critique,* it would be generally conceded, I believe, that persons "have" such sensations: that is, we passively undergo them or passively enjoy them. Hearing pleasant sounds, smelling agreeable odors, or seeing pleasant colors involves undergoing or succumbing to something from which pleasure is passively derived. Though pleasure and pain are often conceived as opposites, "pain" more frequently designates sensations, such as back pain or headache, than does "pleasure." Physical sensations may be described as "spasmodic" or "persistent." Rarely, however, is pleasure a sensation in the sense of being

localizable or temporal. In playing a musical composition one might describe one's state as one of enjoyment, but rarely as "having a pleasant sensation." If there were a difficult trill or figure one had tried to execute, one might have a "pleasant sensation" at the moment that one finally achieved its execution. At such a point a certain localizable pleasure might occur—a tingle down the spine, an involuntary smile, an electric shock passing under the scalp. Such pleasant sensations might last for only a short period and could be located in time.

When Kant speaks of "agreeable sensations," however, it is clear from his examples that agreeable pleasures are not specifically sensations, any more than displeasures are specifically bodily pains.[107] Though sensations of pleasure and displeasure can be extremely acute—sexual orgasm or appendicitis—Kant is not describing such a continuum of sensations when he argues, in an important passage in "The Analytic of the Sublime," that all the workings of imagination and understanding may be related to the feelings of pleasure and pain:

There is no denying the fact that all representations within us, no matter whether they are objectively merely sensible or wholly intellectual, are still subjectively associable with gratification or pain, however imperceptible either of these may be. . . . We must even admit that, as Epicurus maintained, *gratification* and *pain* though proceeding from the imagination or even from representations of the understanding, are always in the last resort corporeal, since apart from any feeling of the bodily organ life would be merely a consciousness of one's existence, and could not include any feeling of well-being or the reverse.[108]

Though one might be aware of only an "imperceptible" painful sensation, or even put such a sensation "out of one's mind," the sensation would still be present in a certain part of the body. Such a sensation would have continued even though one had refocused one's attention. But "getting pleasure or displeasure from something" is not the same as "having" or "undergoing" certain pleasant or unpleasant sensations. Kant's brief discussion of the "agreeable" leads to another member of the hedonic family.

2. Getting pleasure or displeasure from something has an active ring to it, as if, to use Kantian terms, the powers of imagina-

tion were being called upon and the understanding were in active play. It might be helpful to distinguish two different sorts of "getting pleasure or displeasure," though this distinction is not explicitly made in the third *Critique*. First, some sorts of "getting pleasure from something" involve deriving satisfaction from something; for example, many persons obviously derive satisfaction from utilitarian pursuits, or what Kant calls in section four of the third *Critique* "the useful."[109] But pleasure might also be gotten from something, in the sense of deriving satisfaction from it, that is intellectual in aim. What may be of importance to notice is that "getting satisfaction from" and "taking aesthetic pleasure in" seem to be in friction or incompatible. The natural picture of "getting or deriving satisfaction" from listening to music would be, I submit, the picture of someone personally involved—say economically, or by way of family pride—in listening to the music. Getting pleasure in the sense of deriving satisfaction seems to imply an antecedent desire craving to be satisfied, or a need in search of fulfillment. Whatever Kant's final conception of "disinterested pleasure" may be, his meaning does not involve notions of antecedent need or desire requiring active manipulation of the environment to be satisfied.

A second sort of "getting pleasure from something" differs from the sort just described only in being wholly "imperceptible," that is, subconscious. For example, perversely subconscious satisfactions might seem odd because they are not "felt," and a pleasure unfelt seems a contradiction in terms. What I shall call "the subconscious pleasures of satisfaction" are clearly not "disinterested," in Kant's sense, for the same reasons just given concerning conscious kinds of "getting pleasure" or satisfaction from something.

3. A third member of the hedonic family might be "having a sense of accomplishment," say physical, intellectual, or artistic. Such a sense of accomplishment is pleasurable, but the pleasure is grammatically described in the past tense: "having a sense of" is the culmination of past activities and accomplishments. Kant's description of the sense of human dignity, and of one's superiority to the demands of phenomenal Nature as evinced in the sublime,[110] seems to be an instance of the pleasures of "having a sense of ac-

complishment." Accomplishment, if genuine, is predictive: the accomplished will tend to act in the future in the same manner. No one would deny that artists might have the pleasures of accomplishment; but Kant's "disinterested pleasure," linked as it is to "pure" will, or to the absence of any particular interest, is fundamentally different from the pleasures of accomplishment. Delight might be taken in the forms of technical prowess, but Kant would maintain that such delight involves a standard of perfection. It might not be exaggerated to say that by excluding what I have called the pleasures of accomplishment or virtuosity, Kant relocates much of the artist's pleasure in his craft, as well as much of the beholder's pleasure. Yet, in Kant's favor, it would not generally be held that pleasure in aesthetic form is the same as pleasure taken in artistic accomplishment.

4. Another kind of pleasure, about which Kant has strong views in the third *Critique,* might be described as "entertaining pleasurable feelings about." Kant is as fervid in excluding "mere" sensation as he is in condemning "mere" emotion, or what I have called "entertaining pleasurable feelings about." Kant is at his most stern when he says: "Emotion—a sensation where an agreeable feeling is produced merely by means of a momentary check followed by a more powerful outpouring of the vital force—is quite foreign to beauty. . . . A pure judgment of taste, has, then, for its determining ground neither charm nor emotion."[111]

What Kant condemns is sentimentality in art: the limply pathetic, the maudlin, the self-indulgences of nostalgia and romanticism. Kant separates "pure" aesthetic judgment from personal and adventitious evocations that art might summon up in the beholder. In the "Analytic of the Sublime," Kant catalogues various sorts of such "affections":

On the other hand, affection of the LANGUID TYPE (which converts the very effort of resistance into an object of displeasure (*animus languidus*)) has nothing noble about it, though it may take its rank as possessing beauty of the sensuous order. Hence the *emotions* capable of attaining the strength of an affection are very diverse. We have *spirited*, and we have *tender* emotions. When the strength of the latter reaches that of an affection they can be turned to no account. The propensity to indulge in them is sentimentality.[112]

What I have called "entertaining pleasurable feelings about" might be described better by drawing an obvious distinction between feelings expressed and feelings evoked by art. It is feelings of the latter sort that Kant inveighs against in the passage just quoted. Kant does not draw the distinction between expressed and evoked feelings, but it is hardly at variance with his doctrine of "pure" aesthetic judgment to do so.[113]

A melody can be melancholy without the composer's being so when he composes it: music is neither autobiography nor confession. Though art might be revelatory of the artist's emotions, it can be expressive without expressing his own emotions, just as it can express without evoking emotion in the beholder. Art can of course stir up feelings, such as patriotism, religious fervor, or social protest. But evoking or causing an emotion, pleasurable or otherwise, or playing upon the emotions, leads to "entertaining feelings about"; perceiving the expression of a painting is like understanding the expression of a face. Though short shrift must not be given to the complexities of aesthetic perception, my present purpose is only to point out that Kant's exclusion of evoked feelings from "pure" aesthetic judgment does not entail that such judgment is therefore devoid of expression. Kant's doctrine of art as moral symbol closely links expression to the aesthetic.[114] Expressed feelings seem to be a type of representation. As Gombrich remarks: "With the question of personal style we have reached the frontier of what is usually called representation. For in these ultimate constituents the artist is said to express himself. But is there really such a sharp division between representation and expression? The results of our last chapter have made us doubt it."[115]

5. In the passage just cited from the "Analytic of the Sublime" in which Kant defines "sentimentality," he points to yet a further member of the hedonic family. After describing "romances, maudlin dramas, shallow homilies, which trifle with so-called (though falsely so) noble sentiments,"[116] Kant writes of the feeling of "respect for the worth of humanity in our own person and the rights

of men (which is something quite other than their happiness)."[117] Such respect belongs to what he calls "beauty of mental temperament."[118] If such feelings are thus linked with the beautiful, it follows that they are linked with pleasure, given Kant's aesthetic theory. From Kant's description, such pleasure might be called "feeling just contentment with" something. Such serenity of feeling is difficult to describe further, except that it need not be linked to any of the other types of pleasure already mentioned. Such pleasure seems to require personal commitment to a particular world view or *Weltanschauung*. Thus, Kant's moral theory might form the basis of such pleasure that gives "calm of mind all passion spent."

6. Kant would evidently distinguish such pleasure from happiness, which marks another hedonic type. The pleasure of happiness might be described as "feeling good" or "having a sense of well-being." One is tempted to describe (6) as *eudaimonia*, except that "feeling good" or "having a sense of well-being" might be illusory or not rooted in reality, for example, in drug-induced euphoria or the self-created happiness of delusion. At least the Aristotelian *eudaimonia* is a permanent activity, based upon the moral and intellectual virtues. The pleasure of "feeling good," however, need not imply pleasures of type (5), nor need (5) imply (6). (5) would involve what Kant calls in his pre-Critical ethics true or genuine happiness that must "be derived from an *a priori* basis approved by reason." Pleasure of type (5) has intrinsic value, for its "inherent value consists of the fact that it is we who creatively produce it . . . it brings with it self-sufficiency."[119]

7. Kant seems to claim that "disinterested pleasure" is common and peculiar to aesthetic judgment. Before turning to this claim, however, I submit that "disinterested pleasure" is a type of a larger hedonic species which might be characterized as "taking pleasure in" something. Such pleasure demands activity of or participation from imagination and understanding. Kant's theory of the free play of the imagination in accordance with indeterminate concepts appears to indicate that what distinguishes "disinterested pleasure" from other types of (7) is that they require the active employment of determinate concepts. Kant might intend that non-

aesthetic pleasures of type (7) require precise concepts or procedures; for example, the pleasures taken in playing or watching an elaborate game, like chess; or the pleasures taken in solving puzzles or intellectual problems. The implication seems to be that "disinterested" or aesthetic pleasure is of type (7), but that imagination and understanding enjoy a kind of freedom not present in any other pleasure of type (7). At the same time, "disinterested pleasure" does not degenerate into pleasure of type (1)—the merely agreeable, or of type (4)—the emotional. "Disinterested pleasure" is markedly not of type (2)—the pleasures of deriving satisfaction, or of (3)—pleasures of achievement. "Disinterested pleasure" seems to have in common with type (5) intrinsic value, though for Kant only the good will has absolute or noncontingent goodness. "Disinterested pleasure" also shares with (5) a kind of universal validity, which Kant tries to establish, it will be remembered, in the fourth "moment" of the "Analytic of the Beautiful." What sharply distinguishes "disinterested pleasure" from type (5) is that the former lays claim to subjective, while the latter, to objective universality.

Kant's "disinterested pleasure" might be further linked with type (5), for at the end of Part One of the third *Critique*, Kant argues that "only when sensibility is brought into harmony with moral feeling can genuine taste assume a definite unchangeable form."[120] Equally, it appears that "disinterested pleasure" might be part of type (6) but need not be; "being happy" or "having a sense of well-being" might include, as one of its constituents, "aesthetic pleasure." Kant implies that pleasures taken in the fine arts, and in Nature, is part of genuine humanity, or the "*social spirit* of mankind, in contradistinction to the narrow life of the lower animals."[121]

For Kant, aesthetic judgment is itself pleasant or unpleasant; that is, aesthetic judging, given that it involves the free play of the cognitive faculties, is itself a pleasurable activity. Judgments of the aesthetically ugly or grotesque, considered as positive traits, simply exhibit a certain piquancy of pleasure. Aesthetic judgment of actual displeasure would exhibit pain felt at the inept, the shabby, the defective, or the frigid. Judging or perceiving figure or interplay of color, sound, movement, or idea—as in poetry and the novel—is itself pleasurable.

Kant does not need to maintain that such pleasure is sharply conscious in judgment; he might have made use of Leibniz's suggestion that many perceptions or feelings are below the threshold of consciousness. Leibniz argued that subliminal consciousness, or what he called *"les petites perceptions,"* forms the basis of certain types of pleasure:

Music charms us, although its beauty only consists in the harmonies of numbers and in the reckoning of the beats or vibrations of sounding bodies, which meet at certain intervals, reckonings of which we are not conscious and which the soul nevertheless does make. The pleasures which sight finds in proportions are of the same nature.[122]

As a complement to Kant's conception of "disinterested pleasure," I might suggest the notion of a continuum of pleasure, ranging from purely passive sensation to the full and determinate employment of the understanding. I do not need to add that such a continuum is nowhere to be found in Kant's writings on aesthetics; but before turning to a critical appraisal of his claim that the aesthetic must be hedonic and a construal of this crucial "must be," I shall attempt a brief restatement of the Kantian theme of the free play of imagination and understanding.

In reveries, drugged states, and even hallucinations, quasi-aesthetic experience sometimes occurs; a distance obtains between ourselves and the state we are undergoing, as if the experience belonged to someone else. Such experience is often intense and sensual—the stuff of unformed or undisciplined art. In such states one might feel aesthetic delight and exuberance in colors, sounds, textures, or odors. To speak in a Kantian way, no determinate concepts or rules discipline or regulate such judgment. The experience flows, convolutes, reaches heights, and then dissipates into nothingness, leaving behind neither form nor structure. Such experience might be placed on the borderline between clearly aesthetic experience of the fine arts and purely passive sensation, which completely lacks form.

At the active end of the hedonic continuum from nonconcepts

to concepts, lies what might be called determinate pleasure. Art with "a message," ideological or tendentious art, imposes a strict and unwavering interpretation upon the mind. The Kantian "disinterested pleasure," however, lies between the two extremes. Imagination is not permitted vagaries of self-absorption but is disciplined by the form of the object, which both allows and fosters free play of the cognitive faculties.

There is a sense in which art can be so bad that it is not really art. Apart from the obvious reason of technical awkwardness, the Kantian meaning of "bad art" would seem to be art that imposes a particular concept, or stereotype, upon the cognitive faculties: the object can be identified or "seen as" one and only one sort of thing. Characters, for example, degenerate into mere caricatures; the musical theme is only heartbreak or sentimental response. "Kitsch" art demands nothing from the beholder, but "informs" him what to feel and perceive.

At the nonconceptual end of the continuum, imagination is so unformed and directionless that though certain sensations might be intensely enjoyable, they can only be ordered in a linearly temporal way. There is no criterion of fittingness or rightness of sequence. The criteria of structure and correctness, anticipation and resolution, tension and harmony do not obtain in the pleasures of sensation and admit of only a limited application in borderline aesthetic judgment like wine tasting and cuisine.

Whatever my suggestions about such a hedonic continuum might be worth, let us now examine Kant's claim concerning the necessary relationship between aesthetic judgment and the hedonic. Even taking into account that many eighteenth-century philosophers wrote of "pleasure and pain" in a way that closely parallels the contemporary usage of "likes and dislikes," it appears that it is always an open question whether someone is interested in an object aesthetically because he believes that he does or will take such pleasure in it. It also seems to be an open question whether someone aesthetically judging also likes the object, or dislikes it, or remains indifferent to it. Whether the motive or reason for engaging in judgment was hedonic (in any of the seven senses previously distinguished in this section) seems also a matter that cannot be decided a priori or prejudged. Like many other objects in the world, a work of art can hold the attention without likes or dislikes being summoned to the scene. It is not that there is anything wrong with pleasure; most people wish they had more of it. It is simply that aesthetic judgment is broader than feeling pleasure or displeasure; judgments of aesthetic mediocrity or indifference are no less aesthetic judgments for being concerned with what is neither pleasurable nor unpleasurable. Moreover, aesthetic judgment is often engaged in discernment or detection just as much as in enjoyment and delectation. If one is interested in something—even "disinterested" in Kant's sense—it does not necessarily follow that one must be interested hedonically, even allowing for the wide range of pleasure already described.

Although it is clear that aesthetic pleasure or displeasure admits of degree and might be extreme or minute, there is a neutral point at which one is neither pleased nor displeased: one neither likes nor dislikes the object. It would seem that Kant must exclude such judgment from the aesthetic. Moreover, he appears to rule out the possibility of neutral feeling entirely: "There is no denying the fact that all representations within us, no matter whether they are objectively merely sensible or wholly intellectual, are still subjectively associable with gratification or pain, however imperceptible either of these may be."[123] If "associable" here means "may be so associated," Kant's claim is true, though not startling; if "associable" means "must be so associated," that is, that the final explanation of human motivation and interest must be broadly hedonic, then his claim seems false. For if it is an open question whether someone did what he did, or judged as he did, because the hedonic was an ultimate factor, then it would seem to follow that though aesthetic judgment often involves likes and dislikes, it need not conceptually do so.

The most obvious characteristic of the fine arts is their diversity: one is interested in or intrigued by one painting for one reason, and interested in another painting because of something quite different. Though no one could deny that paintings often exhibit striking similarities, it appears that if Kant's claim concerning the aesthetic and the hedonic were true, then the extraordinary diversity of aesthetic judgment—even with the stipulation that such judgment is "pure"—must be subsumed under "disinterested pleasure." At this point, however, "pure" aesthetic judgment appears to be defined in terms of "disinterested pleasure" taken solely in aesthetic form. Many a reader might have an uneasy feeling of circularity.

Kant's view that pleasure is a kind of feeling, or a characteristic defining a kind of feeling, was common among eighteenth-century philosophers who divided the mind into three "faculties" of cognition, will, and feeling. As is evident merely from the fact that each of the three *Critiques* bears a direct relation to one of the three "faculties," Kant adopted the same tripartite scheme developed by earlier German philosophers such as A. G. Baumgarten and Moses Mendelssohn. Their general view of pleasure was that it is an "element" of consciousness immediately felt simply because it is such an element, and that it cannot be analyzed into constituent parts. A felt pleasure, as opposed to the physiological sensation that might be its basis or support, is like a felt warmth, a heard sound, or a perceived color: each must be directly experienced to be known; in Kant's language, judgment must include an empirical intuition of each for knowledge of it to be possible. It is clear that Kant in no way equates pleasure with sensation.[124] Pleasure might "attach itself" to sensation just as readily as to any of the other six types of the hedonic distinguished in this section. Thus, Kant would admit that pleasure could attach itself to "things" as different as the color green and a sense of one's own moral worth or dignity. Though no pleasure is free floating, the ways in which pleasures are related to their "objects" are as different as the model of stimulus-response is from Kant's model of "free play of the cognitive faculties."

What Kant calls "the key to the Critique of taste" in the "Analytic of the Beautiful"[125] is the answer to the question: does taking pleasure follow from or precede judgment of taste? If the pleasure taken in an object were the basis of aesthetic judgment, then, so Kant argues, such judgment could not lay claim to universality. But, given that aesthetic judgment is a kind of belief, it makes an implicit commitment for all persons constituted like ourselves. Just as the possibility of learning language depends upon the shared universal capacity for communication, and just as the validity of moral law postulates the priority of the good will, so aesthetic judgment postulates a certain kind of mental state for which all persons have the capacity. The pleasure taken in such a state, that is, the "free play of the cognitive faculties," is logically consequent to "pure" aesthetic judgment.

In the first *Critique*, Kant distinguishes two cognitive faculties: imagination, or the faculty of gathering together the disparate elements given through sensation; and understanding, or the faculty of unifying the representations into concepts. In practical and theoretical reason, the imagination is brought under determinate rules or concepts; in mere passive enjoyment of sensation, no determinate concepts of the understanding are employed, though the imagination, as the servile gatherer of sensation, must be at work. The imagination and the understanding must be generally harmonious or compatible, or knowledge would be impossible. In cognition, imagination is held in bondage by concepts; in mere passive sensation, the imagination is given no free play: it simply gathers in the sensible manifold. In aesthetic judgment, given that the object is "pure" form or the interplay of figure or "play," the faculties are put out of gear, so to speak, and are allowed to idle freely. Gombrich describes this "state" in a highly Kantian way: "Our twin nature, poised between animality and rationality, finds expression in that twin world of symbolism with its willing suspension of disbelief."[126] Such a state is described by Kant as "pure," by which he means that neither sensation, nor emotion, nor determinate interests are represented. Such a "state" is therefore free of ordinary impingements upon judgment; the resulting free play of the two faculties is pleasurable:

The cognitive powers brought into play by this representation are engaged in a free play, since no definite concept restricts them to a particular rule of cognition. Hence the mental state in this representation must be one of a feeling of the free play of the powers of representation in a given representation for a cognition in general.[127]

Human beings are at least individuals in the sense that each has his own nervous system. Each person, therefore, has his own pleasures, though he might be either vaguely or intimately related with the pleasures of someone else. Kant's argument in section 9 and elsewhere assumes that it makes sense to speak of persons' having "the same pleasure," and in aesthetic judgment, the same "disinterested pleasure." Kant seems to assume that aesthetic pleasure cannot be based upon sensation or emotion, for it is empirically apparent that person's reactions to sensational and emotional stimuli are conditioned by their own constitutions, as well as by conventions of society, and even by their individual caprices. But judgment of "pure" form is not so conditioned. Kant would conclude, then, that the capacity of "disinterested pleasure" rests upon the a priori forms of cognition and the *sensus communis*.

In the previous section, concerning Kant's doctrine of form, I tried to show the relevance of work such as Gombrich's in the theory of aesthetic perception to Kant's doctrine of aesthetic judgment. It is clear that Kant does not intend the "mental state" of free play to be construed empirically. But beyond giving the topography of the hedonic in Kant's aesthetics, I would exceed the confines of this study by examining the claims of gestalt theories of aesthetic judgment and perception.

The Possibility of Erroneous Aesthetic Judgment

Unless one adopted a radical scepticism concerning aesthetic judgment, one would assume that, like any other kind of judgment, it must be either true or false, well or ill founded. It is clear that Kant believes aesthetic judgment or belief to be a kind of knowledge claim. Given Kant's analysis of aesthetic judgment as I have so far expounded and interpreted it, I should now like to ask whether such judgment could be erroneous. How can a "pure" aesthetic judgment, as defined by the four "moments" of the beautiful, be mistaken?

I shall begin with the most trivial cause: mere verbal confusion. Independent of all succor from philosophical theory, someone might not know how to use "work of art" or "beautiful" or some other word characteristic of aesthetic discourse. Such a mistake would not reveal an error in aesthetic judgment, but rather an ineptness in language. Again, a simple mistake might result from using the wrong name or title of a work. More to the point would be mistakes arising from reference to the sensuous or emotional aspects of art. Judgment might seem aesthetic, though upon scrutiny it concerns only the emotional or sensuous import. Again, these are trivial, though Kantian, ways of making a mistaken aesthetic judgment.

Perhaps a more interesting source of error follows from Kant's distinction between *pulchritudo vaga* and *pulchritudo adhaerens*, or "pure" and "dependent" beauty. The former presupposes no concept of what the object judged actually is or ought to be, whereas the latter depends upon criteria of perfection. Judgments about flowers, arabesques, musical fantasies, and filigree, Kant says, do not rest upon determinate concepts: we are content with contemplating the exuberant confusions of Nature or the orderly vagaries of imagination. When we judge of the beauty of a man, a horse, or a church (to use Kant's examples), we employ criteria of definite purpose and perfection. Thus aesthetic judgment might err, Kant warns, by confounding the two sorts of beauty:

This distinction enables us to settle many disputes about beauty on the part of critics; for we may show them how one side is dealing with free beauty, and the other with that which is dependent: the former passing a pure judgment of taste, the latter one that is applied intentionally.[128]

One wonders whether this kind of mistake is often made; in a sense one wishes that it were made more frequently, so that expectations of what a thing should be were not satisfied. A church (to take Kant's example again) must look one way, a public building another. Although one would not want to tamper seriously with the beauty of the human form, still the conventional distinctions between the sexes can often be a source of tedium. There is no reason to assume that essences or determinate concepts must shape aesthetic judgment, for such concepts are often no more than atrophied conventions, or reveal the lapses of creativity in search of new expression. However this might be, confusion of "pure" with "dependent" beauty is a confusion of reference: such judgment is mistaken because it is based upon mere sensation, emotion, utility, morality, or—to use the rationalist term of Wolff and Baumgarten—perfection. Judgment of "dependent" beauty is disguised intellectual judgment of perfection.

Another source of error follows from Kant's distinction between "autonomy" and "heteronomy" of taste. Taste must be "autonomous," for it is not worth having if it is not one's own; genuine aesthetic judgment must be based on one's own sensibilities. When we permit someone to take over our moral conscience, we forfeit our dignity; and when we permit someone to dictate our taste, we lose part of our individuality. "Hence it follows that the highest model, the archetype of taste, is a mere idea, which each person must beget in his own consciousness, and according to which he must form his estimate of everything that is an Object of taste, or that is an example of critical taste, and even of universal taste itself." [129]

Heteronomy of taste is always a report upon other persons' sensibilities, for example, those of a great critic. Kant refers in this regard to Lessing and Batteux, and leaves unmentioned "critics of even greater fame." [130] He doubtless intends Aristotle and Horace. Most forms of heteronomy are based upon what is accepted by someone of note who holds sway over the socio-aesthetic scene; other forms of heteronomy draw their strength fom a small elite or coterie, like "*le petit noyeau*" of Proust's Madame Verdurin.

Other than by what I have called verbal mistakes, confusions of reference, and heteronomy of taste, it is difficult to understand how Kant could explain erroneous aesthetic judgment. Although the varieties of aesthetic heteronomy are vast, they do not account for what seems to be the greatest source of mistaken aesthetic judgment: ignorance. Because Kant maintains that aesthetic judgment cannot be based upon determinate concepts (which include concepts of style, school, and genre), he places himself in what seems to be a paradox. On the one hand, if aesthetic judgment concerned, for example, the styles of Florentine or Sienese painting in the Renaissance, or the subtle changes in figure-painting in ancient Greek pottery, then such judgment would be, for Kant, not "pure," but either technical or even theoretical judgment. In effect, any judgment based upon definite or determinate knowledge of artistic style or manners of composition, in any of the fine arts, would involve judgment of "dependent beauty." On the other hand, if aesthetic judgment is "pure," based solely upon form and indeterminate concepts, then the possibility of error would seem to be confined to one of the three sources mentioned above. If determinate concepts were not required in aesthetic judgment, the danger of confusing form with subjective mood and feeling might become all the greater.

It seems obvious that much aesthetic pleasure, as described in the previous section, depends intimately upon knowledge: discernment of style, of historical influence, and of pattern of composition. Kant is undoubtedly correct in saying that "hardly any one but a botanist knows the true nature of a flower, and even he, while recognizing in the flower the reproductive organ of the plant, pays no attention to this natural end when using his taste to judge of its beauty."[131] To use Kantian language, only highly indeterminate concepts are required for judgment of natural beauties; but aesthetic judgment more frequently requires knowing artistic conventions, having conceptual anticipations, and being familiar with the historical period in which the work was produced.

Kant would concede that aesthetic judgment of "dependent beauty" does involve determinate concepts, or definite standards of perfection; therefore, "nonpure" aesthetic judgment may be erroneous because of inadequate or false belief. The question might arise, nevertheless, whether aesthetic judgment of "free beauty" might not be erroneous in some way other than the three already mentioned.

Given that "pure" aesthetic judgment must be founded solely upon "disinterested pleasure" and form, it might be asked whether such pleasure be known by introspection or reflection. Introspection, however, is hardly an infallible avenue to self-knowledge. We have no privileged access to our actions simply because they are our own; we might dissimulate our motives to ourselves as well as to the world. Yet the feeling of pleasure is not ordinarily the type of "mental datum" that demands introspection to be known. "Introspecting" one's pleasure might arise when it is a question of forbidden pleasure or of perverse satisfactions derived from what either society, or one's own moral standards, or both, condemn. Again, anxiety might be "introspected," but either as genuine moral guilt or as neurotic restlessness. Yet Kant describes aesthetic judgment as "reflective." It is apparent that he does not mean "introspecting" feelings of pleasure, but simply subsuming a particular representation under the feelings of pleasure and displeasure. One might doubt *whether* one feels a certain feeling, when it is a feeling so ambiguous that we are incapable of describing or "giving a face" to it. One might need to introspect such feelings further. Still, errors attributable to self-deception evidently form a class quite distinct from errors of aesthetic judgment of "free" beauty, or, for that matter, of "dependent" beauty as well.

In the *Foundations of the Metaphysics of Morals*, as I have already noted, Kant states that "it is in fact absolutely impossible by experience to discern with complete certainty a single case in which the maxim of an action, however much it may conform to duty, rested solely on moral grounds and on the conception of one's duty."[132] Although Kant maintains that certain knowledge of complex states of affairs in the physical world is possible, as well as certain knowledge of human behavior, yet the "strictest examination" of our own motives can never lead to the absolute certainty that our motive was the "pure" good will. "A secret impulse of self-love"[133] might always mislead us into self-deception. Acting out of a pure sense of duty is the sole ideal of ethical worth; it could be instantiated only if it could be known that respect for the moral law was the sole motive of action. Introspection, however, can never afford such absolute certainty.

I suggest that a similar explanation of the source of error may be given for "pure" aesthetic judgment, although Kant does not himself draw the parallel. The restriction of "pure" aesthetic judgment to form is an ideal that may be approached in perception, though one can never be certain that any perception or judgment is free from all empirical admixture. Just as Kant describes inclinations and the "promptings of self-love" as impediments to the pure sense of duty, so he describes sensations, emotions, and determinate concepts as hindrances to pure judgment of form. Although Kant opposes inclination to duty, and the sensuous to form, he does not, I believe, systematically pit "self-love" against duty; for though one's immediate interests sometimes collide with those of others, on the whole most interests of the individual are socially interwoven with those of other persons. It is only the idiosyncratic or isolated case that pits private interest against public.

Though Kant nowhere says that aesthetic form is the analogue of moral duty, still the parallels between the two, both as pure ideals and as universally binding, are striking. Again, just as introspection of motives might well disclose motives other than duty, so reexamination of the aesthetic object might disclose much that is gratuitous and sensuous rather than formal.

CHAPTER 3

The Analysis of the Sublime

The Distinguishing Characteristics and Presuppositions of the Kantian Sublime

A twentieth-century reader might ask, with a certain smile, whether the sublime really needs an analysis. Such a reader might even wonder what sublimity is, and whether it can be spoken of in a general philosophical manner. Kant, however, along with many other philosophers of the eighteenth century, thought that sublimity could and should be explicated, for the concept was held to contain much of both ethical and aesthetic importance. But as an aesthetic category with roots in our own culture, the sublime seems largely irrelevant. There still remain persons who profess to find sublimity in Nature—the ocean wracked by a storm, mountains looming in the distance, and the stars in their infinitude; such phenomena also struck Kant with great awe. In an early pre-Critical work, *Theory of the Heavens*, he gives vent to a passionate aside, which cannot but surprise anyone with a stereotyped conception of Kant as the dry, pedantic Pietist of Königsburg:

When we follow the Phoenix of Nature, which burns only in order to revive again in restored youth from its ashes, through all the infinity of times and spaces . . . in order to fill eternity as well as all the regions of space with her wonders, then the spirit . . . sinks into profound astonishment. But unsatisfied even yet with this immense object, whose transitoriness cannot adequately satisfy the soul, the mind wished to obtain a closer knowledge of that being whose Intelligence and Greatness is the source of all . . . and with what reverence must not the soul regard even its own being, [which] . . . is destined to survive all these transformations.[1]

It appears that the more Nature is explored and understood, the less mysterious she becomes; the less mysterious, the less inclined we are to refer to Nature as more than can be described by purely mechanical laws. "She" becomes "it," and Nature is reduced to a vast set of elements and relationships. In the passage just quoted, however, it is evident that Kant fully subscribed to the scientific principles of a universal mechanics as described by Newton. The passage also reveals a highly romantic conception of Nature, which Kant was not to develop in detail until the third *Critique*. This conception implies that because Nature cannot account for the moral ends of mankind, Nature must be a kind of visible symbol occasioning feelings of the sublime. The aesthetic-moral category of the sublime leads ultimately to a moral proof of God's existence, as well as of the existence of a soul "destined to survive all these transformations." Even in his pre-Critical writings, Kant never opposes scientific knowledge to moral knowledge, or even to the aesthetic feeling of the sublime. He clearly does not accept the Wordsworthian fear that knowledge hinders feelings, or the contention that we have had

> Enough of science and of art:
> > Close up these barren leaves;
> Come forth, and bring with you a heart
> > That watches and receives,

as Wordsworth expresses the romantic contempt for science in "The Tables Turned." In his *General History of Nature and Theory of the Heavens,* Kant argues that science is not only conducive to genuine feelings of sublimity, but in fact necessary for an accurate aesthetic-moral appreciation of the universe. Thirty-five years later, when the third *Critique* was published, Kant further argues that moral knowledge is presupposed by feelings of the sublime, as opposed to mere outbursts of enthusiasm or swoonings. Just as the feeling of *Achtung,* or moral respect, logically follows from the thought of the moral law, so the feelings of the sublime follow from certain cognitive states. How Kant describes these states will be dealt with later in the present section. It is important to remark at the outset, however, that though there are many "romanticisms," to employ Professor A. O. Lovejoy's term,[2] both in Kant's pre-Critical writings and in the mature views of the third *Critique,* there is never a trace of dislike of science or a mistrust of the fruits of technology.

At certain points in the third *Critique*, Kant does appear to exclude from the sublime anything in Nature which presents an orderly or balanced whole; the sublime does not exist in "things of nature, that in their very concept import a definite end, e.g., animals of a recognized order, but in rude nature merely as involving magnitude."[3] It is not that the scientific and aesthetic are at odds, but rather that in the aesthetic feeling of the sublime our attention is focused elsewhere than on matters of fact or relations holding between them:

Similary, as the prospect of the ocean, we are not to regard it as we, with our minds stored with knowledge on a variety of matters . . . are wont to represent it in thought . . . for in this we get nothing beyond teleological judgments. Instead of this we must be able to see sublimity in the ocean, regarding it, as the poets do, according to what the impression upon the eye reveals, as let us say, in its calm.[4]

What further distinguishes the Kantian from other contemporary accounts of the sublime is Kant's concern for its epistemological basis. In neither his ethics nor his aesthetics does he appeal to mystical intuition as a way of knowledge: man is not possessed of any privileged access to what might lie beyond the world of appearances. Kant never wavers on this point. Even in his earliest writings he expresses his concern for providing a rational support for his belief, which also never wavered, in the spirituality of man as a being who must evolve to higher realms of perfection. The third *Critique* was intended to solve certain problems of justification that had been foreshadowed in the *Theory of the Heavens:*

I am not so devoted to the consequences of my theory that I should not be ready to acknowledge that [it] cannot entirely escape the reproach of its being undemonstrable. Nevertheless, I expect from those who are capable of estimating degrees of probability that such a chart of the infinite, comprehending, as it does, a subject which seems to be destined to be forever concealed from human understanding, will not on that account be at once regarded as a chimera, especially when recourse is had to analogy.[5]

Although Kant attempts in the third *Critique* to give a philosophical or, in his own language, a "transcendental" analysis of the sublime, he is by no means introducing an aesthetic category unfamiliar to eighteenth-century sensibility. The taste for the sublimities of the wild and formless aspects of Nature had already been encouraged by the third earl of Shaftesbury, who had also introduced a notion of the "moral sense." He had argued that the "moral sense" was a faculty especially adapted to the cognizance of both ethical and aesthetic relations.[6] Kant's reluctance to postulate any sort of special insight into such matters kept him from following Shaftesbury, though Kant records a certain admiration for both his and Hutcheson's writings in his letters. Postulating such a sense seemed a case of either begging the question, flouting the demands of philosophical economy, or both. Nonetheless, Kant's exposition of the sublime in the third *Critique* follows many of the vogues of the day and makes use of a number of stock images: the ocean, the Alps, the Basilica of St. Peter's. Though Kant reworked his account into the transcendental mold, he derived many of his quasi-empirical observations from the heritage beginning with Longinus and Lucretius and extending to Edmund Burke, whom Kant mentions and praises highly.[7]

Young philosophers often begin by following the philosophical vogues of their time and by writing on the current topics of discussion. Kant was no exception. His *Observations on the Feeling of the Beautiful and the Sublime*, which appeared in 1764, reveals that philosophical discussions of the sublime were not merely a matter for flighty dilettantes but could also be undertaken by someone who would prove to be the greatest philosophical mind of his epoch. Kant's views on aesthetics were to develop markedly from this youthful and somewhat literary essay. In particular, his attempt to ground both ethical and aesthetic judgment in the a priori realm was not evinced until his Critical period. In the *Observations*, Kant distinguishes moral principles from inclinations simply by asserting that the former mark a more constant and unchangeable feeling and require a universality of application. The same rather cavalier assurance of a universal sensibility, at least among the well-educated and enlightened, so reminiscent of Hume, is revealed in what Kant has to say about the differences between the beautiful and the sublime. He calls both "finer feelings" and proceeds to give physiological, ethnic, and historical examples of both categories. He employs the "humors"—the sanguine, the melancholy, the choleric, and the phlegmatic—which were well worn even in the eighteenth century; he regales his readers with his observations concerning the leading European nations and their aesthetic bents and prowesses. These observations could not have helped but strike many a reader in both France and England as singularly commonplace. In the second section of the *Observations,* concerning the general characteristics of the sublime and the beautiful, Kant describes the understanding as "sublime," along with the male, power, and the night; wit is said to be "beautiful," along with the female, delicacy, and the day. The intended audience of the *Observations* is unclear; it was evidently no one of any philosophical acuity. Felicities of style apart, Kant's first treatise on aesthetics is of the same fiber as Addison's essays in the *Spectator.* Kant does imply, however, that moral principles and virtues are founded on a feeling of the beauty and dignity of human nature. Ethics and aesthetics are not sharply distinguished, as was often the case among the Neoplatonists of the period, such as Shaftesbury. But because of the many eclectic strands in Kant's exposition of the sublime, I shall defer the more detailed discussion of his philosophical heritage until later in the chapter.

Kant excluded everything man-made from the category of the sublime, though he seems to hesitate at a few points in his analysis. Before turning to his theory of the sublime, and before asking whether it might consistently be expanded to include the fine arts as well, I might suggest why the entire enterprise of an "Analytic of the Sublime" appears so artificial and antiquated to contemporary sensibility.

It would be helpful in this regard to have a history or phenomenology of sensibility, as distinct from a formal aesthetic treatise. Though readers are accustomed to political and economic histories, the main access to the past, at least in regard to sensibility, remains imaginative literature, especially the novel. The film occasionally gives us an acquaintance of a past epoch, by showing us people's attire, their appointments, their modes of transportation, their forms of speech. The novel has a far greater sense of interiority and draws one into the most intimate deliberations and nuances of character. Other kinds of history have bordered upon what I have called a phenomenology of sensibility; indeed, it is often necessary to do so to give an adequate explanation of historical events. The Goncourt brothers' works on eighteenth-century sensibility, especially those on the role of the woman, are good examples of the phenomenology of sensibility.[8] To lay down the ground rules of such histories, however, would exceed the narrow scope of this book. I mention the possibility of this breed of history only to suggest that part of the remoteness of Kant's analysis of the sublime in the Second Book of the third *Critique* results from extirpating his philosophical analysis from its cultural and aesthetic milieu.

To the twentieth-century sensibility, almost nothing could be more remote than Kantian sublimity. It is no longer in vogue to write about the sublimities of Nature, as did so many writers in Kant's time, like Rousseau and Bernardin de Saint-Pierre. Apostrophes to Nature by later writers, such as Chateaubriand and Stendhal, fill the general reader with embarrassment, unless they are approached as literary symptoms of a vanished epoch, or as "camp." Kant's own rhetorical descriptions of the sublimities in Nature tend to strike the reader in the same way. As for sublimity in the fine arts, the modern sensibility might be moved by it in the art bequeathed by earlier civilizations: the Parthenon, Notre Dame, *King Lear*, Mozart's *Requiem,* Tolstoy's *War and Peace.* We might go to the trouble of understanding it, analyzing its forms; we might follow revivals of a certain composer, like Monteverdi, and try to be faithful interpreters. Still, art produced in the twentieth century is far removed from the world view that gave rise to the Kantian sublime.

A modern writer might mock the sublime, as Pirandello did; or he might try to invert it, subvert it, or simply dissipate it, as Beckett and Ionesco do. As aesthetic categories of the twentieth century, at least in capitalistic countries, it is the absurd, the grotesque, the convoluted, the narcissistically self-aware that hold sway; one should add another, nameless, aesthetic category: it is in part nostalgic, in part embittered, and at the same time self-bemused, eclectic, mannered, and dyspeptic. To continue in this vein, however, would be to launch into a phenomenology of contemporary sensibility; such a work should attempt to eschew or "bracket" all theories and preconceptions. But the point here is simply that the Kantian sublime cannot but sound a little remote: its ethical and religious preconceptions have so little currency.

In my exposition of the Second Book of Part One of the third *Critique* (§§23–30), I shall deal with the following principal questions: (1) How does Kant describe and analyze the sublime? How is it related to certain of his metaphysical and ethical doctrines? (2) Is Kant's account internally consistent? Does it adequately explain the range of phenomena which, according to Kant's examples, were considered in his own time "sublime"? (3) Who were the chief philosophical progenitors of Kant's analysis, whose works might further clarify it?

Kant begins his account by asserting that the sublime, like the beautiful, does not presuppose a judgment of sense or a logically determinant judgment, but rather one of reflection. That is, a judgment concerning sublimity is not equivalent to an autobiographical account of a private emotion, no matter how awesome or elevated it might be. Neither does such a judgment depend upon a definite concept, or upon a clear-cut cognitive conception. Kant never altered his opinion on this latter point.

To see in a slightly different light what Kant means by calling the judgment of the sublime "reflective," we might turn to the "General Introduction to the Metaphysic of Morals." Desire or aversion is there described as always connected with pleasure or pain; still, one can experience the latter two feelings without any antecedent desire or aversion. Kant says that a "mere mental representation" can also afford us feelings of pleasure or pain.[9] He proceeds to say that taste is "contemplative pleasure" or "passive gratification."[10] Kant entitles the Second Book of his *Anthropology*, concerning the feeling of pleasure and displeasure: "Concerning the beautiful, that is, the partly sensuous, partly intellectual pleasure of reflective judgment, or taste." In the same section he says: "Beauty exclusively belongs to taste; the sublime also belongs to the powers of aesthetic judgment, but not to taste."[11] In the third *Critique,* Kant asserts that the sublime is "directed merely to the feeling of pleasure and not to a knowledge of the object."[12] Both the judgment of the beautiful and the judgment of the sublime are logically singular in form, though universal in purport. Indeed, many of the claims Kant makes for the sublime are familiar to us from "The Analytic of the Beautiful."

Kant asserts, however, that many important differences hold between the beautiful and the sublime. It might be best to begin with the most obvious. Beauty is formal, limited, and related to the discursive and sometimes even playful understanding. Sublimity is formless, wild, and invokes the quasi-intuitive ideas of reason. Beauty encourages the furtherance of life; sublimity arrests it. We have a dalliance with beauty, but a respect for sublimity. The most striking difference is that beauty, of its own accord, seems to adapt itself to our sensibilities, whereas the sublime is jarring and performs an "outrage on the imagination."[13] The sublime forces us to abandon our merely empirical sensibility and draws us up into a higher realm.

Oscar Wilde's well-known comment that Nature imitates art was anticipated by Kant: "*Simplicity* (artless finality) is, as it were, the style adopted by nature in the sublime."[14] Kant is implying that when we consider Nature from the aesthetic point of view we inevitably employ painterly or artistic concepts such as balance, form, composition, and harmony. These concepts, Kant says, belong to beauty, or "to nature regarded as aimless mechanism, but also to nature regarded after the analogy of art."[15] Only insofar as Nature imitates art can Nature appear as an object of beauty to us—a conclusion consonant with Kant's entire Critical philosophy. Nature can only count as beautiful for us if we have aesthetically devised it ourselves.

The relations between the sublime and the beautiful are more intricate; the sublime breaks forms, throws us into chaos, and overturns every ordinary standard of greatness and magnitude. The sublime seems to deny the purposefulness of Nature, leaving us in bewilderment. We are necessarily thrown back upon ourselves and our own moral resources: "For the beautiful in nature we must seek a ground external to ourselves, but for the sublime one merely in ourselves and the attitude of mind that introduces sublimity into the representation of nature."[16]

Kant assumes that the judgment of the sublime must have the same "moments" as the judgment of the beautiful: the "delight" from the sublime must be universally valid in quantity, independent of interest in quality, subjectively final in relation, and necessary in modality. To put part of Kant's point in a linguistic way, it appears that sentences like "The Alps are sublime" must, for a priori reasons, hold for everyone. The philosophical underpinnings of such judgments are quite different from those of the beautiful, in part because the beautiful is founded upon form, whereas the sublime rests upon formlessness.

The dangers, or at least the temptations, of drifting into a psychological or physiological account of the sublime are even greater than in "The Analytic of the Beautiful." For example, in the passage just quoted, Kant speaks of "the attitude of the mind." Elsewhere he describes the sublime as breaking down the faculty of the imagination.[17] He mentions "feeling . . . the inadequacy of . . . imagination"[18] and "a feeling of the effort towards a comprehension that exceeds the faculty of the imagination."[19] Before turning to Kant's account and the difficulties entailed by such apparently psychological language, it is important to notice a division in the Kantian sublime which has no parallel in the beautiful.

The beautiful is contemplative: the mind is at rest. The sublime "involves as its characteristic feature a mental movement combined with the estimate of the object."[20] In point of quantity, though both the sublime and the beautiful demand universal accord, the former aesthetic category entails a limitlessness in the representation, while the latter category entails limitedness. Given that the judgment of the sublime is aesthetic, the movement must be a *felt* movement, or a feeling which the imagination refers either to the faculty of cognition or to desire. An object might be called "sublime," then, because it unhinges the faculty of desire: Kant calls this type the "dynamically sublime." If an object stirs up the faculty of cognition, the object counts as the "mathematically sublime." After defining "sublimity" in general, Kant proceeds to explicate these two species.

In ordinary practical affairs, calling something "great," "huge," or "massive" involves applying a certain standard of measurement. "A great diamond," "a huge tumor," or a "massive petroleum field" are evidently comparative notions. Kant defines the sublime in general as that for which there exists no standard of comparison. It is not that the Alps seen from Megève, for example, could not be measured, or that the view of the Atlantic from some bleak promontory could not be surveyed; it is rather that ordinary standards of measurement fail to do justice to the feelings of infinity and grandeur awakened by such vast scenes in Nature. Although any object in Nature can be considered small in relation to some still greater object, and any small object considered immense in relation to infinitely smaller objects, the sublime is beyond all comparison. As Ezra Pound remarks, "The ant's a centaur in his dragon world."[21]

Because an object is called sublime when all standards are inappropriate to it and the object is great beyond comparison, Kant argues, the source of sublimity is not in the world of sense, or in Nature, but must reside in certain Ideas shared by humanity. According to Kant, "sublime" does not really refer to objects or things external to us, but rather to a certain "disposition of the soul," that is brought about, or occasioned, by an object which engages "the attention of the reflective judgment" in a certain way.[22]

The feeling of the sublime arises in part because the object occasioning it does not exhibit the form and harmony that the imagination would freely dictate. Kant's central notion of the cognitive faculties dictating to Nature is once again at work. In the beautiful, the imagination recognizes forms that would follow from its own laws; but in the sublime, because the object is either formless, or too immense, or overpowering, it is the nature of humanity itself that is outraged. An accord is consequently awakened between imagination and reason by means of the "supersensible substrate." I shall put off until the end of this section most of the discussion of the Ideas; suffice it to say that the Ideas are supposedly awakened in a quasi-emotional, quasi-cognitive way. It should not be surprising, given Kant's penchant for triadic schemes, that the Ideas are three in number. In general, Ideas are concepts of reason, bearing the same relationship to reason that concepts have to the understanding, and that intuitions have to the sensibility. The pure Ideas, Kant adds, with a certain touch of pedantry, also correspond to the three types of syllogistic reasoning—categorical, hypothetical, and disjunctive. To describe the three Ideas very briefly: the first concerns the soul; the second, the cosmos; and the third, God. Kant calls them, respectively, the psychological, the cosmological, and the theological ideas. What they share in common is that they can be neither confirmed nor disconfirmed by empirical science. Moreover, to argue for their truth or falsity by means of deductive reasoning must beg the question. Given that the three Ideas cannot be proved empirically or logically, but also given that they are required to bring the totality of experience into harmony, the Ideas must be established transcendentally.

The further link that Kant attempts to establish between the beautiful and the sublime cannot be examined until his theory of the sublime has been given in full. Nevertheless, it might now be observed why Kant supposes the sublime to be aesthetically parasitic upon the beautiful. By way of recapitulation, it should be recalled that the form of the beautiful depends upon the harmony of imagination and understanding; taste thereby emerges as a sort of discipline, or regulative "faculty." Examining the content of taste, we recognize the products of reason which supply moral depth to the understanding of a work of art, or to the appreciation of Nature. From the aesthetic point of view, reason supplies the link between imagination and understanding. Without the moral influence of reason, Kant suggests, the fine arts would degenerate into empty virtuosity. Reason introduces "aesthetic ideas"[23] which further illustrate the purposive coordination of the faculties. To oversimplify part of Kant's point on this score: imagination and understanding without reason give rise to either more artistic cleverness or barren sensuality; reason without imagination and understanding gives rise to only an echo of art, or to its necessary conditions.

As we have seen, Kant argues that form is essential to the beautiful, whereas reference to our moral nature is essential to the sublime. He was aware, however, that taste is also involved in the sublime, as well as our susceptibility to ideas; raptures in front of a mass-produced seascape, for example, however sublime our feelings might be, would count as evidence for lack of taste. Kant implies a new paradox: a genuine judgment of the sublime may itself be in bad taste. He shows the way out of the paradox in the Second Book of his *Anthropology:*

The representation of the sublime might and in fact ought to be in itself beautiful; for otherwise the representation is uncouth, barbaric, and in bad taste. For even the presentation of the evil or ugly (as in the form of death in the personification which Milton gives it) can and must be beautiful.[24]

To clarify the relationship further, a few paragraphs later Kant asserts that the sublime is the counterweight but not the contrary to the beautiful:

The effort and attempt to raise oneself to the apprehension of the object brings about in us a feeling of our own greatness and power; still, the representation of the mental activities in a description or picturing can and must be beautiful. If this were not the case, then the effect of our astonishment would be repulsion, which is quite different from admiration as a kind of estimating in which we do not grow weary of astonishment.[25]

As aesthetic categories, then, the sublime and the beautiful are mutually compatible; true and false sublimity are distinguished by the dependence of the former upon a beautiful expression or form. An object can be beautiful without awakening feelings of sublimity, though even a beautiful object indirectly presents the morally good: "only when sensibility is brought into harmony with moral feelings can genuine taste assume a definite unchangeable form."[26] Kant further implies that the false sublime might rest upon a merely sentimental ethics, or upon vague and mawkish feelings of sympathy.

The textual link between the beautiful and the sublime is further enhanced by the section entitled "The Ideal of Beauty,"[27] in which Kant describes the beautiful representation of the human form. Evidently with Greek statuary in mind, Kant asserts that a beautiful form would represent an ideal which would itself give rise to feelings of the sublime. Formally, the beautiful is opposed to the sublime and is the object of our critical or analytic reflective judgment. The beautiful expresses "aesthetic ideas" which themselves may occasion sublime feelings. The sublime, then, is the object of our sympathetic reflective judgment. That is, in the sublime, we are overwhelmed or even intimidated by the object in its entirety.

Kant implies, then, that the ugly, as a positive aesthetic value, depends upon a beautiful representation of something that is intrinsically repugnant, defective, or terrifying. To explain how such a tension generates the sublime, or how such feelings arise in Nature, where there is no representation of an object at all, calls for a more detailed examination of Kant's theory.

There are four parts to Kant's definition of "the sublime." The genus (1) is "a certain disposition of the soul" which is (2) evoked or occasioned by a particular representation (3) which engages the attention of the reflective judgment, and (4) the thinking of which evidences a faculty of mind transcending every standard of sense. It is best to postpone the discussion of the "genus" of sublimity until we have examined the two species, the mathematical and the dynamical. About (2), it is best to postpone objections to Kant's definition in regard to the terms "evoked" and "occasioned." In brief, Kant assumes that the natural scene or object, or to be more strict, the representation or image given to us by the productive imagination, is the *occasion* of a certain feeling evoked in our affective nature. The meaning of (4) will emerge in the discussion of the two types of sublimity. A few words about (3) are in order here.

To know whether something is painful or pleasant to us, no

reflection is required. Our memory might fail to report accurately how something struck us in the past; and though we generally know ourselves best, we might be mistaken in predicting how something will strike us in the future. As Kant explains later in his analysis, the judgment of the sublime rests upon a certain kind of composite pleasure, though the first intimations of the sublime are painful. The sight of the object is too vast or too overwhelming for us to cope with; hence we are confronted with our own finitude and weakness as phenomenal beings. The feeling of pain evoked by the sublime is not a sensation, like the effect of an external stimulus, but rather a mental state with which we are acquainted by a kind of rumination or emotionally tinged discernment.

Painful sensations are directly given to us: we need not analyze them either to be aware of them or to describe them as, for example, "piercing," "burning," or "throbbing." A doctor might ask us to describe the painful sensation in a certain way; because we are acquainted with the language, we can name or describe the sensation immediately, as if naming the primary colors. Again, painful sensations are located in a particular part of the body; they endure for a certain length of time. But the kind of painfulness or displeasure that the sublime evokes is neither directly given, nor located in the body, nor temporal. For similar reasons, one would imagine, Kant says that the sublime first arouses a feeling of displeasure which "engages the reflective judgment." Opposed to such judgment are the passive and physiological reception of external stimuli.

The sublime also engages the *attention* of the reflective judgment, by which Kant appears to mean that we linger over and scrutinize the object which occasions the sublime. In brief, we apperceive it instead of merely perceiving it. It makes no sense to speak of a painful sensation's engaging our attention, though the pain might be excruciating and long-lasting. In such cases we usually find that we have no power of attention of all: we cannot attend to anything. This does not imply that our attention is entirely absorbed or taken up by the painful sensation, for attention is active, aimed at or directed to an object. In acute pain we are passive; though we might be acutely aware of our pain, we do not say that our attention is engaged by it.

To explain Kant's category of the mathematically sublime, it is helpful to recall certain epistemological terms in the *Critique of Pure Reason* and to make some attempt to translate them into more ordinary parlance. Three such terms which occur in "The Analytic of the Sublime" require elucidation. Kant says that:

To take in a quantum intuitively in the imagination . . . involves two operations of this faculty: *apprehension* (*apprehensio*) and *comprehension* (*comprehensio aesthetica*). Apprehension presents no difficulty: for this process can be carried on *ad infinitum;* but with the advance of apprehension comprehension becomes more difficult at every step and soon attains its maximum, and this is the aesthetically greatest fundamental measure for the estimation of magnitude. [28]

By "intuitively" in this passage Kant means the direct and immediate way in which sense data are presented to the sensibility. Such data are therefore empirical intuitions, or perceptions. A perception, it is to be recalled, is the immediate awareness of appearances, or of the phenomenal. The productive imagination (*Einbildungskraft*), or the power of forming images, bridges the gap between sensibility and understanding. Imagination focusing its powers directly upon perceptions is described as involved in apprehension.

An apprehension is simply the synthesis or bringing together of a number of particular perceptions into a single image, or to use Kant's word, *Vorstellung* (representation). As Kant asserts in the passage just cited, apprehension can go on indefinitely: unit after unit can be presented to the imagination. It is only when we attempt to hold a number of perceptual units together in the imagination, or apprehend them at the same time, that the limits of the imagination are strained. Comprehension is the operation of holding one or more apprehensions together. Kant uses the term "*aesthetica*" in connection with comprehension to indicate a sensuous "bringing together," as opposed to an intellectual or logical "comprehending."

To give a simple illustration of Kant's basic notion so far, we might imagine that a single brick (an apprehension) is placed before us on a long table, then another brick, and so on. We can readily move our eyes successively down the line, keeping up with every new brick placed before us. When we try to take in a certain number of units in one perceptual swoop (aesthetic comprehension), we become aware that our perceptual grasp is limited and depends upon our proximity to the line of bricks. If we are far enough removed from the line we can take them all in perceptually, but each particular apprehension is then obscured. The line presents itself as a single unit. Although powers of "aesthetic comprehension" probably vary from person to person, there exists a middle range, just as in normal sight.

Anticipating by 122 years Edward Bullough's famous theory of "psychical distance,"[29] Kant says that "we must avoid coming too near just as much as remaining too far away."[30] In the mathematically sublime the imagination is staggered and bewildered by an object which is perceptually too great, too extended, or too immense for us to bring together in our perceptual grasp. Seen from a certain point, the Alps could form one apprehension, like one brick. Seen from Megève, for example, the imagination can begin to bring part of the Alps together, or aesthetically "comprehend" them; however, we are soon staggered by their extent. It is at this point, Kant argues, that in witnessing the limitations of our imagination as a mere productive and reproductive faculty—to be distinguished much later from the creative imagination—we recoil.[31] We then "succumb to an emotional delight."[32]

Before explaining the way in which such a delight is supposed to lay claim to an intersubjective validity, Kant concerns himself once again with the autonomy of the aesthetic, in particular, the "purity" of an aesthetic judgment of the mathematically sublime. If any particular purpose is implicit in an object, for example, in a building or even in a natural object that occupies a particular place in the natural order, then a judgment of its sublimity is not "pure." Kant implies that sublimity in art is never as aesthetically "pure" as in rude Nature. Although he instances St. Peter's Basilica as an example of an object too perceptually great to be "aesthetically comprehended," he might do so only to show some of the attendant feelings of the sublime—bewilderment and perceptual perplexity.

If we observe Kant's vacillations carefully, we shall notice a hierarchy of the sublime developing, closely parallel to that described by Plotinus.[33] The hierarchy begins with works of art and ends with a certain "disposition of the soul." At one point Kant refers to "the sublime in works of art, e.g., buildings, statues and the like."[34] Later he speaks of "the sublime and beautiful in the human form,"[35] for which it is a necessary condition that each part be teleologically adapted for the whole to be sublime. Even so, the judgment must be free, in the sense that it is not based upon a concept of what the object ought to be. Even higher than the human form is the sublimity of Nature in her most ragged, gigantic, and undisciplined moods. No notion of what the object should be is even a necessary condition of the feeling of the sublime: "rude nature merely as involving magnitude (and only in this so far as it does not convey any charm or any emotion arising from actual danger)."[36] Finally he says: "Sublimity therefore, does not reside in any of the things of nature, but only in our own mind, in so far as we may become conscious of our superiority over nature within, and this also over nature without us."[37]

When the extensive magnitude of an object presented to us is so great that it cannot be aesthetically comprehended, we are reminded of our limitations as phenomenal beings in the world. Because we can nonetheless conceive of what the whole must be, we see our superiority as noumenal beings. The mathematically sublime forces us beyond the narrow confines of our sensibility and into the "supersensible substrate" which is "great beyond every standard of sense."[38] Just as in the judgment of the beautiful a free play occurs between the imagination and the concepts of the understanding, so in the judgment of the sublime a conflict occurs between imagination and the Ideas of reason. In both cases, concepts and Ideas remain indeterminate, that is, they are not brought to bear in a full and articulate manner. Moreover, just as the feeling of the free play of the cognitive faculties gives rise to a feeling of pleasure, so the conflict between them produces a feeling of displeasure because we are unable as phenomenal beings to grasp the magnitude presented to the imagination. The displeasure, which is a feeling of our incapacity to fulfill what is nevertheless a moral and intellectual law for us, becomes a feeling of respect for ourselves as rational beings. From the feeling that we somehow transcend the world of sense, and from the realization that the Ideas of reason have no equals in the phenomenal world, a rarefied feeling of pleasure arises. As Kant says, "the object is received as sublime with a pleasure that is only possible through the mediation of a displeasure."[39]

In Kant's final description of the mathematically sublime he employs the term "subreption," by which he means the attribution of a subjective feeling to an object. In effect, sublimity is an instance of what was later to be called "the pathetic fallacy": "Therefore the feeling of the sublime in nature is respect for our own vocation, which we attribute to an Object of nature by a certain subreption."[40]

The dynamically sublime consists in an appreciation of the all-powerfulness of Nature, which, if the spectator were not in a secure position, would overcome him. Kant's definition of the dynamically sublime, as well as the instances he gives of it, pertains exclusively to Nature, and Nature in her most awesome moments:

Bold, overhanging, and, as it were, threatening rocks, thunderclouds piled up the vault of heaven, borne along with flashes and peals, volcanoes in all their violence of destruction, hurricanes leaving desolation in their track, the boundless ocean rising with rebellious force, the high waterfall of some mighty river, and the like, make our power of resistance of trifling moment in comparison with their might.[41]

At no other point in his writings does Kant's prose strive to imitate the grandeur of what he is describing. The ardor of his feelings for Nature is paralleled during the Enlightenment only by Rousseau's. It is curious to remember that Kant himself saw very little of Nature, except what presented itself in the forty-five-mile radius around Königsberg. Though his descriptions of sublimity in Nature are sometimes archly literary, and the epithets he employs are often stock, still the profundity of his feeling, derived as it is from his ethical theory, is undeniably genuine.

The dynamically sublime is also described as revealing our noumenal superiority to Nature. We recognize our helplessness and weakness as objects in the phenomenal world; we see the vanity of riches, health, and the phenomenal life. At first the dynamically sublime terrorizes us, fills us with pain and displeasure at our feebleness; but we recognize that humanity in our own person cannot be violated or humiliated. As noumenal beings we are invincible. When Kant uses the word "humanity," he does not merely mean that the human species will survive all temporary outrages committed against it, but that each person in some inexplicable way survives the phenomenal world. Our personal immortality, together with "the idea of the sublimity of that Being which inspires deep respect in us,"[42] fills us with a pleasure and an elation which lead us to call the object of Nature which occasioned it "sublime." Subreption, or the pathetic fallacy, is again at work.

Kant in no way intends to deify human nature in his exposition of the mathematically sublime. His opinion of humanity as a phenomenal entity is remarkably low and reveals a distrust of human motivation worthy of Calvin or Melanchthon: "for human nature does not of its own proper motion accord with the good, but only by virtue of the dominion which reason exercises over sensibility."[43] In *Religion Within the Limits of Reason Alone*, Kant amplified the theme of man's natural depravity. Man is not so much demonic as he is selfish, perverse, or frail. Instead of taking the moral law as the unique motive of acting, man tends to conform externally to the moral law. Kant finds such behavior the essence of "bourgeois morality," a theme to be developed in detail by Hegel. Reminiscent of St. Augustine's moral opposition of the lower to the higher, Kant asserts that man's constant temptation is to follow the sensuous biddings of inclination rather than the maxims determined by the Categorical Imperative. The result is actions that "reserve the ethical priority among the incentives of a free will."[44] Not only does man err by frailty, that is, by being too weak in observing the moral law; but also by impurity, by hybridizing moral with prudential or nonmoral motives. Kant speaks of positive wickedness, which is not a mere euphemism for human ignorance or carelessness. Wickedness is the conscious and deliberate choice of evil maxims that are known as such to the chooser. Kant implies that such knowledge, in the case of the wicked, even acts as a further motive for following them.

Yet as a son of the Enlightenment, Kant must hold to the perfectibility of man, the necessary improvement of human society, and the paramount importance of education—themes that he lauds in his pamphlet "What Is Enlightenment?"[45] As is well known, Kant also tries to give a moral argument for the immortality of the soul by claiming that since "ought" implies "can," and since the injunction to perfect oneself is universally valid, the soul must therefore have eternity to fulfill the obligation. The sublime in Nature, so Kant argues, gives us murmurings of such immortality as noumenal beings. As phenomenal beings we have little time; as noumenal, we have eternity before us. Kant is quick to stipulate that our personal immortality is a heuristic idea.

To explain the modality of the judgment of the sublime, or its peculiar form of necessity, Kant leaves the aesthetic and turns to our capacity to entertain what he calls "moral feelings." In certain philosophico-psychological treatises on aesthetics with which Kant was perhaps acquainted, such as the works of Shaftesbury and Hutcheson, judgments of the sublime are usually said to be based on "finer feelings." In *Observations on the Feeling of the Beautiful and the Sublime*, Kant uses the same term: "The finer feelings, which we are now going to discuss, are above all of two sorts."[46] It is to be remarked that Kant often employed terminology and arguments from the British moral-sense school in his early writings on ethics as well as on aesthetics. That is, however, a historical aside that cannot be developed in the present book. What is of immediate importance is that in the third *Critique*, Kant finds the epithet "finer feelings" "senseless." For, he argues, if it be assumed that all feelings are entirely empirical, then the sublime could at best be distinguished from others only by its rarity or complexity. The feeling of the sublime would not be fundamentally different from what Kant would call "merely empirical" fear or inclination. However, if we say of someone that he fails to appreciate the sublime, we assume, Kant argues, that he also lacks moral sensitivity. It is not a question of liking or disliking the object, but rather the capacity to be morally elevated by it, that betokens the sublime. Because of the intersubjective validity of such judgments, Kant insists, their analysis cannot be given by empirical psychology, but only by transcendental philosophy. The ultimate principle that must be invoked is finality: even the most undisciplined and chaotic manifestations of Nature must be conceived of as if they had a purpose. Their purposefulness or finality consists in their awakening in us a sense of our vocation as moral beings. All rational agents, Kant concludes, have the capacity to have moral feelings, such as sympathy or communion with others, and respect or *Achtung*. Consequently, the sublime rests upon neither convention nor acquired feelings, but upon an innate capacity:

This, now, is the foundation of the necessity of that agreement between other men's judgments upon the sublime and our own. . . . For just as we taunt a man who is quite unappreciative when forming an estimate of an object of nature in which we see beauty, with want *of taste,* so we say of a man who remains unaffected in the presence of what we consider sublime, that he has *no feeling.*[47]

Both species of the sublime lead Kant to a description of human character decidedly Stoic in tone. "*Chara*," or the rational elevation of the soul, as described by Marcus Aurelius and by Seneca, is at the root of Kant's analysis of sublimity. Moreover, both species involve a reference to a physical object which occasions the feeling, and also to the content of what is aroused in us. The physical object is either of great magnitude or of great power; the content is not given by Nature, but rather by human nature. It is not the material object which is sublime, but rather our own moral feelings, called into indeterminate play. Both species spring from a feeling of apparent disharmony between the imagination and reason; yet by the very disharmony a sense of greater harmony is forced upon us, for we become aware of ourselves as possessing a power of self-sufficient reason. Self-preservation makes out its claim to the noumenal world.

Unlike the finality of the beautiful, by which the form of the object seems preadapted to accommodate itself to our sensibility and cognitive powers, the finality of the sublime consists in our awareness of belonging to the realm of moral ends, or as being of intrinsic worth. Although Kant says that the material object is in some way "fit" to occasion or arouse the feelings of the sublime, the inadequacy of any sensible presentation of the Ideas reveals our personal finality as moral agents in the Kingdom of Ends.

Kant asserts, consequently, that the judgment of the sublime requires no deduction: its exposition suffices to justify its claim to universal validity. Because the ultimate harmony of sensibility with reason is revealed in the analysis, no reference to the physical object which occasions sublimity need be made. The harmony of sensibility with reason is an a priori principle of subjective finality. However, a deduction is necessary for the judgment of the beautiful because a reference to the form of the object must be made:

Consequently the Exposition we gave of judgments upon the sublime in nature was at the same time their Deduction. For in our analysis of the reflection on the part of judgment in this case we found that in such judgments there is a final relation to the cognitive faculties, which has to be laid *a priori* at the basis of the faculty of ends (the will), and which is therefore itself *a priori* final.[48]

Before turning to a critical estimate of Kant's several claims concerning the sublime, we might try to give a more sympathetic account of the content and force of Kant's Ideas. The psychological Idea, like all three Ideas, is "pure," that is, nonempirical, and "regulative," that is, used to bring reason into harmony with itself. Kant asserts that nothing positive can be said about the self or the "soul"; we cannot, for example, show that it must be a kind of substance, or immortal, or simple—attributes which many philosophers, both before Kant's time and during the eighteenth century, firmly assigned to the "soul." The psychological Idea merely affirms the unconditioned unity of the thinking subject.

The cosmological Idea, also described as "transcendental," designates the totality of phenomenal conditions or antecedents. Applied to the moral life of man, or of practical reason, it affirms the freedom of moral actions from all empirical antecedents. According to Kant, the freedom of the moral agent, or the cosmological Idea as applied to moral behavior, is the most important postulate of practical reason.

The theological Idea is sometimes described by Kant as the Ideal of pure reason, or the transcendental Ideal. It designates the unconditioned unity or synthesis of the conditions—the logical and empirical presuppositions—of any thought whatsoever. As a postulate of ethics, or of practical reason, the theological Idea gives foundation to the belief that the economy of the universe is ultimately moral. Happiness will ultimately be commensurate with virtue, and all ills ultimately rectified. The chief role of God, therefore, is as the final moral arbiter.

I have tried to point out in this exposition of the Kantian sublime that part of its remoteness, and perhaps its irrelevance to contemporary sensibility, should be explained by the desuetude of the notions of God, freedom, and immortality. I simply mean here that they exert less influence upon the ordinary man than they did in Kant's time, and that discussion of such topics is far less prevalent today in philosophical circles and of less philosophical urgency and interest. It is of course true that a few professional writers on philosophy still deal with subjects relating to the theistic basis of the Kantian sublime, but they tend to do so from a linguistic or "ordinary language" point of view.

What cannot help striking anyone familiar with Kant's ethics is the profoundly moral tone of the Kantian sublime. It parallels the tension between Kant's Wolffian rationalism and Newtonian materialism, and his almost fundamentalist Pietist leanings. Kant reveals his consanguinity with Swedenborg in the repeated descriptions in the third *Critique* of the "intelligible world" and the ineffable manner in which all persons belong to a universal, supersensible "community."[49] The immediate corollary for aesthetics from Kant's vision of the concordance of all moral wills is not simply the a priori homogeneity of taste, but the notion that each aesthetic sensibility is a support and help to others.

Kant's abhorrence of metaphysics was revealed as early as the *Dreams of a Spirit-Seer*, in which he says that the existence of an intelligible world of spirits is a "futile dream" and a "fairy-tale from the fool's paradise of metaphysics."[50] Kant never maintains that the sublime gives privileged access to the noumenal world, or that it can be cultivated into "intuitive knowledge." The Ideas stand outside the world of cause and effect and are therefore think-able, but not knowable. They are to be used only regulatively and analogically, even though Kant's rhetorical tone never leaves a doubt in the reader's mind that at least Kant believes in "such a ground of the world."[51] To pursue Kant's aesthetic treatment of the Ideas, and of what I might call the moral mandate of mankind, would again lead us into his elaborate discussion of "aesthetic ideas," which became more and more central to the entire Kantian aesthetics.

From the point of view of the literary historian, nothing could appear more egocentrically romantic than Kant's pleas for the aesthetic necessity of God's existence: we must think and act *as if* God existed in order to bring about harmony among the faculties of our own minds. Kant not only implies that man must judge God morally, but also that man must view Nature as if it were remolded by his own moral nature. Without man's aesthetic sensibility, Na-ture would have only scientific interest. Without man's ethical commitments, God would only be someone to whom prudence dictates obedience.

So many anticipations of romantic sensibility occur in the Kantian sublime that it would require an entire study to show what Kant bequeathed to poets, novelists, painters, and musicians. Fundamental to so many "romanticisms" appears to be a kind of symbiotic relationship between mind and Nature, implying some-thing profoundly true about both. These lines from Wordsworth seem to be in order:

> Yea, what were mighty Nature's self
> Her features, could they win us,
> Unhelped by the poetic voice
> That hourly speaks within us?[52]

Defects and Inconsistencies in the Kantian Sublime

The most evident difficulty with Kant's theory of the sublime resides in the supposed universal validity of judgments concerning it. To put the problem in an old scholastic way, Kant's theory lacks a *principium individuationis,* or a principle for distinguishing one judgment on the sublime from another. Given Kant's theory, all judgments of the mathematically sublime would mean: "The infinite is sublime"; and all judgments of the dynamically sublime would come to: "Man's moral nature is sublime." To make this criticism more evident, let us trace through the relevant parts of Kant's analysis so far. (1) No deduction for the sublime is needed because the aesthetic judgment on the sublime makes no reference to an object; the exposition, or analysis of the meaning of sublimity, reveals the a priori element in the judgment needed to justify universality. (2) Therefore, an object in Nature is only the occasion of a judgment; the object is not sublime, for sublimity attaches to the feeling aroused in the spectator. (3) The feeling is one which necessarily follows from man's moral nature, which can be presupposed to be identical, *in potentia,* in all rational beings. (4) Although the feeling of the sublime is more rare than the harmonious feeling of pleasure from the beautiful and consequently requires moral education to bring it about, still, the sublime is a feeling which everyone has the capacity to entertain.

When we say "This is sublime," "this" obviously refers to something independent of us—the ocean, the Alps, the Basilica of St. Peter's. Kant would concede this point, but only as a grammatical observation. "Sublimity, therefore, does not reside in any of the things of nature, but only in our own mind."[53] The "things of nature" divide themselves into the very powerful and the greatly extended, but they have only a causal efficacy in producing the "disposition of the soul." We cannot therefore say that any particular object in Nature must be sublime, and a fortiori, it makes little sense to say that everyone *ought* to find it so. It is only an empirical truth that certain objects cause or tend to cause such feelings. A judgment about them would be assertoric or "fact-stating," not necessary. Moreover, if a judgment of the sublime makes no reference to a particular object but still lays claim to the universal appropriateness of certain feelings occasioned by types of natural objects, then it is an obvious empirical truth that different sorts of things occasion such feelings. Nor does it seem likely, as one commentator on Kant's aesthetics maintains, that "it is a necessary truth that if an object can be used by one rational being to evoke a feeling of the grandeur of reason or of man's moral destiny, it can be freely used by all who properly prepare themselves."[54] The "necessity" of this truth consists merely in its circularity.

It makes sense to say that all rational beings employ the same logic or mathematical presuppositions; it makes sense to say that all rational beings, given their social nature and their common problems of self-preservation, must assume fundamentally the same moral point of view. But given the evident variability in persons' imaginations and powers of resistance, it is false to say that all rational beings find the same object sublime. Though Kant admits that we cannot always expect factual agreement upon such matters, we can demand that everyone develop his capacity of moral feeling.

Even if Kant means that we should demand universal agreement concerning the occasion of our feelings, he states that the universality in question resides wholly in the subject. The link between the object in Nature and ourselves is causal and contingent. If Kant means that what occasions the feelings is so just *for me,* then the sublime would be a private affair, although one could say, given Kant's additional theories concerning the Ideas: "I know what you *mean* by calling it sublime, but the object doesn't affect me in the same way." If, however, the occasion is not represented as the object of universal agreement, then there is no particular to be subsumed under an indeterminate rule. In that case it is difficult to understand how a judgment of the sublime is an instance of reflective judgment.

If Kant had tried to show that the displeasure from the sublime, together with the particular object which occasions it, must be a priori the same for all persons, then he would have needed a deduction for the sublime. Kant argues that no such deduction is required. He is consequently forced into a dilemma: if there is no deduction for the sublime, then the object that occasions it is irrelevant, for any object that occasions such a feeling would do. Without reference to a particular object, the sublime becomes singularly vacuous.

Kant's theory aside, it appears that what we require agreement about concerns the sublimity of the object—a particular work of art or some aspect of Nature. Once the "material object" becomes only a springboard for feelings, or the mere "occasion," then the only way of distinguishing one judgment on the sublime from another is lost. The question "What is sublime about the object?" would always revert to a description of our moral feelings, or of the moral vocation of man. All that could be said about the object that occasions such feelings is that it is either infinite in magnitude or overwhelmingly powerful.

Once Kant relegates the object to the position of an "occasion" it is difficult to understand how a judgment on the sublime can be called "aesthetic." For if the experience of the sublime is not directed to an object independent of us, then the sublime is not an object that we apprehend, let alone one that we aesthetically comprehend. The object which occasions the feeling is by definition formless; it is also described as something independent of sensation. We are left, then, with some vague object, like Locke's "abstract ideas," that exhibits great magnitude—like the stars overhead on a clear night—or a perceptual abstraction that embodies great power—like the force of wind in a hurricane. What seems to be "aesthetic" about such "occasioning objects" is merely that they reawaken moral feelings. "Aesthetic," then, is being used in such a wide sense that anything that awakens such feelings—acts of benevolence or charity, heroism, martyrdom, death, birth, love—should also be termed "aesthetic." What Kant has failed to distinguish adequately are the two predicates "morally sublime" and "aesthetically sublime." By failing to delimit the scope of "is sublime," his analysis systematically confounds the two. An object might evince both sorts of sublimity but need not. There is nothing aesthetically sublime, for example, about a prisoner who steadfastly refuses, under severe torture, to divulge secrets to the enemy. But his action does give ground to "moral sublimity." Clearly, what we mean by calling the façade of a building or a work of music "sublime" rests chiefly upon the structure and complexities of the particular object, though moral feelings are sometimes part of the explanation. Our interest in the sublime is in the object, not in ourselves. The colonnade of the Louvre, for example, or the Pantheon, or the dynamic juxtaposition of forces in baroque music, as in Handel's Dettingen *Te Deum,* are instances of the structurally sublime. The sublime has its form, though based upon elements quite different from those of the beautiful. "Form" admits of a far broader connotation than that given to it by the Kantian neoclassicism. Even the most revolutionary or unconventional artist attempts to impose form; though his work might appear artless, random, or even a repudiation of form itself, a sense of structure is discoverable. Kant has confused an explanation concerning the subject's feelings with what it is about the particular object that makes it sublime.

It will be recalled that Kant analyzed the beautiful as subjective because form must be referred to feelings of pleasure or displeasure for the judgment to count as aesthetic. The sublime, however, is doubly subjective: the "occasion" is referred to our feelings of pleasure or displeasure, but because of the magnitude or great power of the "occasion," other feelings—the moral—are thereby awakened.

At certain points in the third *Critique,* Kant implies that his two principal aesthetic categories are incompatible, as indeed the predicates "is being possessed of form" and "is formless" doubtless would indicate. But when he concedes that man-made objects might to a degree be sublime, as "in a tragedy in verse, a didactic poem or an oratorio,"[55] he implies that the result might be more powerful, but less aesthetically pure. Clearly what Kant once again has in mind as paradigmatic of aesthetic objects are "designs *à la grecque,* foliage for framework or on wallpaper . . . [for] they represent nothing . . . and are free beauties. We may also rank in the same class what in music are called fantasias. . . . all music that is not set to words."[56]

It would hardly be an understatement to say that the most troublesome and Protean concept in "The Analytic of the Beautiful" is form. It might further understanding of the term to contrast it with formlessness. As is well known, one of the standard doctrines of the *Critique of Pure Reason* is that the mind imposes form, or unity, upon the manifold of sensibility. It would therefore follow that to count as experience for us, the object of our experience must be unified:

But appearances are only the representations of things which are unknown as regards what they may be in themselves. As mere representations, they are subject to no law of connection save that which the connecting faculty prescribes. Now it is imagination that connects the manifold of sensible intuition; and imagination is dependent for the unity of its synthesis upon the understanding, and for the manifoldness of its apprehension upon sensibility.[57]

If, then, the two predicates "is formless" and "is totally lacking in unity" are synonymous in connotation, then it is obvious that the sublime, as Kant defines it, could never logically be the object of human experience. It must be, then, that formlessness as a positive aesthetic predicate (as opposed to mere confusion, daubs, or lack of discipline) entails a specific kind of form. But to maintain the symmetry of his argument and to avoid a deduction for the sublime, Kant resists this conclusion. Yet since the sublime must in some way be unified (given that it is not the same as mere chaos and is evidently a "good-making" trait of an object), it follows that the formlessness of the sublime is simply another kind of form. It is at this point that Kant's distinctions between the dynamic and the infinite contribute to understanding the kind of form evinced by the sublime. Because of the inordinate weight Kant gives to the moral effects of sublimity, he leads the reader into further confusions: "In fact, without the development of moral ideas, that which, thanks to preparatory culture, we call sublime, merely strikes the untutored man as terrifying."[58] The "untutored man" might fail to appreciate or respond to the sublime, but he hardly need be terrified by it. Again, as we saw in the previous section, the "moral ideas" of which Kant speaks are specific in content, if not parochial. It is at least curious that much sublime art rests upon moral ideas at complete variance with those cited by Kant. Greek tragedy, for example, is essentially godless, rooted in a conception of fate or μοῖρα, and devoid of the notion of personal immortality. A strong case could be made for the absence of the Kantian moral underpinnings in Shakespeare's tragedies as well as in those from Racine's prebiblical period. Often a feeling of awe is closer to our feeling of the sublime than is anything tinged with morality.

Kant's analysis also appears to confuse the feelings that might be evoked by an object with the feelings that the object might contain. A novel might move someone to tears, but it might in itself be maudlin. Recognizing the emotional content of a work of art is like recognizing someone's mood by looking at his face. In aesthetic recognition it is not that we are not *seriously* entertaining an emotion: we are not entertaining an emotion at all. Kant's way of describing the aesthetic look of things is misleading:

> But we look upon an object as *fearful,* and yet not be afraid *of* it, if, that is, our estimate takes the form of our simply *picturing to ourselves* the case of our wishing to offer some resistance to it, and recognizing that all such resistance would be quite futile. . . . it is impossible to take delight in terror that is seriously entertained.[59]

His stipulation that we must be in a secure position to feel the sublime—an observation that Lucretius makes in *De Rerum Natura*—is of course true, but true of so much in addition to the sublime that it is hardly a distinguishing mark. It is misleading to say that we must be safe from something sublime in order to feel it, for if one is safe from it, then it is at least possible that one could be endangered by it. But one might ask whether the sublime could endanger anyone.

What is further dubious about Kant's analysis, whether it be construed psychologically or transcendentally, is the implication that the feeling of the sublime begins at the point where the efforts toward comprehension flag and give way. This is a mechanistic description, implying process; but the sense of the sublime is present phenomenologically from the beginning, as in one's field of vision, or in sound. Although discernment of the sublime might expand or, for that matter, be undercut and collapse into the ridiculous, the scholastic distinction between *apprehensio* and *comprehensio* is inexact both as psychological description and as philosophical analysis.

Despite the high transcendental apparatus that Kant gives his analysis, he occasionally seems so unsure of his way that his argument can only be considered empirical or psychological. After admitting that "The Analytic of the Sublime" seems too far-fetched and subtle to be the basis of aesthetic judgment, he says:

"But observation of men proves the reverse, and that it may be the foundation of the commonest judgments, although one is not always conscious of its presence."[60] Not only has he reduced the sublime to the moral, thereby surrendering aesthetic autonomy, but he has in effect given a psychological explanation for that which requires an aesthetic explanation.

To correct his psychologizing, or at least to palliate it, Kant repeatedly insists that the judgment of the sublime must be pure or "unmixed with any teleological judgment."[61] Our judgment must not be based upon anything cognitive or utilitarian; it must be "bracketed," to use Husserl's term, and considered without any link to human ends or utility. We are not permitted to consider the sublime even under the general head of Nature's purposefulness, which was required by the beautiful. The sublime is too chaotic and irregular to portray even a vague sense of the teleology of Nature, or more precisely, to be interpreted as if it were purposeful. As we have seen, the only purposiveness that Kant allows the object that arouses the sublime is subjective: it serves to bring about moral feelings. The judgment must be pure in the sense that it concerns only the impression we have of an object. Curiously, Kant gave one of the essential tenets of impressionism long before it found its way into painting and literature: "We must be able to see sublimity in the ocean, regarding it, as the poets do, according to what the impression upon the eye reveals, as let us say, in its calm, a clear mirror of water . . . disturbed . . . threatening."[62]

Although Kant was as concerned to guarantee the autonomy of aesthetics as that of ethics, he draws numerous parallels between aesthetic categories and the autonomy of the moral agent. The beautiful is a civilizing and social force, based upon form; but form is common to etiquette, civil law, religion, and even the moral law. The form of civil law is determined by legislative act, whereas that of religion is determined by tradition and the analogical imagination. The form of the moral law is dictated by the Categorical Imperative, or the requirement that maxims must be universalized for all persons in relevantly similar situations. Aesthetic form parallels the Kingdom of Ends, or the set of all moral agents in a community who are freely bound by the forms of morality just as the understanding and imagination are freely controlled by aesthetic form.

By contrast, the sublime is divisive: each man recoils upon his own noumenal self, struck by the realization of his personal dignity, for man is not only a social animal but a being in his own right. The sublime throws into relief the individuality of the moral agent, whereas the beautiful reveals his sociability:

Simplicity (artless finality) is, as it were, the style adopted by nature in the sublime. It is also that of morality. The latter is a second (supersensible) nature, whose laws alone we know, without being able to attain to an intuition of the supersensible faculty within us—that which contains the ground of this legislation.[63]

In the passage just cited, we might ask why Kant assumes that there must be a "supersensible faculty within us" to account for the moral laws that we know. I suppose that his first argument would be similar to the one given for the necessity of the noumenal. In brief, he argues that there could not be appearances (phenomena) without something which appears (noumena). His argument might be put as a rhetorical question: How could something have appearances if there were not *something* that had appearances? So, too, how could there be moral laws unless there were a giver of them? The source of moral laws, or the will that commands them, is neither God, nor religious exemplars, nor the political state. The source is rather each man willing the moral law for himself. Given that the moral law has the same form for all rational beings, what one man wills a priori must necessarily cohere with the legislation willed by all others.

The argument based upon "appearances," however, makes only a grammatical point; it hardly precludes the obvious alternative that the notions of aesthetic rightness and fittingness might not be based entirely upon the empirically given. In a perceptual gestalt we often perceive what is out of place, unfitting, or "not right." The pillars, for example, might be too low for the pediment, or an episode in a novel might anticipate too strongly the development of a character which should be kept in suspense. Had Kant argued that form exhibits a perceptual necessity, he might have given a more convincing explanation of the intersubjective validity of aesthetic judgment. The "necessity" or exemplary worth of aesthetic objects would thus be a function of their organization and structure.[64] Aesthetic form, like truth, is not always easy to detect or discern. Because Kant denied that the sublime was based upon form, he could only demote the aesthetic category to a handmaid of morals.

The sublime is also claimed to awaken a feeling of respect for "the supersensible faculty within us—that which contains the ground of this legislation."[65] We know the moral law, but we cannot "attain to an intuition of the supersensible faculty within us."[66] Having thus defined the supersensible faculty, Kant means that it is a theoretical impossibility to have cognitive access to it. He occasionally appears, however, to grant a kind of emotional or quasi-religious access to such a faculty. The supersensible faculty is sometimes described as a theoretical entity helpful in contemplating ethical law. As a theoretical entity, it admits of neither cognitive nor emotional access; however the "faculty" is described as some positive entity that must elude our cognitive grasp because of our epistemological structure. Kant hints that in the sublime one might become aware, by a kind of religious or numinous experience, of the supersensible faculty; still, we can no more articulate our "findings" than the mystic can bring back reports from his visions. The reports might, however, have analogical or metaphorical value in providing a poetic bridge to the noumenal. Yet it must be stressed that Kant only hints at such a possibility. The feeling of the sublime and the elevation and awe that attend it are the highest feeling of which man is capable; they do not, however, afford any privileged access to the noumenal. "Thus the sublime must in every case have reference to our way of *thinking*, i.e., to maxims directed to giving the intellectual side of our nature and the ideas of reason supremacy over sensibility."[67]

What Kant left as a faint hint, the Sturm und Drang movement picked up as a manifesto. Herder, for example, in his *Kalligone*,[68] argued that the experience of the sublime breaks down the epistemological distinction between phenomenal and noumenal, thereby thrusting one bodily into an experience of high universal values and making one a denizen of the supersensible. Herder also rejected the notion that pain or displeasure must precede the experience of the sublime. Because the supersensible was so vague and mysterious, and promised to satisfy fantasies that were stifled or ridiculed in the phenomenal world, romantic philosophers and artists were to make much of it. The transpontine realms of the noumenal seemed all the more idyllic because of their inaccessibility. The metaphor was to become a way of bridging the sensible gulf between the world of sense and the world of idea. The poet would become mystic, seer, and not quite of this world. Kant, however, in spite of his nascent romanticism, would have been strongly opposed to later romantic interpretations of the sublime that claimed him as their spiritual father:

This pure, elevating, merely negative presentation of morality involves, on the other hand, no fear of fanaticism, which is a *delusion* that would will some VISION *beyond all the bounds of sensibility:* i.e., would dream according to principles (rational raving). The safeguard is the purely negative character of the presentation. For the *inscrutability of the idea of freedom* precludes all positive presentation.[69]

Neither does Kant mask his contempt when he alludes to what must have been the new Sturm und Drang school: "For not a few leaders of a newer school believe that the best way to promote a free art is to sweep away all restraint, and convert it from labor into mere play."[70] Although Kant foresaw the excesses of the romantic interpretation and rejected them, his distinction between the noumenal and the phenomenal was just as crucial to his analysis of the sublime as to the rest of the Critical enterprise. I shall defer further discussion of that distinction until we turn to Kant's antinomy of taste.[71]

As a final observation concerning the link between the noumenal and the sublime, one might wonder how Kant can argue that moral law is universal and necessary, and at the same time imposed by the will, like civil and legal law. Yet he systematically describes the supersensible faculty as "legislating," not only in the third *Critique,* but in the *Critique of Practical Reason* and in the *Fundamental Principles of the Metaphysics of Morals.* The argument against Kant's position appears to be the following: Moral laws are either apodictic or they are not. If they are not, then Kant would not have needed to invoke the supersensible faculty of legislation in his analysis of the sublime. If moral laws are in some sense apodictic, then they resemble mathematical laws at least in the respect that both are discoverable and not in any way dependent, except historically, upon anyone's will. For example, early Christians believed that they had made moral discoveries which marked an advance over the legalistic and retributive ethics of the Pharisees. The Pauline virtues of faith, hope, and charity were construed as eternal values, though discovered at a certain point in time. Some early writers, like Tertullian and St. Augustine, did give a voluntaristic interpretation of such virtues, though they implied that even God's will would not be sufficient to vouch for moral validity, unless God were omnibenevolent. Given that moral law is in some sense discoverable, it is theoretically independent of any will whatsoever. It is misleading to say, as Kant does, that part of the validity of moral law depends upon the will of each autonomous agent. Mathematical laws can of course be applied to the "phenomenal" world or used practically, as in engineering or accounting. But what it would mean to *impose* mathematical laws is as unclear as to *impose* moral laws, especially given Kant's frequent claim that moral laws are pure a priori.

In the "General Remark," the sublime finally emerges unabashedly as an ethical category, stripped of both particularity and sensuousness:

We have no reason to fear that the feeling of the sublime will suffer from an abstract mode of presentation like this, which is altogether negative as to what is sensuous. For though the imagination, no doubt, finds nothing beyond the sensible world to which it can lay hold, still this thrusting aside of the sensible barriers gives it a feeling of being unbounded. . . . Perhaps there is no more sublime passage in the Jewish Law than the commandment: Thou shalt not make unto thee any graven image, or any likeness of anything that is in heaven or on earth, or under the earth etc. . . . if we divest this representation of everything that can commend it to the senses . . . and the unmistakable and ineffaceable idea of morality is left in possession of the field.[72]

As we observed in the previous chapter, Kant did not give a satisfactory explanation of mistaken or erroneous judgments of the beautiful. A similar difficulty arises with the sublime, the autonomy of which is completely undermined. If we asked how a judgment of the sublime could be false, given Kant's analysis, it could only be that the judgment inadequately records a certain subjective feeling. Given that we judge only of the *impression* that the object leaves upon us, together with the feelings "occasioned" by it, we could err only through self-deception.

Of all human weaknesses, self-deception is surely one of the most pervasive. Though it has often been the theme and burden of art, self-deception presents little danger to the experience of art. An artist might deceive himself about the worth of what he has made; members of a school might deceive themselves about the merits of their master. But when both conscious and subconscious motives are absent, self-deception is eliminated by definition, and aesthetic experience is free from motive. Once self-deception is ruled out, no way remains for a judgment of the sublime to be false. If the judgment cannot be false, neither can it be true. Yet judgments which are neither true nor false seem drained of their cognitive force. The logical positivists happily accepted such a conclusion and extended it to aesthetic judgment in general. Both the early Wittgenstein and A. J. Ayer, for example, argued that aesthetic and ethical judgments are neither true or false. That a judgment of the sublime is to be construed as an exclamation or an imperative is of course antithetical to Kant's method and purpose in the *Critique of Judgment.* Yet the conclusion strictly follows. Although we are not thereby argued into accepting an analysis similar to that of logical positivism, we are forced to conclude that Kant's theory of the sublime is not only logically untenable but seriously distorted in its details.

The Kantian Sublime and Its Ancestors

Ideas, like families, have histories which members of the family often do not know, but by which they are nonetheless influenced. Kant's ideas on the sublime can be traced to a number of writers in the eighteenth century: Shaftesbury, Addison, Silvain, Pope, Dryden, Burke, and Lord Kames. Certain of these writers claim parentage from Boileau, and all ultimately hearken back to Longinus (or Dionysius), author of the brief treatise "On the Sublime," which was written during the last century B.C.[73] How many of the lesser writers who wrote on the subject with whom Kant would have cared to admit acquaintance cannot be known: great philosophers often like to give the impression of having none but the most illustrious ancestors. The history of an idea can be helpful in gaining an understanding of its texture, as opposed to its validity. Kant's theory of the sublime incorporated many of the commonplaces of his day, though he reworked them to fit into his metaphysical system.

It should not be surprising that Longinus draws upon certain distinctions made by Plato; they have curious but vague parallels in Kant's theory of the sublime. That art imitates, or ought to imitate, not the objects of sense ($\alpha\iota\sigma\theta\eta\tilde{\iota}\acute{a}$), but rather the truths known by mind ($\nu o\eta\tilde{\iota}\acute{a}$), is the axiom of Plato's aesthetics. The poet enjoys a supersensible cognition which his genius embodies, with the help of his craft, in sensuous form. The power of art is a form of ecstatic fascination exercised upon the soul, a psychic manipulation ($\psi\nu\chi\alpha\gamma\omega\acute{\iota}a$). Although Plato loved art, he loved the state more. The only emotions aroused by art that he would countenance were moral. Emotions that were divisive were to be condemned; those that united men as political and moral beings were to be fostered. Although Plato does not speak of sublimity in art as a distinct category of the aesthetic, he does speak of the highest or only true form of art, which he invariably links with a power of strengthening the moral fibers of the soul.

In his brief treatise, Longinus asks two questions about the sublime, chiefly with reference to literature: (1) What is the quality which makes a work great, or sublime? (2) How can the quality be produced? Longinus has much to say about the rhetorical devices for bringing about the feeling of the sublime; like Kant and many later romantic philosophers, he assumes that sublimity is a disposition of the soul. The necessary conditions of the disposition are the ability to grasp "great conceptions" and to harbor strong and impetuous passions. Longinus assumes that these two attributes can be presupposed in all sentient beings and are in some sense innate. The artist, by either his craft or rhetorical skill, brings about a feeling of ecstasy. The soul recognizes an affinity with the supersensible and feels as though it had created the object itself. Longinus defines "sublimity" as "the note which rings from a great mind":

I wrote elsewhere something like this: "sublimity is the echo of a noble mind". This is why a mere idea, without verbal expression, is sometimes admired for its nobility. . . . Words will be great if thoughts are weighty. . . . It is our nature to be elevated and exalted by true sublimity. Filled with joy and pride, we come to believe we have created what we have only heard.[74]

In the introduction that Boileau wrote for his translation of Longinus, he draws a distinction between the sublime and the sublime style. Rhetoric gives us the latter; only "high thought" or spirited feeling gives us the former. In Boileau's introduction, the credo of neoclassicism resounds: the greatest thoughts must be expressed in the simplest language; images must be few or nonexistent. Even the sublime must not violate propriety. In Silvain's *Traité Du Sublime* (1732), elements from both Boileau and Longinus are brought together into something strongly Kantian. The sublime is said to reawaken in the soul feelings of its own grandeur and nobility.

To appreciate Kant's decided preference of Nature to art, we must turn to England, and first of all to the third earl of Shaftesbury.[75] Two pecularities of Shaftesbury's conception of the sublime should be noted because of their variance with Kant's theory. Art and Nature are both called artifacts, because to appreciate Nature leads to witnessing the work of the supreme artist, God. Moreover, the sublime and the beautiful are not to be contrasted; the latter is a variety of the former. Shaftesbury closely identified the sublime with Nature; his examples are often those later given by Kant: raging torrents, cliffs, the starry heavens, and the ocean. Though Shaftesbury was hardly the first to write about the "sublimities" of Nature, he was the first to describe it in philosophical tones and to give an explanation decidedly pre-Kantian: the vastness of Nature is too immense for us to comprehend perceptually. Thrown back upon our own finitude we are reminded of the infinite.

A minor writer of the period, Thomas Burnet, had more than hinted at Kant's theory a hundred years before the third *Critique* presented a "transcendental" explication. Burnet wrote:

The greatest objects of Nature are, methinks, the most pleasing to behold: and next to the great Concave of the Heavens, and those boundless Regions where the Stars inhabit, there is nothing that I look upon with more pleasure than the wide Sea and the Mountains of the Earth. There is something august and stately in the Air of those things that inspires the mind with great thoughts and passions; we do naturally upon such occasions think of God and his greatness, and whatsoever hath but the shadow and appearance of INFINITE, as all things that are too big for our comprehension, they fill and overbear the mind with their Excess, and cast it into a pleasing kind of stupor and admiration.[76]

Once he had been revived in the seventeenth century, Longinus did not have to wait long to be popularized. One of the first men to do so was Joseph Addison, who took over, in a distorted manner, the distinction between what is expressed and how it is expressed. He also distinguished the false from the true sublime; the former is greatness of bulk, the latter greatness of manner. In the *Spectator*, Addison remarks that the Aristotelian unities do not go far in explaining the sublime, which is something that "elevates and astonishes the fancy, and gives a greatness of mind to the reader." The Gothic might be confused with the sublime because of its immense size; but because of what Addison calls its "meanness" of style, the Gothic is only barbarous.[77]

Kant shared the common eighteenth-century attitude toward the Gothic; his taste in general was conventionally correct for an eighteenth-century philosopher-gentleman. In the *Observations*, Kant wrote:

If, in conclusion, we survey the course of history, we find man's taste, like Proteus, assuming ever-changing forms. The ancient times of the Greeks and Romans gave clear evidence of a genuine feeling for beauty as well as for the sublime, in poetry, sculpture, architecture, legislation and even in morals. The reign of the Roman Caesars transformed both the beautiful and the sublime in their simplicity into splendor and then into spurious glitter. . . . The barbarians, once established, introduced a certain perverse taste which is called the Gothic, and which culminated in the grotesque. . . . In our own day we see beginning to flourish a true taste for the beautiful and the sublime, in the arts and sciences, as well as in morals.[78]

However, given Kant's definition of the sublime, surely a Gothic cathedral would have satisfied his conception. Addison, who was more of a classicist than Kant, describes even the sublime, which he sometimes calls "greatness," as quite orderly:

Such are the prospects of an open champion country, a vast uncultivated desert, of huge heaps of mountains, high rocks and precipices . . . with that rude kind of magnificence which appears in many of these stupendous works of Nature. Our imagination loves to be filled with an object, or to grasp at anything that is too big for its capacity. We are flung into a pleasing astonishment at such unbounded views, and feel a delightful stillness and amazement in the soul at the apprehension of them.[79]

Like Shaftesbury, Addison does not contrast the beautiful with the sublime but asserts that it is one of the species of the beautiful, along with uncommonness or novelty. Both writers are impressionistic and phenomenological in their descriptions: they are more interested in describing the content of our experience than in giving a psychological or physiological explanation of it.

It awaited Edmund Burke to give the first reasoned and systematic account of the sublime, which he presented in his *Philosophical Enquiry Into the Origin of Our Ideas of the Sublime and Beautiful*.[80] Kant cites a passage from it, but only to show "where a merely empirical exposition of the sublime and beautiful would bring us."[81] The parallels between Burke's and Kant's analyses are so striking that often a mere adverb separates them: Burke will have it "physiologically" and Kant, "transcendentally."[82]

Romantic aesthetics first appeared in English letters in a politically reactionary stance. Maintaining the importance of tradition in art and in politics, Burke could argue for the revolution in

America and condemn the revolution in France because he believed the former to be a just and legitimate extension of traditional rights, and the latter a subversion of fundamental class structures. Though a romanticist, Burke detested Rousseau and remained at heart traditionally religious.

As Kant argued much later, Burke held that the rationalistic aesthetics of clarity and perfection was profoundly mistaken, for whatever stretches the imagination to its limits, like the infinite perceived in the ocean, can be neither clear nor distinct. The imagination is moved to its greatest heights by what it cannot comprehend. Art must always hint or suggest, and remain veiled in mystery, to have its greatest effect. It is fear or obscurity, not knowledge or complaisance, that gives rise to the sublime.

The description that Burke gives to his aims in the "Introduction on Taste"[83] closely parallels Kant's avowed purpose in the third *Critique*. Burke intends to discover an intersubjectively valid standard of taste, by which he means "no more than that faculty, or those faculties of the mind which are affected with, or which form a judgment of the works of imagination and the elegant arts."[84] Burke claims "that the standard both of reason and Taste is the same in all human creatures," and that by a kind of physiological and phenomenological analysis he can discover "a logic of Taste, if I may be allowed the expression,"[85] which will raise aesthetic matters, or taste, out of the realm of the subjective. Agreeable sensations might be "positive" or involve "the removal or diminution of pain."[86] The sublime belongs to the latter type but also hinges upon the passions connected with self-preservation, or the passions related to pain and danger. Such passions "are delightful when we have an idea of pain and danger, without being actually in such circumstances. . . . Whatever excites this delight I call *sublime*."[87] The analysis of the sublime begins with what Burke calls "astonishment," or "that state of the soul, in which all its motions are suspended, with some degree of horror." The mind is overpowered, filled with the immensity of the object contemplated; we are transfixed, unable to move. Burke appears more sensitive to the varieties of sublimity than Kant and distinguishes various grades of sublimity ranging from astonishment and horror to "admiration, reverence, and respect."[88] Fear of pain or of death is linked as a necessary condition of sublimity: "Whatever is fitted in any sort to excite the ideas of pain, and danger, that is to say, whatever is in any sort terrible, or is conversant about terrible objects, or operates in a manner analogous to terror, is a source of the *sublime;* that is, it is productive of the strongest emotion which the mind is capable of feeling."[89]

The sublime appears to be at variance with the neoclassical aesthetic virtues of order, proportion, clarity of line, and perspicuity of structure. Burke argues that though the beautiful rests upon harmony and the cooperation of the mental faculties, still the sublime, which arouses the deepest feelings of the soul, is based upon disunity and conflict of faculties. At first the conflict produces pain, which causes the organism to recoil and the muscles to tighten. All laws seem to be broken; but rather than succumb, we feel exalted and strengthened.

The sources, or at least the anticipations of Kant's analysis, become more striking in the details of Burke's early work. Sublimity is said to remove the finitude of the self, not by crushing it, but by revealing its own boundlessness. Confronted by the sublime in art or Nature, we become aware of our own personal freedom; we witness our limitations as other objects in a deterministic world only to revel in our freedom as transcendent beings. As members of society, we are enchained in numerous ways; the beautiful helps us accept the bondage of society by imparting the forms of civility and morality. The sublime throws us back upon our selfhood. The beautiful unites and civilizes by means of form; the sublime is divisive and formless, but it arouses the profoundest moral feelings.

Burke's inventory of the causes of the sublime is far more exhaustive than Kant's distinction between the mathematical and the dynamic. Because ignorance is usually at the foot of admiration, obscurity is a necessary condition of the terrible aspect of the sublime. Ignorance being part of the human condition, the sublime will exist as long as man. The chief factors of sublimity are greatness of magnitude or extension, great power, and great privation or emptiness. "To see an object distinctly, and to perceive its bounds, is one and the same thing. A clear idea is therefore another name for a little idea."[90]

Kant concedes that these "psychological observations . . . of our mental phenomena are extremely fine,"[91] though he gives Burke short shrift: "But if we attribute the delight in the object wholly and entirely to the gratification which it affords through charm or emotion, then we must not exact from *any one else* agreement with the aesthetic judgment passed by us."[92] To give Burke a fairer hearing, and to conclude this historical sketch, the following intimation of the Critical philosophy might be in order:

On the whole it appears to me, that what is called Taste, in its general acceptation, is not a simple idea, but is partly made up of a perception of the primary pleasures of sense, of the secondary pleasures of the imagination, and of the conclusions of the reasoning faculty, concerning the human passions, manners and actions.[93]

CHAPTER 4

The Metaphysics of Criticism

The Antinomy of Taste

Anyone acquainted with Kant's reflections on other branches of philosophy would naturally expect a dialectic and an antinomy in Kant's aesthetics. The first two books of Part One of the third *Critique* deal respectively with the "Analytic of the Beautiful" and the "Analytic of the Sublime." Parallel to the division that Kant draws in the first *Critique* between "Analytic" and "Dialectic," the "Analytic" of the beautiful attempts to explicate its "transcendental logic" and its functions in aesthetic judgment; similarly, the "Analytic of the Sublime" gives the logical structure of the second major "category," sublimity. Both parts of the "analytic" attempt to relate the two aesthetic "categories" to experience. Just as the first *Critique* attempts to show how pure concepts have objective reference, so Part One of the third *Critique* attempts to explain the subjective reference of the beautiful and the sublime. Just as objective knowledge would be impossible without the pure concepts, so aesthetic judgment would be impossible without the "concepts" of beauty and sublimity. And finally, just as the first *Critique* attempts to show the proper use of a priori concepts, so the third *Critique*, Part One, explains the proper use of aesthetic concepts. It is for this reason that I have entitled this chapter "The Metaphysics of Criticism"; as I interpret Kant, one of his main purposes in the Dialectic is to lay down the "ground rules" of criticism of the fine arts.[1]

The Transcendental Dialectic in the first *Critique* gives the appearance of negative criticism of the traditional, dogmatic metaphysics. In the light of the "Analytic," Kant exposes the sophistries and illusions of what he deems constitutive, or "school" metaphysics. At the same time, he tries to map out the correct or regulative employment of theoretical reason. A similar attempt lies at the base of the "Dialectic of Aesthetic Judgment" in the third *Critique.* Very broadly, before entering into the details of his argument, I shall simply note that Kant attempts to criticize what I might call dogmatic criticism, or rationalistic aesthetics. At the same time, in a purely regulative way, he tries to chart the course of regulative ideas in aesthetics. A large part of the negative presentation of the "Dialectic" includes the antinomy of taste. Like the antinomies in the first *Critique,* the antinomy of taste presents an apparently insoluble paradox, which must nevertheless be solved to bring "reason into harmony with itself."[2]

Although one sometimes feels that Kant forces philosophical issues into his preconceived critical mold, the apparent arbitrariness of his distinctions between "Analytic" and "Dialectic," and the perhaps even grotesque conception of the antinomy of taste, reveal by the very vigor of his argument much that might remain inert under the hands of a more impressionistic and gentle-minded philosopher. Kant claims to find a paradox in judgments of taste which only the Dialectic and the principles of critical philosophy can resolve: "For a power of judgment to be dialectical it must first of all be rationalizing; that is to say, its judgments must lay claim to universality, and do so *a priori,* for it is in the antitheses of such judgments that dialectic consists."[3]

Kant argues that a judgment of taste must in some manner be conceptual, though the role of concepts in such judgments must be carefully construed. If judgments of taste were almost nonconceptual, they would be solely autobiographical reports upon subjective feelings of pleasure and pain.

Kant distinguishes "private taste," or what might be called "judgments of preference," from aesthetic judgment. We might prefer one work of art to another without having to say that the one is better than the other. Preferences, which often run counter to aesthetic judgment, are not to be universalized. "And in so far as each person appeals merely to his own private taste, even the conflict of judgments of taste does not form a dialectic of taste—for no one is proposing to make his own judgment into a universal rule."[4] A judgment such as "This is an instance of sulphur" is clearly conceptual because the concept of sulphur—its atomic weight or some less technical definition—is adduced. Again, in line with Kant's fond examples of "flowers, blossoms, even the shapes of plants as a whole,"[5] the botanical judgment "This is a good example of a spadix" is conceptual because the judgment draws upon the notion of what a perfect spadix is: a spike with fleshy or succulent axis, usually enclosed in a spathe—like a jack-in-the-pulpit. If aesthetic judgment were based upon determinate concepts, then judgments as different as "This is a good Petrarchan sonnet" and "This is a good poem" would be verified in the same way. Just as the necessary and sufficient conditions of the Petrarchan sonnet can be explicitly stated, so the necessary and sufficient condition of being a good poem could be laid down. Yet the rules of the Petrarchan sonnet can be learned from a handbook on prosody, whereas there are no comparable rules for "a good poem." This does not imply that one cannot study the art of poetry, but it does imply that aesthetic education does not consist in amassing determinate rules or even techniques. For the present I shall defer Kant's discussion of aesthetic education.[6]

The reader might have been struck by my tentative use in the present section of both "concept" and "category" as I attempted to explain the beautiful and the sublime in Kant's "Dialectic." Neither the beautiful nor the sublime, however, seems to be a category or an a priori concept; for neither of these two aesthetic "categories" is required by the cognitive faculties for knowledge, nor are they as "pure" as the mathematical categories of quantity and quality, or the dynamical categories of relation and modality. Yet one hesitates to call the beautiful or the sublime empirical concepts: "greenness" and "heaviness" seem to be much further embedded in the sensible manifold than either "beauty" or "sublimity."

If Kant's Copernican revolution of taste is to be taken as more than a flamboyant metaphor, he must intend that aesthetic judgment approach the objects of its experience with the "notions" of the beautiful and the sublime. Kant could not consistently claim that such "notions" are derived by passive abstraction from phenomena, as are the empirical concepts of, say, "greenness" or "hardness."

Before turning to the details of the antinomy of taste, I shall attempt to place the beautiful and the sublime on Kant's logical map, as it were: that is, whether they are a priori concepts, in some sense, or empirical. I shall begin with a very Latinate passage from the first *Critique*, in which Kant attempts to give such a map:

The genus is *representation* in general (repraesentatio). Subordinate to it stands representation with consciousness (perceptio). A *perception* which relates solely to the subject as the modification of its state is *sensation* (sensatio), an objective perception is *knowledge* (cognitio). This is either *intuition* or *concept* (intuitus vel conceptus). The former relates immediately to the object and is single, the latter refers to it mediately by means of a feature which several things may have in common. The concept is either an *empirical* or a *pure* concept. The pure concept, in so far as it has its origin in the understanding alone (not in the pure sensibility), is called a *notion*. A concept formed from notions and transcending the possibility of experience is an *idea* or concept of reason.[7]

From this passage it appears that among the likely classificatory niches for the beautiful or the sublime are (1) an empirical concept, (2) a pure concept, (3) a notion, or (4) an idea. But reasons against Kant's consistently placing the beautiful in any of these four "species" readily come to mind. Other than the general reasons that I have already mentioned, the beautiful could be neither an empirical nor a pure concept, for clearly Kant does not construe singular judgments of the beautiful, or judgments of taste, as connoting "a feature which several things may have in common," for aesthetic judgment would then give objective knowledge, which would undercut Kant's entire aesthetic theory. It is significant to observe, I believe, that Kant does not give an elaboration in this passage of "empirical concept," but does do so for "pure concept."

Elsewhere in the first *Critique*, Kant states that concepts in general are rules of synthesis and, as such, the work of understanding. "All knowledge demands a concept, though that concept may, indeed, be quite imperfect or obscure. But a concept is always, as regards its form, something universal which serves as a rule. The concept of body, for instance, as the unity of the manifold which is thought through it, serves as a rule in our knowledge of outer appearances."[8] It is also clear that the beautiful could not be what Kant calls a "notion"; for if the beautiful is conceptually related to the feelings of pleasure and displeasure, as Kant so strongly maintains, it follows that "the understanding alone" could not give rise to the aesthetic. Finally, if the beautiful were placed in the subspecies that Kant calls "idea," it would be confounded with the concepts of reason, that is, either theoretical or practical versions of the Psychological, Cosmological, or Theological Ideas. Furthermore, to describe the beautiful as a "concept formed from notions and transcending the possibility of experience" would lead Kant to say that aesthetic judgment is not reflective (or determinate), which would also undermine his entire aesthetic.

Kant nowhere presents, to the best of my knowledge, a clear distinction between empirical and a priori concepts. Both are described as spontaneous and synthetic acts of the understanding,[9] as embodiments of cognitive construction. When Kant asserts in the third *Critique* that the "green color of the meadows belongs to *objective* sensation, as the perception of an object of sense,"[10] "greenness" must be taken as paradigmatic of empirical concepts for Kant. As such, "greenness" is a rule, or connotes a rule, concerning the unifying of certain sensible "qualia."[11] The pure concept of quality gives the rules for forming any such empirical concept of color, or any other sensational qualium. Pure concepts, consequently, give what I might call epistemological parallels of *Robert's Rules of Order*: they lay down the complete set (or at least Kant so believes) of the juridical procedures required for any knowledge whatsoever. Empirical concepts are formed, as for their content, out of the workings of the reproductive imagination as it shapes and imposes the "pure" concepts upon the sensible manifold given in perception. Empirical concepts are not simply abstracted in a passive way, but are constructed out of the perceptual manifold. Imagination, which even in the judgment of the sublime is fundamentally lawful, acts—if a flamboyant metaphor of my own be allowed—like Hermes moving between the gods and man, or between the pure concepts and intuition.

In Kant's long inventory of the types of "representation" in the first *Critique*,[12] one subspecies is omitted which is crucial to the understanding of the antinomy of taste. In the "Analytic of the Beautiful," Kant describes "the ideal of the beautiful":

Properly speaking, an *idea* signifies a concept of reason, and an *ideal* the representation of an individual existence as adequate to an idea. Hence this archetype of taste . . . may more appropriately be called the ideal of the beautiful. While not having this ideal in our possession, we still strive to beget it within us. . . . Now how do we arrive at such an ideal of beauty? Is it *a priori* or empirically?[13]

Kant says that an ideal cannot be formed for free beauties, "presumably because their ends are not sufficiently defined and fixed by their concept."[14] Kant argues that only man, because he alone is capable of determining their ends by reason, admits "of an ideal of beauty."[15] Such an ideal, like the tulip mentioned in Dr. Johnson's *Rasselas*, must contain nothing individual or characteristic; moreover, unlike the "normal idea," or the academic norm of the human figure, the ideal of beauty in the human form evinces "moral ideas that govern men inwardly."[16] The "normal idea" is produced out of the manifold in perception. Kant comes as close in the third *Critique* as he ever does to discussing aesthetic relativism: "If, again, for our average man we seek on similar lines for the average head, and for the average nose, and so on, then we get the figure that underlies the normal idea of a beautiful man in the country where the comparison is instituted."[17]

Yet the average or normal idea does not give the "archetype of beauty in the genus."[18] The normal idea gives only an empirically correct concept of a certain genus; the archetype, which omits all reference to the individual, both gives the perfection of the genus and imposes the form of beauty. Kant restricts the "ideal of beauty" to the archetype of man because only the representation of man bears "visible expression of moral ideas."[19]

To return now to my original question: given that the beautiful is for Kant neither an empirical nor an a priori concept, neither a notion nor an idea of reason, and lastly, not an ideal, what, according to Kant, is the genus of the beautiful? As a brief recapitulation, it should be noted that in each of the four "moments" of Kant's definition of "the beautiful" he hesitates to designate any particular genus. Moment (1) "The object of such a delight is called *beautiful.*"[20] (2) "The *beautiful* is that which, apart from a concept, pleases universally."[21] (3) "*Beauty* is the form of *finality* in an object, so far as perceived in it *apart from the representation of an end.*"[22] And (4) "The beautiful is that which, apart from a concept, is cognized as object of a *necessary* delight."[23]

In the light of Kant's four claims and the meanings that he assigns to the various species and subspecies of "representation," it seems obvious to conclude: first, that neither the beautiful nor the sublime connotes representations at all, though the beautiful (as opposed to the sublime) does denote certain representations insofar as they are referred to feelings of disinterested pleasure; and second, that it is misleading to describe either the beautiful or the sublime as "concepts" or "categories," even in an analogous manner. Calling the beautiful a "form" would also be misleading, given the Platonic connotations of the term, as well as the role of the "pure" forms of space and time in Kant's first *Critique.*

Yet, if Kant's Copernican revolution of taste implies that cognitive free play imposes forms such that the understanding and imagination would freely dictate to the sensible manifold, then to describe the beautiful as "form" might not be misleading, though Kant himself does not explicitly do so. In the first *Critique,* in the "Transcendental Doctrine of Elements," Kant says: "That in the appearance which corresponds to sensation I term its *matter;* but that which so determines the manifold of appearance that it allows of being ordered in certain relations, I term the *form* of appearance."[24] In the "Analytic of Concepts," while describing concepts, Kant says, "Concepts rest on functions. By 'function' I mean the unity of the act of bringing various representations under one common representation."[25] Although aesthetic judgment does not involve bringing representations under "one common representation" (which would make such judgment cognitive), aesthetic judgment, according to Kant, does and must bring representations under one common feeling: disinterested pleasure. It might not be misleading, then, to interpret aesthetic judgment as a "function" or even a "disposition" that involves imposing the form of the beautiful upon the sensible manifold by indeterminate concepts, in accordance with feelings of pleasure and displeasure. Such concepts are empirical for the beautiful; for the sublime, the ideas of reason are indeterminately awakened. Just as understanding is at its least free when constructing empirical concepts, so it is at its most free, or autonomous, in aesthetic judgment.

In view of these observations, Kant's paradox or antinomy of taste may now be stated. If aesthetic judgment rested upon concepts, it could be rationally proved; conclusive rules could be adduced for judgment, with either deductive glory or inductive grandeur. Though he was acquainted with Baumgarten's attempts to demonstrate aesthetics "in the geometrical manner" and very probably with Hume's psychology of taste, Kant held that rationalistic aesthetics reduces to barren analyticity, and psychological aesthetics, to relativism of judgment. However, if aesthetic judgment were only faintly conceptual, it would have only autobiographical validity. Yet, for better or worse, literary criticism, and art criticism in general, is one of the oldest forms of verbal discourse.

The antinomy can be stated more formally and formidably: (1) Thesis: the judgment of taste *is not* based upon concepts; if it were, then it could be disputed, and logical argument could be brought to bear: such judgment would be clearly cognitive. (2) Antithesis: the judgment of taste *is* based upon concepts; if it were not, then one could not even contend or quarrel about matters of taste: such judgment would be purely and merely personal.

Of antinomies in general, in the third *Critique*, Kant asserts that their solution "turns solely on the possibility of two apparently conflicting propositions not being in fact contradictory, but rather being capable of consisting together, although the explanation of the possibility of their concept transcends our faculties of cognition."[26] From so loyal a son of the Enlightenment, such a declaration is surprising. One might wonder how explanation of the possibility of a concept could meaningfully transcend the faculties of cognition. A particular person might say that something always "transcends his faculties of cognition," for example, astrophysics. But what such a person does not know is knowable and might in fact be known by other persons. Something might "transcend the faculties of cognition" temporarily because no one has yet found the solution. A truly orthodox son of the Enlightenment, like Voltaire or La Mettrie, would have argued that whatever exists is knowable and that the progress of science proves the cognitive accessibility of reality. Some *philosophes*, like Condorcet, held out the possibility that reality would soon reveal all its scientific and psychological mechanisms.[27] Moreover, it was folly even to intimate anything beyond, behind, or "other than" such mechanisms.

Though Kant was far removed from the mysticism of Pascal, one cannot but be struck by the parallel between Pascal's *pensée* that the ultimate move of reason is to concede many things to be beyond reason, and Kant's mysterious observation toward the end of Part One of the third *Critique*: "The subjective principle—that is to say, the indeterminate idea of the supersensible within us—can only be indicated as the unique key to the riddle of this faculty, itself concealed from us in its sources; and there is no means of making it any more intelligible."[28]

To solve the antinomy, Kant first distinguishes between disputing and contending. Persons might reasonably contend with each other, as opposed to merely bantering, even though a determinate concept cannot be articulated. In a dispute in mathematics or in physics, or in an applied science like engineering, it is possible to refute or disprove one's opponent by purely rational procedures, or by invoking determinate rules or concepts. Nothing of the sort can occur, Kant claims, in disagreements in aesthetic taste. Someone might prove or disprove the authenticity of a certain painting, but one can never prove its beauty. This is so, not because adequate proof will be forever wanting, but because "proving beauty" is, according to Kant, a contradiction in terms. He implies, therefore, that the realm of rational disagreement is broader than strict proof and disproof. Disagreements in matters of taste are neither irrational, nonrational, nor subjective in the sense that judgment is biased or prejudiced.

Kant becomes somewhat tentative about his solution of the antinomy of taste. He writes that the "determining ground lies, perhaps, in the concept of what may be regarded as the supersensible substrate of humanity."[29] Later, his tone is almost diffident and apologetic:

If, however, our deduction is at least credited with having been worked out on correct lines, even though it may not have been sufficiently clear in all its details, three ideas stand out in evidence. *Firstly*, there is the supersensible in general, without further determination, as substrate of nature; *secondly*, this same supersensible as principle of the subjective finality of nature for our cognitive faculties; *thirdly*, the same supersensible again, as principle of the ends of freedom, and principle of the common accord of these ends with freedom in the moral sphere.[30]

In spite of his hesitations to invoke the supersensible to solve the antinomy, Kant maintains that only the noumenal can make good the claim of aesthetic judgment to universal validity. As I have already noted, Kant invoked the supersensible in the first and second *Critiques* in hopes of quelling philosophical disturbances, many of which, it might be suggested, were of his own inciting. It would hardly be appropriate to review here all the criticism that has been brought against Kant's conception of "the thing-in-itself," most of which has been leveled against the epistemological and ethical roles that Kant assigned to the noumenal. In general, one wonders how theoretical difficulties can be solved, or even rendered more palatable, by relocating them in a logically possible sphere. Given that one of the pure categories is existence, and that Kant holds the categories to be applicable only to the phenomenal, existence could not even be predicated of the noumenal. To speak of something that *may* exist entails conceiving of what it would be like if it *did* exist. Moreover, the noumenal could not be called a theoretical entity of heuristic value. Theoretical entities, which are perhaps a species of poetic metaphor, are tolerated in science or in practical life as long as they are fecund and useful. Theoretical entities decay and fall into desuetude, like religious myths, when they no longer aid the imagination in solving practical or theoretical problems. Yet no possible change in the affairs of the world could possibly lead to the desuetude of the noumenal. The notion seems not only self-contradictory, but tinged with a sort of fideistic absurdity recalling Tertullian.

It must be noted, however, in Kant's defense (if inconsistency be granted as a kind of defense), that sometimes he implies that it is quite meaningless to speak of the thing-in-itself,[31] or the noumenon, as the cause of appearances. In the negative, or regulative sense, the noumenal designates an epistemological object insofar as it exists independent of any possible knowing subject constituted like ourselves. Given that the human knower must always judge from a particular perspective, his aesthetic judgment must also record a limited point of view. The thing-in-itself is the "nonperspectival" object, about which nothing positive can be known. Revealing his early attraction to Swedenborg, Kant implies that if we had a purely intellectual faculty of intuition, then the thing-in-itself could be known.

Kant's distinction between noumenal and phenomenal, which has an ontological parallel to the epistemological, might be construed as a distinction between two ways of speaking or describing one and the same object. It would therefore be pointless to speak of the noumenal as "causing" the phenomenal or as being the ontological ground for the realm of appearances. For example, human behavior might be described or talked about, from the phenomenal point of view, as a set of causally interacting forces. From the noumenal point of view, moral behavior might be described in terms of rational causation, that is, in terms of nonconstraining causes, or grounds of actions in the light of which the moral agent chooses. If my suggestion of interpreting the noumenal-phenomenal distinction as one involving kinds of discourse is tenable, then neither kind of discourse would in any absolute sense have priority over the other. In some contexts it is important to know whether the cause is "an intelligible cause," that is, a motive or reason for someone's behavior. In moral and legal assessment it is a question of determining what kind of cause is present, rather than trying to prove the absence of a "phenomenal" cause.

Given that Kant's general doctrine of the noumenal appears so untenable, and given that he believes practical reason to lay claim upon the noumenal, perhaps any interpretation of Kant's doctrine of the noumenon can be undermined by a quotation from Kant himself. Against the interpretation of two forms of discourse, Kant states in the first *Critique:* "The concept of a noumenon is thus merely a limiting concept, the function of which is to curb the pretensions of sensibility; and it is therefore only of a negative employment."[32] Perhaps if Kant had distinguished between kinds of causes, he would never have tried to reconcile the determined "phenomenal" self with a teleological, free, and "noumenal" self. Hence, it would never have been necessary to speak of curbing "the pretensions of sensibility." For, in human behavior, nonfree causes might be attributed to factors as various as compulsion, psychosis, political constraint, or excusable ignorance; free causes might be described in a thoroughly Kantian way as those involving consistency, autonomy, and respect for any other moral agent. Moreover, if both types of discourse concerning human behavior were founded in the "phenomenal" world, the entire enterprise of the third *Critique* might have been rendered otiose. In the "First Introduction" to the *Critique of Judgment*, Kant states that in both aesthetic and teleological judgment a sort of bridge is formed between theoretical and practical reason, between the noumenal and the phenomenal.

Rather than continuing these general criticisms of the noumenal, it would be more in order, and more sympathetic to the *Critique of Judgment,* to try to make Kant's notion of the aesthetic supersensible more plausible. What Kant was trying to explain might be dealt with more simply and understandably. I should like to mention a few considerations which might prepare the way for something like the supersensible, though Kant himself does not enlist their aid.

Many words employed to characterize or describe aesthetic experience do not directly refer to properties of objects, but rather to "properties" that supervene upon or pervade the object. To describe a painting as "monochromatic" or as "representing a family of three standing on the beach" is to refer to properties that are directly given: they are not inferred on the basis of other properties, nor are they the results of critical interpretation. To describe the same painting as "melancholy" or "forlorn" characterizes the work or gives it an aesthetic "physiognomy." The language of aesthetic discernment, unlike the language of categorization, relies heavily upon perceptual schematism and formal ambiguities.

Historical and sociological descriptions of art might be said to refer to the "phenomenal" aspect of art. I am not using "phenomenal" in Kant's sense of the word, but to refer to positivistic or scientific properties such as color, subject matter, provenance, or whatever might be substantiated by what Kant calls "determinate" empirical concepts.

Aesthetic properties are "noumenal," not in Kant's strict sense, but rather in the traditional and etymological meaning of "noumenal": an "aesthetic property" is an intelligible property supervening upon purely physical properties. The "noumenal" is thus a hybrid between human sensibility and the physical object. Although Kant does not distinguish between the directly given or positivistic properties of art and those that I have called "supervening," still he often speaks of art as a "visible expression" or as a symbol of morality.[33] If "noumenal" and "phenomenal" were used in Kant's strict sense, then both directly given and supervening or expressive properties would be species of the phenomenal. Yet because the etymological meaning of "noumenal" implies "apprehending," "conceiving," or "being intellectually aware of," it seems appropriate to speak of apprehending or being intellectually aware of expressive qualities and of aesthetic form, rather than seeing or hearing them. Expressive qualities of art might then be termed "noumenal," whereas nonexpressive qualities might be termed "phenomenal."

Philosophers are as much prey to the ambiguities of words as are other mortals. Though Kant gave "noumenal" a technical definition, the atavistic meanings of the term might have influenced his conception of the supersensible in aesthetic judgment. An aesthetic object seems especially "outside the phenomenal world" because, for Kant, it is not paradigmatically a practical or cognitive object, nor a mere stimulus for gratification.

One sometimes reaches a curious impasse in guiding another into acquaintance with an object of art. A historical background might be provided, along with a detailed analysis of the work and even the biography of the artist. Everything even remotely relevant to helping someone appreciate the work, as opposed to knowing mere bookish things about it, might be conjured up, and still one fails to impart an appreciation of it. There might be something in the aesthetic realm which parallels moral blindness. Without entering into the problems of ethical intuitionism, we might not be surprised that a comparable view, with comparable difficulties, is arguable in aesthetics. There comes a point at which one can only say, "But don't you see? It's a great work of art for just the reasons you are trying to bring against it." When the impasse occurs, however, other roads than the somewhat facile one of intuitionism remain open. Yet the language of intuition is cousin to the language of the noumenal, and the difficulty of imparting an appreciation of the fine arts might be their common parent.

The language of criticism reveals a parallel with certain aspects of the old controversy between vitalism and mechanism. Words that mark disapproval or disliking of aesthetic objects tend to fall under the rubric of the mechanical; words that mark approval tend to fall under the vital. We speak of a "dead," or a "wooden," or a "mechanical" interpretation of a piece of music, as opposed to one that is "alive," "supple," or "inspired." Genuine, as opposed to spurious or academic art, is often described as "living," "vital," and "fecund." Without going into the details of the controversy between vitalism and mechanism, it might not be amiss to cite Aristotle's *On the Soul* and *On the Generation of Animals* as expressing some of the chief notions of vitalism which have a loose analogy in aesthetic judgment. Aristotle says that the *psyche* of an organism is its life principle. Purposive activity, organic unity, and the power to develop autonomously—given correct conditions—are the salient characteristics of the living. Again, understanding the functions of the parts involves taking into account their relation to the whole organism. The *psyche*, moreover, acts upon the organism not as efficient cause, but as formal cause.

Aesthetic judgment might be characterized as "vitalistic"; for genuine art, or a genuine performance, is supposed to have a "soul" that gives life and validity to experience of it. When Kant attempts to define the "faculties" of the mind that constitute genius, he uses a number of vitalistic notions:

'Soul' [*Geist*] in an aesthetic sense, signifies the animating principle in the mind. But that whereby this principle animates the psychic substance [*Seele*]—the material which it employs for that purpose—is that which sets the mental powers into a swing that is final, i.e., into a play which is self-maintaining and which strengthens those powers for such activity.[34]

A genuine novel, for example, might be described as an organic unity with its own power to develop its plot and characters. A kind of "entelechy" in the conception gives an overriding purposiveness to the work. To understand a particular episode in a novel or in a piece of music, one must relate it to the *psyche* of the whole. In dead art there is only a collection of parts; in contrived art the parts are mechanically forced to relate to each other. Like any other mechanism, such a work is roughly a system of parts; a change in some of the parts causes changes in most of the others. Such an aggregate of connected changes fulfills a "determinate" concept; the parts are discrete, and the articulation of the whole is designated to effect something external. Some such contrast between "the mechanical" and "the vital" seems to be implicit in the "Analytic of the Sublime" and in Kant's distinction between the aesthetic and the logical:

There are, in fact, two modes (*modi*) in general of arranging one's thought for utterance. The one is called a *manner* (*modus aestheticus*), the other a *method* (*modus logicus*). The distinction between them is this: the former possess no standard other than the *feeling* of unity in the presentation, whereas the latter here follows definite *principles*. As a consequence the former is alone admissible for fine art.[35]

Although I do not mean to imply that the distinction between the mechanical and the vital must be made as a general claim, I do suggest that at least for Kant's aesthetics there is an interesting parallel between, on the one hand, the vital and the supersensible, and on the other, the mechanical and the phenomenal world. Kant often describes the phenomenal world in a purely mechanistic way and speaks of the moral or rational agent as a free and self-actuating being. Kant introduced the supersensible and the noumenal into aesthetic judgment because he assumed that "beauty as the symbol of morality"[36] would be impossible in the phenomenal world as explained by a mechanistic physics or by an empirical or associationist psychology.

Kant's solution of the antinomy, however, even within the framework of his own philosophy, seems untenable. Kant introduces the supersensible to explain the universality of aesthetic judgment; he also describes the beautiful as that which pleases by virtue of its form, independent of interest. Kant seems to be caught in a definitional embarrassment; for if it is impossible to say anything about the supersensible, it does not seem convincing to describe the capacity of disinterested pleasure taken in aesthetic form as "somehow related" to the supersensible substrate of humanity.[37]

Of the three conceptions that Kant relegates to the noumenal in the three *Critiques*—the necessary foundations of knowledge, the freedom of the moral agent, and the aesthetically supersensible —the last is the least comprehensible. The noumenal, by definition, is antipathetic to the aesthetic. As Kant employs "aesthetic" in the third *Critique*, judgment that both is aesthetic and lays claim to the supersensible seems like a contradiction in terms.

Kant often gives the impression while describing the supersensible that if something is describable in either natural language or in mathematics, or again, if something is discoverable or reducible to empirical law, it is phenomenal. He also appears to believe that if something is theoretically undescribable, or not reducible to empirical law, and also required by morality or even art as a symbol of morality, then it must be noumenal. Yet I submit that in the experience of music, for example, much is understood that cannot be described in any sense, except perhaps by analogy. If someone does not understand a piece of music, the first and best step is to play it again. Then the work might be musically analyzed or compared to other works. Though music exists in the realm of the "phenomenal," such analysis does not seem to be in the realm of the linguistically or mathematically describable. To explain why a certain passage in music fits or fails to fit, or why a word is out of place in a line of poetry, or why an area in a painting is compositionally required, recourse to neither psychological explanation nor the Kantian supersensible is required. Yet as Kant describes criticism of the arts, to give reasons for aesthetic judgment is tantamount to giving causal explanation concerning why some things please and others do not: "As an art, Critique looks to the physiological (here psychological), and, consequently, empirical rules, according to which in actual fact taste proceeds . . . and seeks to apply them in estimating objects."[38]

The picture of aesthetic taste that seems to emerge from Kant's solution to the antinomy would be as follows: as phenomenal beings described by physiology or psychology, persons have various and sometimes capricious tastes. Insofar as one attends strictly to aesthetic form, then given that "pure" aesthetic judgment of taste is universalizable, a supersensible "dimension" must be postulated. As rational beings, we have "faculties" that are rooted in a noumenal substrate that must be the same for everyone as the ground of intellectual, moral, and even aesthetic rightness. "But the mere pure rational concept of the supersensible at the basis of the object (and of the judging Subject for that matter) as Object of sense, and thus as phenomenon, is just such a concept."[39]

Kant's solution of the antinomy of taste leads to an examination of Kant's latent conception of art criticism or what I might call, with a little pomposity, his metaphysics of criticism.

Autonomy and the *Sensus Communis*

In his earlier work on aesthetics, *Observations on the Feeling of the Beautiful and the Sublime,* Kant gives many examples of what I have called "substantive" aesthetics[40] concerning the various merits and defects of contemporary poets and novelists; he also discusses the aesthetic taste of certain western European nations. In the third *Critique,* Kant entirely eschews criticism of the fine arts; nonetheless, he is concerned with showing the possibility of art criticism, and its *raison d'être.*

At first glance, it would seem that Kant has already ruled out the possibility of criticism:

A proof *a priori* according to definite rules is still less capable of determining the judgment as to beauty. If any one reads me his poem . . . which, all said and done, fails to commend itself to my taste, then let him adduce Batteux or Lessing, or still older and more famous critics of taste, with all the host of rules laid down by them. . . . I would prefer to suppose that those rules . . . were at fault, or at least had no application, than to allow my judgment to be determined by *a priori* proofs.[41]

That aesthetic judgment is not to be coerced by abstract reasonings from above, or seduced by blandishments of sensation from below, is part of what Kant means by the autonomy of aesthetic judgment. But Kant also demands that aesthetic judgment be subjective, that is, founded upon the feelings of pleasure and displeasure. At the same time, as we have seen, Kant claims "pure" aesthetic judgment to have universal or exemplary validity. The three claims of autonomy, subjectivity, and universality of aesthetic judgment might well lead one into a quandary concerning what the critic can possibly do. If criticism depended upon "determinate" rules, either a priori or empirical, then Kant would call such criticism a form of science; if the critic did not appeal to "determinate" rules but based his judgment solely upon pleasure and displeasure without aspiring to universality, then the result would seem to be only confessions of a man of sensibility. In order to understand Kant's conception of art criticism, it might be best to begin with his requirement that aesthetic judgment be autonomous. I shall then ask whether the other two requirements, universality and subjectivity, are compatible with autonomy.

Because Kant's interest in the aesthetic is centered upon the beautiful, his concern with aesthetic autonomy also centers upon judgments of taste, rather than on judgments of the sublime. Kant appears to concede that "pure" judgments of the sublime are not autonomous: they are founded upon morality. Though a judgment of the sublime can be "impure," that is, based upon the purpose of the object or intermingled with sentimental emotions, the sublime is not aesthetically autonomous. For Kant, "autonomy of aesthetic judgment" refers uniquely to "pure" aesthetic judgments of taste.

Because Kant's ethics is generally much better known than his aesthetics, I shall once again have recourse to observing some parallels between his conceptions of ethical and aesthetic autonomy. Though Kant rarely draws such parallels himself, and though the two kinds of autonomy naturally differ in a number of details, I find a strong underlying similarity between Kant's general epistemology and his theory of value: his analysis of belief often runs side by side with his analysis of both ethical and aesthetic judgment. Perhaps part of the support for this claim will be revealed in my exposition of Kant's meaning of "aesthetic autonomy."

Kant's morality is humanistic in that it places the entire burden of moral judgment upon the natural reason of the individual and his powers of self-legislation. Religious values or doctrines have a transcendent, not an immanent, position in the Kantian ethics; yet at the same time, as I have tried to underscore in the Kantian sublime, both Kant's ethical and his aesthetic orientation is profoundly religious. A tension prevails in Kant's aesthetics between the autonomy of the judge who must base his aesthetic judgment solely upon his own feelings, and the implicit appeal that such a judge must make to extra-aesthetic or ethical values.

The tension between Kant's ethical formalism and his doctrine of personal immortality has often given rise to the criticism that the postulates of practical reason undermine the absolute autonomy of the moral agent. A similar tension between form and enjoyment in his aesthetics might lead to a similar criticism: insofar as aesthetic judgment is "pure," judgment is autonomous, but at the price of empty formalism; insofar as aesthetic judgment rests upon sensuous interests, it is enjoyable, but at the price of heteronomy. For my own part, however, I do not see an irresolvable tension in either Kant's ethics or his aesthetics in this regard. What gives a moral agent autonomy is his legislating the moral law for himself; a law that he has himself constructed and imposed upon his behavior evinces his superiority over sensuous inclinations and impediments. In a similar way, aesthetic judgment is autonomous because it imposes forms of the understanding and imagination upon the sensible manifold. The "matter" of such judgment is not hostile to or incompatible with the "form" of aesthetic judgment; rather, autonomous aesthetic judgment organizes and "informs" the sensible manifold. Similarly, the freedom and autonomy of the moral agent do not reside in his power to subvert or collide with sensuous feelings or with happiness, but rather in his ability to order sensibility and inclinations in the light of moral law. As Kant says in his *Lectures on Ethics*, the demands of moral autonomy and happiness are neither incompatible with nor inimical to each other: "to renounce happiness is to differentiate it from morality in a transcendental and unnatural way."[42]

The autonomy of the moral agent is further secured by relinquishing the belief in a God as the basis of moral obligation: "But whence do we have the concept of God as the highest good? Solely from the idea of moral perfection which reason formulates a priori and which it inseparably connects with the concept of a free will."[43] Similarly, aesthetic judgment is autonomous by being familiar with "the classics," though not dominated by them. Autonomous aesthetic judgment must spring from one's own sensibility, just as autonomous ethical judgment is produced from one's own will: "Taste, just because its judgment cannot be determined by concepts or precepts, is among all faculties and talents the very one that stands most in need of examples of what has in the course of culture maintained itself longest in esteem."[44]

Kant is not arguing for aesthetic isolationism: we are not to cut ourselves off from what critics or qualified persons might say about a work of art. Neither is he arguing that art should not be enjoyed. He maintains instead that enjoyment and natural attraction cannot be the determining grounds of aesthetic judgment. In his ethical theory, Kant does not oppose duty to inclination but contrasts them; one might actually enjoy doing what one believes to be obligatory. Yet the motive of the action, if it is to have moral worth, can only be the sense of duty, not desire for our own pleasure or even that of other persons. In his aesthetic theory a similar contrast is drawn between aesthetic discernment of form and enjoyment. At the risk of pedantry, I shall describe four possible cases of aesthetic judgment: (1) we both perceive the form and enjoy the work; (2) we perceive the form, but do not enjoy the work; (3) our attention is not centered upon the form of the object, but we are simply taken in by its sensuous or nonaesthetic aspects, such as its moral message, its ideological import, or perhaps snob value; (4) we are left indifferent on both accounts.

If any one does not think a building, view, or poem beautiful, then, *in the first place*, he refuses, so far as his inmost conviction goes, to allow approval to be wrung from him by a hundred voices all lauding it to the skies. Of course he may affect to be pleased with it, so as not to be considered wanting in taste. He may even begin to harbour doubts as to whether he has formed his taste upon an acquaintance with a sufficient number of objects of a particular kind. . . . But, for all that, he clearly perceived that the approval of others affords no valid proof, available for the estimate of beauty.[45]

Ethical autonomy also requires that the judge be impartial; when Kant writes, "Act as though the maxim of your action were by your will to become a universal law of nature,"[46] he means that genuine moral judgment is a commitment of each person for all persons: the impartial moral agent must disregard both his own phenomenal person and the empirical objects of desire of all other persons. Thereby the moral agent seems to be asking himself: What sort of moral legislation must be actualized if all persons are to be treated as ends withal and the greatest potentiality of human perfection is to be equitably maximized?

Kant's conception of aesthetic autonomy requires a similar disregard of one's own likes and dislikes, at least so far as judgment claiming exemplary validity is concerned. The artist, then, might be conceived (though Kant does not himself make this comparison) as someone creating formal structures, in figure or in "play." The artist believes (though perhaps mistakenly) that such forms will have exemplary validity for anyone who judges his art impartially and patiently. Kant's explanation of one of the most salient features of art history—the artist's demand for a public— seems to be that the genuine artist, as opposed to the dilettante or the leader of a voguish coterie, demands that his artistic constructions be valid for everyone. The genuine artist must therefore be prepared for disappointment; yet disappointment at not winning "exemplary validity" is artistically more reassuring than gaining an easy general acceptance.

But if aesthetic judgment is for Kant both autonomous and universally valid, and given Kant's claim that art criticism logically cannot be based upon "determinate" principles or concepts, it would not be an exaggeration to say that Kant is up against a dilemma. His way out of it is contained in Book Two of the "Analytic of the Sublime" in the "Deduction of Pure Aesthetic Judgments," to which I shall now proceed.[47]

Kant of course eschews the rationalistic way of delimiting the aesthetic, employed by certain of his contemporaries like A. G. Baumgarten, who argued that aesthetics rests on ultimate, intuited principles. Baumgarten held that the various branches of knowledge begin with certain fundamental notions which require "intellectual perception" akin to the "direct perception" of mathematical relationships. Kant was aware of the general difficulties of epistemological intuitionism and in particular of rationalistic aesthetic intuitionism. Aside from the obvious objection that the appeal to intuition leaves no way of rationally resolving disagreements in matters of taste, Kant makes the more important objection that to found the aesthetic upon intuited perfection entails giving determinate concepts of aesthetic objects. If perfection were defined in nonaesthetic terms, the autonomy of aesthetic judgments would be sacrificed. To define perfection into other aesthetic terms, such as "harmony" or "coherence," would be evidently circular. Kant argues that no objective principle of taste is possible; for though form is public and universalizable, any attempt to formulate axioms of taste or precise principles of aesthetic value is contradictory:

A principle of taste would mean a fundamental premise under the condition of which one might subsume the concept of an object, and then, by a syllogism, draw the inference that it is beautiful. That, however, is absolutely impossible. For I must feel the pleasure immediately in the representation of the object, and I cannot be talked into it by any grounds of proof.[48]

In seeking to establish the autonomy and universality of aesthetic judgment, Kant is not in search of ultimate aesthetic canons, for they are either so vague and tenuous as to admit of any application, or so confined and strict as to stipulate only what is academically correct.[49] With both sorts of canons, one is confronted with either an infinite regress or an arbitrary stopping point. If certain suppositious aesthetic canons are questioned—for example, that tragedies must embody a hero of moral stature who moves from happiness to adversity—then either a would-be higher aesthetic principle, like unity, is invoked, or some empirical relationship concerning human sensibility is mustered to the fore. In the former case, justification of the "higher" aesthetic canon might arise; in the latter case, the autonomy of the aesthetic would seem to be lost by resting the case upon a supposed empirical fact of human nature.

Kant states the problem of justifying the possibility of autonomous and universally valid aesthetic judgment by asking a question typical of his entire Critical method:

That, now, is what lies at the bottom of the problem upon which we are at present engaged, i.e. How are judgments of taste possible? This problem, therefore, is concerned with the *a priori* principles of pure judgment in *aesthetic* judgments, i.e., not those in which (as in theoretical judgments) it has merely to subsume under objective concepts of understanding, and in which it comes under a law, but rather those in which it is itself, subjectively, object as well as law. It is easy to see that judgments of taste are synthetic, for they go beyond the concept and even the intuition of the Object, and join as predicate to that intuition something which is not even a cognition at all, namely, the feeling of pleasure (or displeasure) . . . so far as concerns the agreement required of *every one*, they are *a priori* judgments, or mean to pass for such. The problem of the Critique of Judgment, therefore, is part of the general problem of transcendental philosophy: How are synthetic *a priori* judgments possible?[50]

Kant's "Transcendental Deduction" concerns judgments of the "beauties" of both Nature and the fine arts; Kant holds that though the fine arts might be formally superior to Nature, yet Nature alone is "able to awaken an immediate interest."[51] That is, aesthetic judgment of Nature does not require training or familiarity with the object, or even interest. Kant seems to imply that interest in the fine arts (which are, after all, a kind of craft) is a learned interest. However this might be, aesthetic judgment of Nature is described as both more spontaneous and "natural"; once again Kant reveals his temperamental kinship with the Rousseau of the *Discours sur les sciences et les arts*[52] and *Emile*.[53]

In my own discussion of Kant's "Deduction," I shall pay most attention to its implications for art and literary criticism. It is plainly pointless to "criticize" Nature, for the critic assumes that the object could have been otherwise; the object of criticism is the result of the artist's intentions or artistic plans. Kant's talk of "principles" of taste would thus apply only to something involving a "craft," like poetry or music. Before turning to the details of the "Deduction," perhaps a brief statement of Kant's own conception of art criticism is in order.[54]

Kant refers with approval to Hume's observation that critics reason more plausibly than cooks, "but they must still share the same fate. For the determining ground of their judgment they are not able to look to the force of demonstration, but only to the reflection of the Subject upon his own state (of pleasure or displeasure)."[55] The chief purpose of criticism is "the rectification and extension of our judgments of taste."[56] The critic can be engaged in either an art or a science; Kant's third *Critique*, by his own statement, counts as scientific criticism, or what I have previously called "analytic aesthetics," which involves the elucidation and justification "of the subjective principle of taste, as an *a priori* principle of judgment."[57]

As Kant describes "analytic aesthetics," it is primarily an epistemological enquiry concerning the nature of taste as an autonomous, subjective, yet universal "faculty." For Kant, art criticism illustrates, by particular examples, how works of art bring about cognitive free play; the critic makes use of psychological rules concerning how "in actual fact taste proceeds . . . and seeks to apply them in estimating its objects."[58] In sum, criticism as art "criticizes the products of fine art" whereas criticism as science, or aesthetics, criticizes "the faculty of estimating them."[59]

After so lengthy a prelude to Kant's "Deduction of Pure Aesthetic Judgment," the reader might be surprised that Kant himself calls the "Deduction" "easy": "What makes this Deduction so easy is that it is spared the necessity of having to justify the objective reality of a concept. For beauty is not a concept of the Object, and the judgment of taste is not a cognitive judgment."[60] Because mankind can communicate both ideas and feelings, it must be the case that the epistemic constitutions of all persons are basically identical. Consequently, Kant claims, when we attend to or judge solely the formal representation of an object, or imaginatively reconstruct both its sensuous and cognitive content, then the pleasure arising from the free play of the cognitive faculties must be such that it can be presupposed in all persons epistemically like ourselves. In a footnote to the "Deduction" (Section 38), Kant gives a succinct resume of his entire argument:

In order to be justified in claiming universal agreement for an aesthetic judgment merely resting on subjective grounds it is sufficient to assume: (1) that the subjective conditions of this faculty of aesthetic judgment are identical with all men in what concerns the relation of the cognitive faculties, there brought into action, with a view to cognition in general. This must be true, as otherwise men would be incapable of communicating their representations or even their knowledge; (2) that the judgment has paid regard merely to this relation (consequently merely to the *formal condition* of the faculty of judgment), and is pure, i.e., is free from confusion either with concepts of the Object or sensations as determining grounds. If any mistake is made in this latter point this only touches the incorrect application to a particular case of the right which a law gives us, and does not do away with the right generally.[61]

It is both an obvious and, I believe, a well-warranted criticism of Kant's "Deduction" to observe that he completely ignores cultural aesthetic differences. In a much earlier passage in the third *Critique*, which I have already commented upon, Kant distinguishes the "normal idea" from the "archetype," and both of these from the "ideal."[62] The implication seems to be that aesthetic disagreement often occurs with what is normal, typical, or ancillary to "pure" aesthetic form; yet such agreement ought not to occur with "pure" aesthetic judgment. But to distinguish peripheral or accidental matters of taste from "formal" matters, as Kant appears to do, is itself question-begging. For the aesthetic or cultural relativist denies any such "essential core" to aesthetic judgment. Though certain styles or forms might be more deeply rooted in a society than others, the relativist denies that any have genuine primacy in aesthetic judgment. Kant would reply that the "Deduction" does not rest upon a weak analogy between the universal communicability of knowledge and the universal communicability of feeling, but aesthetic judgment itself presupposes a *sensus communis*. Before turning to further criticisms of Kant's "Deduction," let me try to clarify what Kant means by the crucial claim: "We might even define taste as the faculty of estimating what makes our feeling in a given representation universally communicable without the mediation of a concept."[63]

The first hint that Kant gives of the *sensus communis* occurs in the "Analytic of the Beautiful," where, it may be recalled, he invokes the notion to help explain the necessity of judgments of taste. Kant there contrasts common understanding with common sense: the former is cognitive and rests upon objective principles and determinate concepts; the latter is noncognitive and rests upon pleasure and pain.[64] Kant's first description of the aesthetic "common sense" is sketchy and negative:

The judgment of taste, therefore, depends on our presupposing the existence of a common sense. (But this is not to be taken to mean some external sense, but the effect arising from the free play of our powers of cognition.) Only under the presupposition, I repeat, of such a common sense, are we able to lay down a judgment of taste.[65]

When Kant returns in the "Deduction" to the notion of taste as a kind of *sensus communis,* his tone might recall the famous opening to Part I of Descartes' *Discourse on Method:*

Good sense is of all things in the world the most equitably distributed; for everyone thinks himself so amply provided with it, that even those most difficult to please in everything else do not commonly desire more of it than they already have. It is not likely that in this respect we are all of us deceived; it is rather to be taken as testifying that the power of judging and of distinguishing between the true and the false, of which, properly speaking, is what is called good sense, or reason, is by nature equal in all men.[66]

Kant of course introduces his "common sense" not to distinguish the true from the false but, it appears, to distinguish "pure" from "dependent" beauty. For if "taste would further be presented as a link in the chain of the human faculties *a priori* upon which all legislation must depend," [67] such a "faculty" would evidently not be required for judging "dependent" beauty, for which "determinate" concepts of ends and perfection suffice. Kant would also allow that psychological feeling is sufficient for determining the agreeable. Kant describes the *sensus communis* as a necessary postulate, or presupposition, of "pure" taste: "by the name 'sensus communis' is to be understood the idea of a *public* sense, i.e., a critical faculty which in its reflective act takes account (*a priori*) of the mode of representation of every one else, in order, *as it were*, to weigh its judgment with the collective reason of mankind." [68]

In the same definition Kant speaks of "putting ourselves in the position of every one else, as the result of a mere abstraction from the limitations which contingently affect our own estimate." [69] *Sensus communis* seems thus related to his conception of aesthetic autonomy as both public and interpersonal. Kant seems to be applying the principle of ethical parity—the principle of treating or judging similar cases similarly, irrespective of particular likes and dislikes—to aesthetic judgment. That Kant construes aesthetic judgment as a parallel to both cognitive and ethical claims appears from his attempt to elucidate the notion of "Taste as a kind of 'sensus communis' ":

While the following maxims of common human understanding do not properly come in here as constituent parts of the Critique of Taste, they may still serve to elucidate its fundamental propositions. They are these: (1) to think for oneself; (2) to think from the standpoint of every one else; (3) always to think consistently. The first is the maxim of *unprejudiced* thought, the second that of *enlarged* thought, the third that of *consistent* thought. [70]

It is not wholly clear, however, whether these three "propositions" do elucidate the "Critique of Taste." The first would evidently be a restatement of the already too familiar Kantian theme of autonomy: aesthetic judgment must be based upon one's own sensibility. For my own part, (2) makes sense in ethical discourse, but not in aesthetic judgment. Though it is a principle of justice as fairness to consider the interests of everyone on a par and not to except oneself from the moral law, yet given that Kant himself claims that there are no aesthetic laws or principles, the notion of excepting one's own judgment from such a law must be vacuous. If Kant means by (2), as applied to his "Critique of Taste," that prejudices or preconceived attitudes inhibit aesthetic judgment, I think no one would quarrel with him. But judging aesthetically "from the standpoint of every one else" sounds dangerously like having no taste of one's own; whereas judging ethically "from the standpoint of every one else" is a rewording of the principle of parity. As for (3), it is brave and good advice in regard to thinking through problems; but since Kant claims that there are no "determinate" concepts in "pure" aesthetic judgment, "thinking consistently" seems only weakly applicable to his theory of aesthetic judgment. Moreover, if "consistently" modifies "feeling pleasure or displeasure" (as Kant's aesthetic theory would lead one to expect), then the advice is either pernicious—do not change your aesthetic feelings—or jejune—do not let ephemeral likes and dislikes warp your aesthetic judgment.

If Kant means by "estimating what makes our feeling in a given representation *universally communicable* without the mediation of a concept"[71] that aesthetic judgment is guided by a principle analogous to the principle of parity, then he would seem to hold that if something is a good reason for one aesthetic judgment, it ought to be equally good in another case, *ceteris paribus*. Yet whether there is any point to or merit in considering works of art as "cases" with repeatable "good-making" characteristics is hardly evident. And Kant's pronounced suspicion of aesthetic principles implies his disbelief in the possibility or even value of strictures about what the artist should or should not do. Informative criticism gives knowledge by acquaintance, of the type that a competent guide or *cicerone* imparts. What Kant means by *"universally communicable* without the mediation of a concept" is not an aesthetic canon or principle which is universally communicable, but rather the subjective feeling of pleasure brought into play by an object: "Only when the imagination in its freedom stirs the understanding, and the understanding apart from concepts puts the imagination into regular play, does the representation communicate itself not as thought, but as an internal feeling of a final state of the mind."[72]

Such a purposive and internal feeling of pleasure, or the capacity for such feelings, is the *sensus communis*. Yet the cultural relativist might ask why the *sensus communis* must respond similarly in all societies and at all times. Aesthetic forms that give pleasure in one society often do not do so in another. Kant would reply that such diversity is empirically true, but only because it is a question of "nonpure" judgment or of "dependent" beauty. The aesthetic relativist might reply by asking why such disagreement cannot occur when it is a question of "pure" judgment. Kant would have only one answer at his disposal: such judgment is uniquely of aesthetic form. As I indicated in my discussion of "form," such a reply would be interesting only if "aesthetic form" could be spelled out in terms of forms of gestalt-type perception, for example, in the manner of Gombrich's *Art and Illusion*. Aesthetic form might thereby be shown to be not only intracultural, but also intercultural. Kant, however, does not attempt to give any content to his notion of aesthetic form, to speak paradoxically. He thus leaves himself open to another complaint from the aesthetic relativist: Why must there be only one "transcendental Deduction" of "pure" judgment of taste? If "pure" judgment is restricted to aesthetic form imposed upon the sensible manifold, then different societies might well impose different forms, though there might be significant overlappings; in any case, however, any number of "transcendental Deductions" might be required. Though it might make sense (pace Kant) to speak of the formal free play of understanding and imagination, with the attendant "disinterested pleasure," still very different forms might be the object of such pleasure in various societies. Even if the cognitive faculties were homogeneous, what affects their free interplay in one society need not do so in another.

Kant might have argued for the necessity of a sole "Deduction" for aesthetic judgment in a way comparable to his argument for a "Deduction" of the "pure" categories in the first *Critique*. Roughly, he might have claimed that just as the possibility of cognitive communication presupposes the same set of categories, so the possibility of critical discourse of the fine arts presupposes certain "ground rules" or ultimate critical canons. Given a shared body of critical agreement, a "Deduction" of the underpinnings or critical presuppositions would be at least conceivable. But it is precisely because Kant denies the possibility of "determinate" principles of taste, and a fortiori their "ultimate presuppositions," that he finds the "Deduction" of pure judgments of taste so "easy": there are no objective principles to justify. Kant thereby cedes much ground to the aesthetic relativist which could only be won back by a perspicuous account of aesthetic form, which, sadly, he never gives.

CHAPTER 5

The Cognitive and Pedagogical
Roles of the Aesthetic

"Aesthetic Ideas" and Genius

It has become one of the commonplaces of contemporary Anglo-Saxon philosophy to distinguish radically facts from values, and the affective from the cognitive. Like many such distinctions, these lend more balance to style than insight into thinking. Although Kant never refers to the celebrated passage in Hume's *Treatise* in which he observes that a proposition containing "ought" cannot be logically inferred from a proposition containing "is,"[1] Kant's distinctions between the noumenal and phenomenal reflect his own way of distinguishing between fact and value.[2] It would not be faithful to the letter of Kant's philosophy, but perhaps within the spirit of Kantianism, to characterize the noumenal as the realm of prescriptive language and the phenomenal as the realm of descriptive language. In his writings on aesthetics Kant never tires of proclaiming that if aesthetic judgment were merely phenomenal, it could not contain the ground of universalizability. What Kant calls "aesthetic ideas" are supposed to form a link between the noumenal and the phenomenal, as well as between the cognitive and the affective. The relationships that Kant draws between artistic genius and metaphor provide the key to his theory of genius and artistic imagination.

Of course, Kant was not the first philosopher to link genius with the capacity to form metaphor. In the *Poetics*, for example, Aristotle states: "It is a great thing to make a proper use of each of the elements mentioned, and of double words and rare words too, but by far the greatest thing is the use of metaphor. That alone cannot be learnt; it is the token of genius. For the right use of metaphor means an eye for resemblances."[3] A history of thought could probably be written on the concept of metaphor, although I am here chiefly concerned with Kant's views on the subject. Having its origins in rhetoric and poetics, the metaphor raises important questions concerning the origins and limits of knowledge, as well as the role of myths and models in religion, politics, and the sciences. A few great philosophers, like Plato, employ myths, or extended metaphors, when it appears that literal language cannot bear the strain of their insights. Or it might simply have been that for Plato, myths were a more economical and moving method of communication. However that might be, Kant appears to maintain that metaphor cannot be recast into literal language and that metaphor is the hallmark of artistic genius.

But many other philosophers warn against the dangers of metaphor. Few writers are so vehement in their condemnation of imagistic language as Hobbes and Locke. As Hobbes traces what he calls the "causes of absurdity" in human discourse and thinking, he reserves a special place for the absurdities caused by analogical language: "The sixth, to the use of metaphors, tropes, and other rhetorical figures, instead of words proper."[4] Locke, describing what he calls "figurative speeches," asserts that "all the artificial and figurative application of words eloquence hath invented, are for nothing else but to insinuate wrong ideas, move the passions, and thereby mislead the judgment; and so indeed are perfect cheats . . . wholly to be avoided."[5]

The early rationalists, like Descartes and Spinoza, were as wary of the metaphor as were the early British empiricists. Metaphorical or figurative language is the most deceptive fruit of the imagination, for pure reason speaks in clear and distinct ideas, choosing the simplest, most literal, and most unadorned language. Mental images, which are another product of the imagination, may be useful in grasping a proof, for example, in geometry; but they are to be discarded as soon as the proof is grasped. The metaphor is at best decorative, and always expendable. The early empiricists, like Bacon and Hobbes, described the imagination as contaning the residue left by physiological motions. The passively received data of the imagination might be combined or recombined; Locke notices that similar ideas have a tendency to consort with each other. But metaphor and the other daughters of "fancy" strictly contribute nothing to knowledge.[6]

Kant exhibits no such fear of the artistic imagination; it is not, for him, the source of unclarity or falsehood. As a further example of Kant's romanticism, his conception of the role of "aesthetic ideas" as actually helping "to bring reason into harmony with itself"[7] sharply distinguishes Kant's "aesthetic ideas" from both rationalist and empirical conceptions of metaphor.

Kant's conception of "aesthetic ideas" is closely related to his entire doctrine of the "regulative" use of ideas. Once the categories of causality, substance, necessity, and the others are removed from empirical application, they can never give rise to "determinate" concepts. Yet, Kant claims, it is possible to construct, by analogy, certain models which aid in the total comprehension of the universe. The idea of God, for example, is such a model of a being for which, as Kant says in the first *Critique*, "we have no concept whatsoever, but which we none the less represent to ourselves as standing to the sum of appearances in a relation analogous to that in which appearances stand to one another."[8] In describing "God" as a metaphorical construct of the "regulative" use of reason, Kant implies that to ask whether God really is "like" our model of him, or whether any other realities are really "like" our metaphors of them, is as wrong-headed as to ask whether light, for example, is "really" wavelike or molecular, or whether the chemical elements "really" resemble the models in elementary books on chemistry. Similarly, the other two models that Kant describes in his ethical theory—freedom and immortality—are also the product of "regulative" intellect; as such, they have only heuristic value. They are, as it were, metaphorical models constructed to elucidate the categorical nature of morality as Kant conceives of it.

Kant's generic term "aesthetic ideas," then, seems to include not only similes, tropes, metaphors, and poetic analogies, but also the postulates of practical reason and the bulk of religious language as well. The imagination as a productive faculty merely combines and rearranges the qualia or data from the senses according to the laws of association. The phenomenal workings of the imagination are therefore wholly determined by Nature and by the laws of empirical psychology. But Kant implies that to gain a sense of freedom from the confines of commonplace experience and to afford a sensuous analogy of the noumenon, the artist remodels experience into something that transcends the empirical laws of understanding and fulfills the higher laws of reason. The poet, for example, gives images that convey part of the meaning of death, or love, or eternity—ideas for which there is a host of indefinite concepts, but for which we can give nothing but crude and unsatisfactory verbal definitions.

By an aesthetic idea I mean that representation of the imagination which induces much thought, yet without the possibility of any definite thought whatever, i.e., *concept*, being adequate to it, and which language, consequently, can never get quite on level terms with or render completely intelligible . . . Such representations of the imagination may be termed *ideas*. This is partly because they at least strain after something lying out beyond the confines of experience . . . no concept can be wholly adequate to them.⁹

It should be recalled once again that when Kant speaks of "reason," he does not have in mind what the contemporary French *philosophe* commonly understood by the term. For Kant, cognition in its broadest sense divides into understanding or *Verstand*, and reason or *Vernunft*. What the French *philosophe* called "*la raison*," Kant calls "*Verstand*," that is, day-to-day thinking about the empirical or phenomenal world. *Verstand* is the province of the physicist as well as the bookkeeper; it is antithetical to the province of the artist or religious man, for whom cognition has a greater depth and transcendence. Kant maintains that although obedience to the rules of the understanding is essential to producing fine art, only genius gives the *Geist* or "soul" to a work; for "we may frequently recognize genius without taste, and in another taste without genius."¹⁰

According to Kant, "aesthetic ideas" are "based on analogy"¹¹ and are quasi-sensuous or aesthetic examples of analogical reasoning. The metaphor, for Kant, is not a mere ornament; it enjoys cognitive value. It would appear that ordinary usage supports Kant on this point, for one does not speak of ornaments as "far-fetched," "implausible," "strained," "profound," or "apt"—all of which adjectives are often applied to metaphor. The language used to describe metaphor and other varieties of analogical imagery is generally the language of cognition and understanding. One speaks of a "pregnant" metaphor, and a "pregnant" idea: both imply a fecundity of cognitive and affective implications.

What is of more importance is that Kant views "aesthetic ideas" as untranslatable into the literal or the "determinate." Apparently unlike metaphorical constructs used in the physical sciences (for which exact rules of the correct interpretation of the metaphor are given), Kant's "aesthetic ideas" are intrinsically indeterminate. Metaphors in the physical sciences and in mathematics have a habit of becoming second nature to the language, thereby losing their metaphorical foreignness. As Kant describes "aesthetic ideas," it appears that they logically cannot be assimilated into literality because they represent a special mode of thinking.

Poetic metaphor is only one species of Kant's "aesthetic ideas," though he tends to give chiefly poetic examples. "Aesthetic ideas" expressed in words are metaphor, myth, or even religious language; expressed in line and color—Kant's "figure"—they become pictorial or plastic images with apparently greater significance and suggestiveness than the objects from which they were derived. Kant implies that "aesthetic ideas" expressed in musical form—or "play" —take on the structures and tensions of highly complex affective states which can be understood and followed *in* music, but not reexpressed *outside* music.

Thus, though the notion of translation strictly applies to language, Kant seems to be opposing the literal or nonaesthetic use of line, mass and sound, as well as language, to their aesthetic reworking by way of "ideas"; moreover, his general thesis is that the nonaesthetic involves the "determinate" and the aesthetic, the "indeterminate"; and lastly, he claims that the latter logically cannot be reduced to or "translated" into the former. The cognitive significance of "aesthetic ideas" lies, for Kant, in their unparaphrasability and their transphenomenal application. It would seem that as a class, "aesthetic ideas" give quasi-intuitive awareness of a type that empirical science can never provide.

Kant is committed to a mimetic theory of art, according to which even the most recondite "aesthetic idea" involves a representation or image, often distorted and greatly altered, that is drawn from ordinary phenomenal experience and "superimposed" upon a given concept. The two elements— the image and the concept—are brought into an indeterminate union for which there exists no law or rule. Artistic genius, Kant claims, is unlike the scientific temper, which always proceeds according to empirical rules. Kant does not discuss the pathology of genius but merely asserts that the genius is "the elect of nature."[12]

Just as the supersensible is the *tertium quid* that harmonizes the dictates of Nature with the commands of morality, so artistic genius, Kant implies, is the link between the world of appearances and the moral world of freedom. The supersensible, and its intrinsic finality, must be postulated to explain how man as a moral agent, destined for perfection, can ultimately achieve his moral goal. In a similar way, "aesthetic ideas" must be construed, Kant implies, as giving an insight into the supersensible, though drawing from the "literal" world. Just as the human form is somehow an expression of moral ideas, so "aesthetic ideas," in the hands of artistic genius, reveal how moral ideas shape or inform the physical world in Nature. Kant admits that such matters are beyond demonstration; yet the overarching purpose of the third *Critique* is to disclose the intimate interrelation between the natural world of the first *Critique* and the moral world of the second *Critique*. The beauties of Nature, then, are to be construed *as if* their form implied "a uniform accordance of its [Nature's] products with our wholly disinterested delight."[13] So, too, "aesthetic ideas" are artistic "ciphers" of moral ideas expressed in nonconceptual or indeterminate ways.

What distinguishes "aesthetic ideas" from daubs, nonsense, or artistic frauds and posturings, is that an "aesthetic idea" is a sort of "cognitive overture," though Kant does not himself use this comparison. An "aesthetic idea" is fertile of thought and suggestion, but in a condensed and "indeterminate" way, just as the overture of an opera contains the elements that are subsequently developed. Nonsense combinations of words are not metaphors, any more than random combinations of notes, however unprecedented, are music. The "aesthetic idea," in whatever medium it might be expressed, not only broadens the understanding, though in an indeterminate way, but also enriches the sensibility:

In a word, the aesthetic idea is a representation of the imagination, annexed to a given concept, with which, in the free employment of imagination, such a multiplicity of partial representations are bound up, that no expression indicating a definite concept can be found for it— one which on that account allows a concept to be supplemented in thought by much that is indefinable in words, and the feeling of which quickens the cognitive faculties, and with language as a mere thing of the letter, binds up the spirit (soul) also.[14]

The representation drawn from experience has a literal or ordinary meaning, just as the terms in a poetic metaphor have a lexical meaning. Although the literal and lexical meanings are played upon in metaphor or in "aesthetic ideas" generally, because of the newness and fecundity of the combination, indeterminate connotations of the terms are brought into play. Though the simile is again not Kant's, in the poetic metaphor it is as if two bodies of discourse came into wedlock: just as only some of the genetic traits of both partners are passed on to the progeny, so only certain associations and connotations of the two terms are selected for their suggestive significance. To indulge myself further in this comparison: just as the child does not simply inherit the combined traits of its parents, but dips back into the genes of ancestors on both sides, so, too, the metaphorical result of the two bodies of discourse is not a mechanical overlapping of two lexical meanings, but enjoys an etymological atavism that goes to the roots of language. The metaphor is not a mere selection from meanings already known; it draws from those held in the subconscious of language as well. This further trait of metaphor also distinguishes it from nonsense combinations of words. For verbal nonsense neither suggests anything about the present or future nor recollects anything from the past; the words are uprooted from their traditions and consequently from the ties that they have by allusion with other literary expressions.

Sometimes the density of a metaphor might make it appear to be nonsense, especially in a modern poem, though Milton's "that two-handed engine at the door" in *Lycidas* is a good seventeenth-century example of the same kind of density. What might seem to be nonsense sometimes gains metaphorical meaning once the context is provided. Kant implies that it would be wrong-headed for the literary exegete to try to translate or paraphrase metaphor into literal language because the function or point of "aesthetic ideas" is to provide a continuous source of indeterminate concepts. Moreover, metaphor and "aesthetic ideas" in general give a sense of subjective freedom as vehicles for the free play of the cognitive faculties which would be lost by spelling out "aesthetic ideas" into determinate concepts. Kant is committed to the claim that because "aesthetic ideas" express the supersensible in a nonconceptual way, they logically cannot be expressed in determinate concepts as objects of sense.

Just as what Kant calls "the productive imagination" reworks elements and suggestions given to it by ordinary experience, so, too, metaphorical language seems to be parasitic upon nonmetaphorical or literal language. An "aesthetic idea" could not be grasped, Kant seems to hold, if knowledge of the world of appearances were lacking; even though the poetic metaphor takes its genesis from literal language, it cannot be reduced to literal language. Though Kant's "aesthetic ideas" take their origin from prosaic experience, he claims that they can no more be translated into ordinary experience than metaphors can be paraphrased:

Poetry and rhetoric also derive the soul that animates their works wholly from the aesthetic attributes of the objects—attributes which go hand in hand with the logical, and give the imagination an impetus to bring more thought into play in the matter, though in an undeveloped manner, than allows of being brought within the embrace of a concept, or, therefore, of being definitely formulated in language.[15]

Whether Kant is right in holding poetic metaphor to be untranslatable into literal language is a question that exceeds the purpose of my study. As I have often mentioned, I mean only to expound Kant and not to defend him. After quoting a short (and rather lame) verse in French by Frederick the Great, Kant comments that the poem "stirs up a crowd of sensations and secondary representations for which no expression can be found."[16] Had he quoted from more of a poet than Frederick the Great, Kant would have greatly advanced his case. However this might be, he seems to be contrasting "aesthetic ideas" with conceptual or "determinate" ideas: the former thrive upon their ambiguity and their freedom of interpretation; the latter thrive upon perspicuousness. Even when images are introduced into scientific discourse—like Darwin's "struggle for existence" and Marx's "infrastructure" and "superstructure"—the metaphors are carefully guarded; ideally they are translatable into more pedestrian terminology. Kant's claim is that poetic discourse is ideally ambiguous. To use a phrase coined by J. S. Mill in another connection than aesthetics, Kant implies that "aesthetic ideas" are cognitively valuable because they are permanent possibilities of reinterpretation.

In the visual field of a painting, for example Da Vinci's *Virgin and St. Anne,* the sensible manifold is so rich that many compositional relationships, ambiguities, and "echoes" can be detected. Metaphor, like facial expression, can be interpreted or seen in a number of different ways. Kant implies that such freedom of interpretation is another sign of the autonomy of aesthetic judgment. Given that the free play of the cognitive faculties is formally controlled by the object of art, aesthetic judgment does not degenerate into mere free association. And given that aesthetic judgment is a form of "reflective judgment," the free play brought about by indeterminate "aesthetic ideas" is itself pleasurable.

Though Kant could claim, therefore, that the attempt to translate metaphor into literal language is wrong-headed, his ultimate support—other than the subjective feeling of cognitive freedom—for the nontranslatability of "aesthetic ideas" hearkens back to his fundamental distinction between the noumenon and phenomenon. When Kant states that an "aesthetic idea" "stirs up a crowd of sensation and secondary representations for which no expression can be found,"[17] I interpret him as intending a logical "cannot";

that is, just as religious symbols, for Kant, express something indefinable that can nonetheless be shared with other rational persons, so "aesthetic ideas" communicate indeterminately the feelings of the supersensible for which, by definition, no determinate "expression can be found."

The chief difficulty in expounding Kant's views on the supersensible as related to "aesthetic ideas" is that the language of the mere expounder inevitably becomes as vaguely grandiose as Kant's. Thus, my pointing out that for Kant religious beliefs and symbols seem to belong to the class of "aesthetic ideas"[18] may be of help to the reader only if he is familiar with what Kant calls the "holy mysteries of religion."[19] It is plain that Kant's doctrine of "aesthetic ideas" is yet another instance of the sharp dichotomy so pervasive in his aesthetics between "determinate" and "indeterminate" concepts.

Kant's picture of poetic metaphor seems to have validity, merely as description, for what I shall call the romantic use of metaphor: imagery that is intended to "get out of hand," to be loose and evocative, obscure, and even mysterious. However, the imagery of Donne, for example, or of Racine, plainly has nothing of Kant's "indeterminacy" about it. When Donne says: "When I died last, and dear, I die / As often as from thee I go," or "And new philosophy calls all in doubt, / The element of fire is quite put out;" his meaning could not be more "determinate," even though metaphorical.[20] Examples of such "determinate metaphors,"[21] as I shall call them, abound in the classical poets of French literature such as Boileau, Charron, and La Bruyère—as well as in the Augustan poets of England.

To conclude my discussion of Kant's "aesthetic ideas," it seems in order to remark that once again Kant's own protoromantic predilections led him into a theory, now of metaphor, that has rather limited application to the fine arts. Kant's theory of artistic genius suffers from similar restrictions in that it is apparently founded upon a sharp distinction between the biological or organic, and the mechanical. Mechanistic principles, Kant claims, are the necessary condition of understanding Nature; yet Nature must also be considered, in regard to biological organisms, as evincing objective finality. Kant maintains that the whole of Nature can be conceived as fundamentally teleological, or as a vast system of ends. Subjective finality (as in the contemplation of beautiful forms and the possibility of a set of interconnected laws of Nature) is not sufficient ground for saying that Nature is actually constituted as teleological. Yet the objective finality of biological organisms, in their symbiotic relationships, cannot be understood other than as a system of means to ends. From this general conception of organic finality, Kant defines *Geist*, or "soul," as a kind of mental faculty which, in the personality of artistic genius, animates or vitalizes the workings of the imagination and the understanding. Kant argues that the fine arts are exclusively the product of genius and that genius itself is exclusively artistic. The man of talent for the arts always proceeds in a mechanistic way, following rules that could be articulated or formulated. According to Kant, even the great scientific inventor is only a man of extraordinary intelligence who develops theories from preceding scientific theories. A person of sufficient intelligence could trace the steps by which a great scientific mind, like that of Galileo or Newton, arrived at his new conception or law. At the base of Kant's radical distinction between artistic genius and other types of intelligence rests the contrast between vitalism and mechanism.

Kant implies that genius, or the "power" of artistic creation, is vitalistic or "organic" in several senses. First, though genius can be educated or subjected to the mechanical rules of academic art, the "power" itself cannot be learned. Second, because artistic genius cannot be learned, it cannot be taught or imparted in a determinate manner to anyone else. The artistic genius might have disciples who imitate his products as models, but he cannot impart determinate rules or even his "know-how." The great scientist, however, can take on students to whom he can impart not only definite procedures, but also clear and distinct problems awaiting solution. In only a technical sense are there artistic problems awaiting solutions. The twelve-tone scale, for example, impressionism, and pointillisme represent technical solutions in the fine arts. Artistic techniques of a certain school or style of art can be learned, but the result is generally mannerism, or the imitation of the singularities of a school without its *Geist*. Third, Kant implies that artistic genius is a special form of the fundamental purposefulness of Nature; the artist "must give the rule to art."[21]

For Kant, *Geist*, or the "power" of the creative genius, consists in the capacity of laying hold of the momentary and transient play of human feelings for which an expressive form is created. Nuances of expression and imagination can neither be predicted nor generated from empirical law, yet by virtue of artistic form they communicate universally. The products of artistic genius serve as exemplars to other artists but not as patterns or forms to be imitated:

Genius properly consists in the happy relation, which science cannot teach nor industry learn, enabling one to find out ideas for a given concept, and, besides, to hit upon the *expression* for them—the expression by means of which the subjective mental condition induced by the ideas as the concomitant of a concept be communicated to others. This latter talent is properly that which is called soul.[22]

Kant's ideal of the creative artist is based upon the general ideals of the Enlightenment: cosmopolitanism, rationality, and the continuous progression of culture. These ideals being universal, it is inevitable that the intensely particular claims of genius sometimes come into conflict with them. In spite of Kant's romantic tendencies that I have observed elsewhere in this study, he says that "where the interests of both these qualities clash in a product, and there has to be a sacrifice of something, then it should be on the side of genius."[23]

What further distinguishes the products of genius from those of scientific talent arises from the idea of progress. Kant holds that because art is a solution to neither a practical nor an intellectual problem, art does not progress by the slow increment of knowledge or of skill. Although there is little trace of Hellenism in Kant's writings, or the devotion to antiquity that became so widespread during the last half of the eighteenth century, yet he maintains that the limit of art "has in all probability been long since attained."[24]

To conclude: given Kant's rigid dichotomy between the aesthetic and the scientific, his restriction of "genius" to art and to the indeterminate workings of "aesthetic ideas" can only appear arbitrary. Kant does not seem to take into account that metaphorical constructs also play an important role in the history of science. Even if it is added that such models in science are more tightly controlled than poetic metaphor, the difference between the two types of analogy would seem to be one of degree, not of kind, as Kant seems to imply. It is to be remarked, however, that in his final brief observations on "genius" in his *Anthropology*, Kant broadens his definition of the term to include any manifestation of "originality in powers of intellectual perception."[25]

Art, Imagination, and Humanity

In the third *Critique*, Kant comes as close as he ever does to giving practical advice to the art critic and to the artist in his doctrine of "exemplary" art. By arguing that the products of genius, or of the creative imagination, must be exemplary, Kant implies that a particular work of art must provide a standard or touchstone for estimating or judging other roughly similar works. Yet, as Kant argued in connection with "disinterested pleasure," an exemplary work of art is not to be confounded with a perfect specimen of its kind, or one that portrays what is common and peculiar to a given species or form.

In line with his notion of aesthetic autonomy, Kant holds that each person must judge for himself whether a given work of art is or is not exemplary. Art education, Kant implies, does not consist in the amassment of canonic examples before which the individual must cower. Just as in his moral theory Kant holds it morally improper to base ethical judgment upon "exemplars"—or the great moral teachers of the past—so in his aesthetic theory Kant holds that it is spurious to base judgment simply upon the so-called classics. Each judge, on the basis of his own sensibility, must in fact determine what is to count as a "classic." Though Kant regards "enlightenment" as "the escape of men from their self-incurred tutelage," still aesthetic judgment seems to be part of the general lawfulness that Kant describes in his essay "What Is Enlightenment": "The touchstone of everything that can be concluded as a law for a people lies in the question whether the people could have imposed such a law upon itself."[26] Kant holds that imitation is to an exemplary work of art what mere discipleship is to an exemplary moral figure. Both are forms of heteronomy—the one of taste, the other of will. Both kinds of heteronomy seem to arise from confusing a particular embodiment of the beautiful or of moral worth with aesthetic or ethical value itself.

Though Kant does not say that art criticism is the parallel of casuistry in morals, both criticism and casuistry concern the particular—either a work of art, or a particular "case" of moral behavior. It should be observed that Kant's few excursions into casuistry, however, are based upon laws or moral imperatives. In the *Foundations of the Metaphysics of Morals,* for example, Kant tries to show how four "cases" of moral behavior—involving, respectively, suicide, making lying promises, failing to perfect one's talents, and indifference to the sufferings of other persons—can be shown to be morally wrong in accordance with all three formulations of the Categorical Imperative. Yet Kant's doctrine of exemplary art seems to imply that no such judging of works of art, in accordance with determinate principles or law, is possible. An exemplary work is not made in accordance with determinate rules that can be stated; neither can a set of rules be derived from such a work that would enable someone to generate another. The exemplary work, Kant holds, serves as an intelligible but indefinite canon of excellence that must act as a regulative but not constitutive rule for artists and critics.[27]

As is his wont, Kant proceeds to ask a transcendental question: What must be the case concerning the employment of the cognitive faculties if exemplary works of art are possible? It appears that the answer to this "critical" question must carry us back to Kant's doctrine of "aesthetic ideas" and imagination.

The "reproductive" imagination in Kant's epistemology is empirical; it corresponds to what Locke, Berkeley, and Hume termed the faculty that acts according to the laws of association. Kant distinguishes another aspect of the imagination, which he calls "productive"; it is nonempirical or "pure." As "productive," the imagination works spontaneously in cognition, actively constructing images and syntheses.

The creative imagination presupposes ordinary experience of the world, or the sensible constructs given to it by the reproductive and productive imagination. The creative imagination selects elements from the productive imagination, not according to a determinate rule, but nonetheless in accordance with a pattern or form. Artistic constructs are vaguely conceptual; yet the artist, unlike the scientist or positivistic thinker, does not render his ideas in a conceptual or discursive manner. Although the artist might restrict his imagination at the outset and is wise to do so for the sake of aesthetic form and coherence, within the restrictions imposed by the artist himself, the purpose is to show rather than to tell. Working through his form, the artist inevitably constructs "aesthetic ideas," or analogical models.

Kant would assume, it is safe to conclude, that in the analogical constructs of the creative imagination, at least the "laws of thought"—identity, excluded middle, and noncontradiction—must be obeyed, even in the most "transcendental" "aesthetic idea." The literary productions of Kant's time, as well as those of the seventeenth century, naturally adhered to the fundamental logical requirements. It has often been a mark of modern literature, however, and of some schools of romantic poetry, to circumvent even logical coherence in "aesthetic ideas." By "modern" we need not mean only twentieth-century literature, for the *Satyricon* is a fair example of a "modern" literary work in its defiance of classical standards of logical coherence and order.[28] Kant, as an ardent neoclassicist, does not consider the possibility of illogical "aesthetic ideas"; in even his most romantic moments, as observed in his "Analytic of the Sublime," "the outrages to the imagination" are brought under a moral aegis.

Neither does Kant consider the possible link between genius and deranged imagination which has been a recurrent theme in Western thought at least since the time of Plato.[29] Aristotle, for example, asserts in the *Problemata:* "No excellent soul is exempt from a mixture of madness"; in his essay "On Tranquility of the Mind,"

Seneca says that "there is no great genius without some touch of madness." Kant's neoclassicism seems again to be under strain while further describing genius:

A certain *boldness* of expression, and, in general, many a deviation from the common rule becomes him well, but in no sense is it a thing worthy of imitation. On the contrary, it remains all through intrinsically a blemish . . . but for which the genius is . . . allowed to plead a privilege . . . a scrupulous carefulness would spoil what is inimitable in the impetuous ardour of his soul.[30]

Kant's analysis of the creative imagination suggests two criteria for distinguishing what might be called "artistic insanity" from madness. Though some poets, like Torquato Tasso, might qualify under both heads, and though some artists might live exclusively in a creative-imaginary world, Kant maintains that there must be technical mastership and even "something mechanical" in the product of creative imagination.[31] Secondly, just as the idea of a private language appears to lead into contradiction, so, too, an "aesthetic idea" with only privately imaginative associations would lack the exemplary validity that Kant demands of genuine art. The psychiatrist might be interested in such private "aesthetic ideas," but for Kant, in line with neoclassicism, such "ideas" are both too individuated and too eccentric to count as more than autobiographical.

Kant, like many other writers on aesthetics, described a system of the fine arts according to which the various virtues of the arts are to be shown. Kant informs the reader that his scheme for the division of the fine arts is only one of many that might be proposed. For example, the arts might be divided according to their media, or according to their social and historical origins. After giving a factual or descriptive division of the fine arts, Kant gives his reasons for comparing and contrasting the arts in point of aesthetic worth. He begins with an obvious but fruitful comparison. Because the fine arts communicate, they have many points in common with the paradigm of communication, speech. Insofar as persons communicate their ideas and feelings to each other, Kant says, such behavior might be classified under three heads:

words, gestures, and tones. To these heads correspond the three types of fine art: the arts involving the word, the arts of "figure," and the arts of the "play" of color and sound. Taking Kant's doctrine of "aesthetic ideas" together with his comparison of art to speech, it follows that the fine arts, in even their most transcendent reaches and esoteric moments, are mimetic.

Beginning with the verbal arts, Kant distinguishes poetry from rhetoric: poetry must give the appearance of being undesigned and spontaneous, whereas rhetoric promises something serious but gives only "an entertaining play of the imagination."[32] Poetry, however, promises only entertainment but "accomplishes something worthy of being made a serious business, namely, the using of play to provide food for the understanding, and the giving of life to its concepts."[33]

The formative arts embody "aesthetic ideas" either in plastic form (like sculpture or architecture), or in two-dimensional portrayals of Nature (like painting), or in three-dimensional arrangements of Nature (like gardening). In sculpture the chief concern is with the expression of "aesthetic ideas," whereas in architecture and the lesser plastic arts like cabinet-making, a functional end is annexed. Painting taken in a broad sense, Kant says, includes landscape gardening, the art of personal adornment and dress, and interior appointments.

Kant's love of symmetrical architectonics seems to lead him into a confusion of thought about the formative arts. Both sculpture and architecture are said to be arts of "sensuous truth"; painting, however, in both the broad and the particular sense, is said to be an art of "sensuous semblance." Kant is quick to add that it might seem odd to include landscape gardening under the head of painting rather than under the plastic arts, along with sculpture. He says that the landscape gardener arranges the products of Nature, taking advantage of their textures and colors, just as the painter portrays Nature itself. Gestures, like verbal forms of communication, can both dissimulate meaning or intention and make it frankly open. But though a work of art might deceive someone into believing something (like a *trompe-l'oeil*) or give the illusion of something without deceiving anyone (like three-dimensionality represented in a painting) or give a straightforward imitation of something (like the sound of water dropping in a cistern in Strauss's *Salome*), these types of "semblance" are as readily found in the three-dimensional formative arts as in the two-dimensional.

Of all the fine arts, music clearly arouses the most ambivalence in Kant; he even implies some doubt as to whether it is to be classified as a fine art at all. Kant complains that music "has a certain lack of urbanity about it. For owing chiefly to the character of its instruments, it scatters its influence abroad to an uncalled-for extent (through the neighborhood), and thus . . . deprives others of their freedom."[34] Kant even compares music to the widespread habit of eighteenth-century gentlemen who carried perfumed handkerchiefs, and spread their odors around them.[35] The arts are the most trivial, Kant implies, when they are the most entertaining; they are to be esteemed when they combine the affective with "culture."[36]

From what has been said concerning Kant's descriptive division of the fine arts, the relative worth that he assigns the various fine arts is at once obvious. "*Poetry* . . . holds the first rank among all the arts."[37] For poetry and the other verbal arts can suggest a greater wealth of "aesthetic ideas" and invigorate the mind with more freedom and spontaneity than any other art. Music moves the mind with greater diversity, Kant says, but it leaves nothing to reflect upon in even a vague or shadowy way. For enjoyment, music is superior to the verbal arts, but it is inferior from the point of view of reason.

Kant seems to be aware that attempts to explain the "meaning" of music in an extramusical sense tend to degenerate into merely personal associations or reveries, or program notes. The explanation, Kant implies, is that "aesthetic ideas" in poetry are controlled by an indeterminate concept. In music the concept is so indeterminate that only a vague emotional epithet can be attached—like "melancholy," "joyful," or "tragic." Music presents a morphological or iconic resemblance to feelings that can be apperceived but not reexpressed discursively. As an agreeable art, music is the highest art, but because it deals in the affective associations of language, music can universally communicate only the broadest and vaguest "aesthetic ideas." After listening to pure music—as opposed to opera or song—one might want to hear the piece again to understand it better from the musical point of view. Nevertheless, Kant says, one is left with nothing to reflect upon or to ruminate over.

"If . . . we estimate the worth of the fine arts by the culture they supply to the mind, and adopt for our standard the expansion of the faculties . . . necessary for cognition,"[38] then the formative arts are superior to music. Music passes from sensations to indefinite ideas; the formative arts, especially painting, occasion more aesthetic thought than stimulation of sensation.

Kant asserts toward the end of his enquiry into aesthetic judgment that "the beautiful is the symbol of the morally good."[39] Kant's particular sense of "symbol" might be made clear by recalling one of the cardinal points in his epistemology: a concept without empirical content to corroborate it is empty, and empirical content without a concept is blind. Intuition, it will be recalled, is either empirical—that is, perception, or "pure"—that is, the forms of space and time. Intuitions of an empirical concept are examples; intuitions of the pure concepts of the understanding are "schemata." The reader hardly needs to be reminded that, for Kant, intuition has nothing in common with a mystical insight into reality or with any sort of Platonic or Bergsonian intellectual insight. Rather, intuition, or *Anschauung*, is simply "a looking at" of an object. Just as examples *illustrate* empirical concepts, and just as the pure categories when subsumed under space and time *produce* the schemata, so a symbol *furnishes* an analogy, or an indirect presentation of an a priori concept.

A symbol, for Kant, bears some likeness to the object evoked, whereas marks or signs bear no such likeness; they are simply linguistic conventions. A symbol of a pure or nonempirical concept carries over some of the associations from one body of discourse to another. To take Kant's own example: if a monarchical state governed by a constitution is symbolized by a living body, then a state is symbolized "as a mere machine (like a hand-mill) when it is governed by an individual absolute will."[40] No resemblance, however, is implied between hand-mills and despotic states, though they function in much the same way and evoke certain of the same associations. Language is rich in such attempts to give abstract and nonempirical concepts a foothold in sense:

Thus the words *ground* (support, basis), *to depend* (to be held up from above), to *flow* from (instead of to follow), *substance* (as Locke puts it: the support of accidents), and numberless others, are not schematic, but rather symbolic . . . transferring the reflection upon an object of intuition to quite a new concept, and one with which perhaps no intuition could ever directly correspond.[41]

When Kant says that "the beautiful is the symbol of the morally good,"[42] he must be taken to mean "morality" in a broad sense. It might be helpful to recall that Aristotle never speaks of ethics as a special form of enquiry, but as "the study of character" or "our discussions of character."[43] "Ethics" etymologically means "the study or science of character," just as its Latin equivalent, *moralia*, as used by Plutarch, Seneca, St. Gregory the Great, and many others, means the study of the customs and characters of mankind. According to Pythagorean and Platonic aesthetics, the beautiful is a symbol of human character. The fine arts—though the distinction between "fine'" and "applied" arts was not drawn in Western philosophy until the eighteenth century—were supposed to be closely linked to moral education. Certain modes of music, according to Plato, are enervating because they conjure up effeminate and undesirable traits of human character. The Pythagoreans argued that music is an embodiment of ethical character, or morality; "right" music was supposed to restore the balance or harmony of the soul.

Kant warns that "where fine arts are not, either proximately or remotely, brought into combination with moral ideas, which alone are attended with a self-sufficing delight . . . they [the fine arts] only serve for a diversion."[44] Kant is not advocating moralizing in art, or putting art into religious bondage. In broadening his meaning of "moral ideas," Kant points out that one often describes natural objects and objects of art by "names that seem to rely upon the basis of a moral estimate":

We call buildings or trees majestic and stately, or plains laughing and gay; even colours are called innocent, modest, soft, because they excite sensations containing something analogous to the consciousness of the state of mind produced by moral judgments.[45]

"Moral" is sometimes used to mean "morally right," just as "morality" is sometimes used to refer to the opposite of "immorality." Kant uses "moral ideas" to refer to the feelings that generally attend moral judgment. For Kant, all human characteristics and values expressed in the fine arts, or ascribed to Nature, fall under the general head of morality. Art expresses the moral traits of humanity, both the ugly and the beautiful, the social and the divisive.

Although Kant has taken care throughout Part One of the third *Critique* to point out the differences between the aesthetic and the moral, he calls attention in the last pages of Part One to four respects in which he holds the two to be analogous. (1) The beautiful and the morally good please *immediately:* the former by means of affective cognition, the latter by means of determinate concepts. (2) Both the beautiful and the good are independent of personal interest: the aesthetic pleases by its form, the moral pleases because of its consonance with the "pure" sense of duty. (3) In aesthetic judgment one is free of sensation and also of determinate theoretical and practical cognition. In moral judgment, the will is free of the dictates of inclination and sense. (4) Both moral and aesthetic feelings are universal, or "valid for every man":[46] the moral by constitutive principles and the aesthetic by regulative principles.

Kant assigns to art a central role both in the life of man and in the political state. In Part Two of the *Critique of Judgment,* the "Critique of Teleological Judgment,"[47] Kant gives a sketch of human history and progress that was later greatly developed by Hegel. In Kant's view of history, moral freedom is the necessary parallel of culture, which can only be realized through violent social strife and evolutionary movement. In his model of history, Kant begins with a large class of workers who provide the material means to and comforts for an elite class. At this stage in the history of culture, the leisured class both directs and produces the arts and sciences. As luxury grows, social antagonism and strife increase: "Yet this splendid misery is connected with the development of natural tendencies in the human race, and the end pursued by nature itself, though it be not our end, is thereby attained."[48] The purposefulness of Nature, as manifested in human history, is directed towards an end higher than the end of any individual human being, yet the only true end of the human species: civilization. The ultimate purpose of Nature is to achieve a moral community founded upon the advancement of science—which regulates man's thinking—and the fine arts—which discipline man's feelings and sensibilities. For Kant, art and science are the two great humanizing forces. Both presuppose a "common sense," the one aesthetic, the other logical. Nature's "secret plan," so Kant maintains in his essay "Idea for a Universal History from a Cosmopolitan Point of View,"[49] is to make use of man's discords and perverse inclinations to bring about, both by natural evolution and "reformative revolutions," "a universal civic society."[50]

Kant gives the traditional doctrine of *felix culpa*—the "happy fault"[51]—a historical twist related to his doctrine of "disinterested pleasure." In his "Conjectural Beginning of Human History," Kant gives a sketch of the progress of humanity from the primitive state to the state of culture.[52] In the first stage of man's development, choice was discovered, together with the power to resist inclination and blind impulse. Man learned which inclinations to serve, but he was left in an anxious state between competing impulses. In the second state, man discovered the powers of imagination that could both prolong ordinary inclinations and satisfy or transmute them by art and by reason. At this stage, Kant holds, the agreeable was transformed into the beautiful, and carnality into love. The aesthetic arose with the advent of the spiritual, just as moral "decency" arose from the desire for the esteem of other persons in the social community. In the third stage, man saw how greatly he could predict the future, but wisdom increased man's sorrow and anxiety. In the fourth stage, man discovered his autonomy as a rational and sensuous being containing within himself the source of all law. Thus, the *felix culpa*, without which neither the arts nor the sciences would have been developed.

Finally, for Kant, exemplary art is the symbol of the moral community, or what he calls in the *Groundwork* "the Kingdom of Ends."[53] In the last pages of "The Critique of Aesthetic Judgment," Kant implies that class struggle occurs when the interests of either the ruled or the rulers, or of both, are not met. Just as complete social restraint leads to political bondage, so, it would seem, a "determinate" form leads to tendentious art that cancels out the free play of the cognitive faculties. Yet art which gives too great an emphasis to what Kant calls "the sensuous" leads to "barbarism." The moral community, like exemplary art, maintains an equilibrium between ideas and feelings, the formal and the sensuous. As is well known, Schiller was the next to pick up such themes of the politics of art in his *Letters on the Aesthetic Education of Man.*[54]

Concluding Remarks

Whether Kant's aesthetics, as I have expounded it in this study, has more than antiquarian or historical interest is for the reader to judge. This question is perhaps related to a broader issue that would take us beyond the limits of Kant's aesthetics: whether philosophical aesthetics, without the tools of the literary or art historian, is a fertile form of inquiry. Whatever the reader might care to conclude about the broader issue, historically at least Kant's aesthetics has influenced not only the majority of philosophers of art from Schiller to Croce, and even later, but psychologists such as Fiedler, Hildebrand, and Herbart. In one guise or another Kant's doctrines have continued to represent the orthodox and traditional point of view in aesthetics, and to a measure, in art criticism as well.

Whether E. H. Gombrich is a Kantian is perhaps not to the point; however, his descriptions of art are frequently in the tradition of Kant. I have already referred to his *Art and Illusion* to expand upon Kant's doctrine of form; to show the continuity of Kant's tradition, a few quotations from Gombrich will suffice. In defining art, Gombrich explains that "the Greek miracle" led to the production of copies of statues and paintings and that "this industry of making reproductions for sale implies a function of the image of which the pre-Greek world knew nothing. The image has been pried loose from the practical context for which it was conceived and is admired and enjoyed for its beauty and fame, that is, quite simply within the context of art. . . . The creation of an imaginative realm led to an acknowledgement of what we call " 'art'."[55] Again, Gombrich implies that aesthetic perception or judgment is not the "ordinary" form of perception, for "we prefer suggestion to representation, we have adjusted our expectations to enjoy the very act of guessing, of projecting."[56] Even highly abstract art and "action painting" have a humanizing force reminiscent of Kant's conception of art as "moral symbol": "If this game has a function in our society, it may be that it helps us to 'humanize' the intricate and ugly shapes with which industrial civilization surrounds us. . . . We are trained in a new visual classification."[57]

Throughout Kant's aesthetics, as well as the restylings of his thought during the past two hundred years, run a number of rigid dichotomies. First, the literal is opposed to the metaphorical.[58] The nonaesthetic use of words, for example, supposedly eschews metaphor, imagery, and ambiguity; the aesthetic use of language thrives upon equivocation and the permanent possibility of multiple interpretation. The contrast between the literal and metaphorical, which is the product of Kant's crucial dichotomy between "determinate" and "indeterminate" concepts, supposedly encompasses all the fine arts. In painting, for example, because of the visual density and ambiguity of the representation, the viewer is not presented with a literal likeness, but rather with a visual field affording the possibility of many structural analogies and interpretations. "Usual" modes of perception require that ambiguities be eliminated; they are never so "complex" or "intense" or "unified" as "nonusual" or aesthetic modes of judgment. It is often supposed that the aesthetic object can be "seen as" a number of various things[59] and that such multiplicity is entertained or "contemplated" (yet another term in the traditional language of aesthetics) for its own sake.

The first dichotomy leads to a second: "usual" modes of experience require active use of cognition, either theoretically or practically; what is called "aesthetic experience" is supposed to be nonpractical, detached, contemplative, or "disinterested." The second dichotomy engenders a third: moral judgment is practical, whereas aesthetic judgment is "reflective" or "gratuitous."[60] The third dichotomy leads to a fourth, which opposes the "mechanistic" to the "vitalistic." The aesthetic object is supposed to be an "organic unity," a term whose parentage is Kant's theory of *Geist* or "soul" in art.

The Kantian and traditional aesthetics also holds that the aesthetic and the hedonic are conceptually linked, although aesthetic judgment is supposed to have more than autobiographical importance. It makes no sense to dispute about mere likes and dislikes, whereas aesthetic judgment, to use contemporary parlance, can be supported by "good reasons."[61]

The traditional Kantian aesthetics also claims that aesthetics, as a "discipline," is autonomous; aesthetic judgment cannot be "reduced" to moral, practical, or cognitive judgment. Moreover, aesthetic questions, though related to psychological,[62] economic, and political questions, are idiosyncratic, or *sui generis*, for the aesthetic supposedly marks some "special attitude."[63]

Because I have not tried to argue in favor of Kant's aesthetics, but merely to expound and sometimes to expand upon his views, I shall not try to support the set of rigid dichotomies that his aesthetics presupposes. My aim has been to place Kant's aesthetics in the wider context of his Critical philosophy and to show the origin in Kant's aesthetics of much current and accepted terminology. Although I have often been critical of Kant's aesthetic doctrines, I have supposed that with a clearer view of these doctrines many of the preconceptions, and perhaps dogmas, of modern aesthetics might be thrown into better relief.

NOTES

BIBLIOGRAPHY

INDEX

Notes

To avoid the frequent repetition of the titles of the central works by Kant referred to or quoted in this study, I have adopted the following abbreviations for the English translations, listed in alphabetical order:

A or B: *Critique of Pure Reason,* trans. Norman Kemp Smith, 1st or 2nd ed. (London: Macmillan, 1933).

CAJ: *Critique of Aesthetic Judgement,* trans. J. C. Meredith (London: Oxford University Press, 1952).

CTJ: *Critique of Teleological Judgement,* trans. J. C. Meredith (London: Oxford University Press, 1952).

G: *Foundations of the Metaphysics of Morals* (the *Grundlegung,* or *"Groundwork"*), trans. Lewis White Beck (New York: Bobbs-Merrill, 1959).

MEJ: *The Metaphysical Elements of Justice* (Part I of the *Metaphysics of Morals*), trans. John Ladd (New York: Bobbs-Merrill, 1965).

MM: *The Metaphysical Principles of Virtue* (Part II of the *Metaphysics of Morals*), trans. James Ellington (New York: Bobbs-Merrill, 1964).

O: *Observations on the Feeling of the Beautiful and the Sublime,* trans. J. T. Goldthwait (Berkeley: University of California Press, 1960).

All references to the German text are to the edition issued by the Royal Prussian Academy, now the German Academy of Sciences, in Berlin. The *Akademie Ausgabe* of Kant's works, which has been published from 1902 onward, is both the canonical and the most available edition of Kant's writings. I have abbreviated it as "*Ak.*," followed by the volume and page numbers. I have tried throughout to cite the most recent and most available translation of Kant into English. So that the reader will have ready access to both the German text and the English translation, where there is one, I have first put the page number of the

(185)

German text, followed by the page number of the English translation. Thus,

CAJ, §35. Ak. V:287; Meredith, p. 143.

means "Critique of Aesthetic Judgment, section 35. Akademie Ausgabe, volume V, page 287; Meredith translation, page 143."

In the quotations from or references to the Critique of Pure Reason, I have followed the traditional practice of citing page numbers from both the 1781 ("A") edition and the 1787 ("B") edition, for example; A 533, B 561.

Preface

1. Kritik der Urteilskraft, first published in Berlin and Liebau in 1790. In Kant's lifetime two revised editions appeared, in 1793 and 1799. There are two English translations: J. H. Bernard, Kritik of Judgement (London, 1892; later republished as Critique of Judgement); and J. C. Meredith, Critique of Aesthetic Judgement (Oxford, 1911) and Critique of Teleological Judgement (Oxford, 1928). Meredith's translations were reissued together as The Critique of Judgement (Oxford, 1952). Although neither Bernard's nor Meredith's translation is particularly elegant, I have consistently used Meredith's, because it is usually the more perspicuous. The pagination of the two-part edition is identical to the pagination in the one-volume edition of 1952.

2. London, 1938.

3. First German edition published in 1932; English edition, Fritz C. A. Koelln and James P. Pittegrove, trans. (Princeton: Princeton University Press, 1951). See especially chap. VII.

4. For readers desiring a general background, in English, to Kant's philosophy, the following commentaries are recommended: S. Körner, Kant (Harmondsworth, 1955); for the Critique of Pure Reason, see N. Kemp Smith, A Commentary to Kant's Critique of Pure Reason (London, 1918; rev. ed., 1923); A. C. Ewing, A Short Commentary on Kant's Critique of Pure Reason (London, 1938); T. D. Weldon, Kant's Critique of Pure Reason (Oxford, 1945; 2nd ed., 1958). For commentaries on the Critique of Practical Reason and Kant's other works on ethics, see L. W. Beck, A Commentary on Kant's "Critique of Practical Reason" (Chicago, 1960); H. J. Paton, The Categorical Imperative (London, 1947); W. D. Ross, Kant's Ethical Theory (Oxford, 1954); P. A. Schlipp, Kant's Pre-Critical Ethics (1938; Evanston, Ill.: Northwestern University Press, 1960). For the Critique of Judgment, see J. C. Meredith's introductory essays concerning both the history of the text and its probable methods of composition in his translation of the Critique of Aesthetic Judgement (Oxford, 1911).

1. Introduction

1. *CTJ*, §5. *Ak.* V:376; Meredith, p. 24.
2. *CAJ*, preface. *Ak.* V:170; Meredith, p. 7.
3. *CAJ*, §57. *Ak.* V:341; Meredith, p. 209.
4. *CAJ*, preface. *Ak.* V:170; Meredith, p. 7.
5. *CAJ*, introduction. *Ak.* V:195; Meredith, pp. 36–37.
6. *CAJ*, §31. *Ak.* V:281; Meredith, p. 136.
7. *CAJ*, introduction. *Ak.* V:191–92; Meredith, pp. 32–33.
8. *CAJ*, introduction. *Ak.* V:196; Meredith, p. 38.
9. *CAJ*, introduction. *Ak.* V:178; Meredith, p. 17.
10. *CAJ*, introduction. *Ak.* V:187; Meredith, p. 27.
11. *CAJ*, introduction. *Ak.* V:178; Meredith, p. 17.
12. *CAJ*, introduction. *Ak.* V:187; Meredith, p. 27.
13. *CAJ*, introduction. *Ak.* V:193; Meredith, p. 35.
14. *CAJ*, introduction. *Ak.* V:192; Meredith, p. 33.
15. *CAJ*, introduction. *Ak.* V:179; Meredith, p. 18.
16. *CAJ*, introduction. *Ak.* V:193; Meredith, p. 35.
17. See *CTJ*, §4. *Ak.* V:372–73; Meredith, pp. 19–20.
18. *CAJ*, introduction. *Ak.* V:193; Meredith, p. 34.

19. In German, *Beobachtung über das Gefühl des Schonen und Erhabenen* (Königsberg, 1764).

20. 1714–62; author of the incomplete tractatus in Latin on aesthetics, *Aesthetica* (first published in 1750), not translated into any modern language. There is, however, a translation of his *Meditations on Poetry* by Karl Aschenbrenner and William B. Holther (Berkeley, 1954) and a German version of a part of his lectures on the Latin work by Bernhard Poppe, *A. G. Baumgarten, seine Bedeutung und seine Stellung in der Leibniz-Wolffschen Philosophie und seine Beziehung zu Kant* (Münster: Borna, 1907). Georg Friedrich Meier developed versions of Baumgarten's works: *Die Anfangsgründe aller schönen Wissenschaften* (1749 and onwards). Further references may be found in Lewis W. Beck, *Early German Philosophy: Kant and His Predecessors* (Cambridge: Belknap Press of Harvard University, 1969).

21. A 21, B 36.
22. Ibid.
23. B xvii.

24. See John R. Silber, "The Copernican Revolution in Ethics: The Good Re-examined," in *Kant*, ed. Robert Paul Wolff (New York: Anchor Books, 1967), pp. 266–90.

25. A 21, B 36, fn.
26. *CAJ*, introduction. *Ak.* V:189; Meredith, p. 29.
27. Ibid.
28. Ibid.

29. *CAJ*, introduction. *Ak.* V:189; Meredith, pp. 29–30.
30. *CAJ*, §22. *Ak.* V:239–40; Meredith, pp. 84–85.
31. *CAJ*, introduction. *Ak.* V:178–79; Meredith, pp. 17–18.
32. *CAJ*, introduction. *Ak.* V:179; Meredith, p. 18.
33. *CAJ*, §22. *Ak.* V:241; Meredith, p. 86.
34. Ibid.
35. *CAJ*, §41. *Ak.* V:298; Meredith, p. 156.
36. *CAJ*, introduction. *Ak.* V:174–75; Meredith, pp. 12–13.
37. *CAJ*, introduction. *Ak.* V:191; Meredith, p. 32.
38. *CAJ*, §58. *Ak.* V:350; Meredith, p. 220.
39. *CAJ*, 22. *Ak.* V:239; Meredith, p. 84.
40. *MEJ. Ak.* VI:230; Ladd, p. 34.
41. *MEJ. Ak.* VI:233; Ladd, p. 39.
42. *MEJ. Ak.* VI:230; Ladd, p. 35.
43. P. A. Schilpp, *Kant's Pre-Critical Ethics* (1938; Evanston: Northwestern University Press, 1960), p. 48.
44. *CAJ*, §53, fn. *Ak.* V:328; Meredith, p. 193.
45. *Anthropologie in Pragmatischer Hinsicht* (*Anthropology from the Pragmatic Point of View*), first published in Königsberg in 1800. See especially First Book, §13, *Ak.* VII:149–50. Portions of the *Anthropology* relevant to aesthetics have been translated by Walter Cerf in *Immanuel Kant: Analytic of the Beautiful* (New York: Bobbs-Merrill, 1963). The firm of Martinus Nijhoff (The Hague) has just published a complete English translation by Mary Gregor.
46. For Burke, see *CAJ*, §29, *Ak.* V:277; Meredith, pp. 130–31. For indications of Kant's acquaintance with Hume, Shaftesbury, and Hutcheson, see the *Nachricht*, trans. P. A. Schilpp, in *Kant's Pre-Critical Ethics*. See also Kant's letters, the most important of which have now been translated by Arnulf Zweig in *Kant: Philosophical Correspondence 1759–1799* (Chicago: University of Chicago Press, 1967).
47. See Keith Ward, *The Development of Kant's View of Ethics* (New York: Humanities Press, 1972).
48. *The Principles of Philosophy*, First Part, Principle XLV, in *The Philosophical Works of Descartes*, trans. E. S. Haldane and G. R. T. Ross, 2 vols. (Cambridge, 1911), I:237.
49. See René Le Bossu, *Traité du Poème Epique* (Paris, 1675), in *Le Bossu and Voltaire on the Epic*, comp. Stuart Curran (Gainesville, Fla.: Scholars Facsimiles and Reprints, 1970).
50. "Defense of an Essay of Dramatic Poesy," in *Essays*, ed. William P. Ker, 2 vols. (1900; reprint ed., London, 1962), I:123.
51. Ibid.
52. See René Descartes, "Passions of the Soul" ("Traité des passions de l'Ame," 1649) in *Philosophical Works*, trans. Haldane and Ross, I:329–427.
53. *Les Beaux Arts Réduits à un Même Principe* (Paris, 1764). See also

my *Aesthetic Thought of the French Enlightenment* (Pittsburgh: University of Pittsburgh Press, 1971) for a more detailed examination of the aesthetics of Batteux.

54. *CAJ*, §58. *Ak.* V:346; Meredith, pp. 215–16.

55. Francis Bacon, *Two Books of the Proficience and Advancement of Learning, Divine and Humane*, in *Works*, ed. James Spedding, R. L. Ellis, and D. D. Heath, 3 vols. (London, 1870), I:343–44.

56. Thomas Hobbes, *English Works*, ed. W. Molesworth, 11 vols. (London, 1839–45), III:1–2.

57. See "Of the Standard of Taste" (1757), in *Aesthetic Theories*, ed. Carl Aschenbrenner and Arnold Isenberg (Englewood Cliffs, N.J.: Prentice-Hall, 1965).

2. The Analysis of the Beautiful

1. First published in 1757.

2. First published in 1709.

3. Apart from Kant's own letters, the main sources for accounts of his life and aesthetic interests are: L. E. Borowski, *Darstellung des Lebens und Characters Immanuel Kants*, R. B. Jachmann, *Immanuel Kant, Geshildert In Briefen an einen Freund*, and E. A. C. Wasianski, *Immanuel Kant in seinen letzen Lebensjahren*, all memoirs published in Königsberg in 1804. Thomas De Quincey relied chiefly upon Wasianski's work for his own *The Last Days of Kant* (*Works*, 1859, vol. XII). Also to be consulted are Ernst Cassirer, *Kants Leben und Lehre* (Berlin, 1921); and Karl Vorlander, *Immanuel Kants Leben* (Leipzig, 1911). For an anecdotal account of Kant's life and temperament as seen through the eyes of W. Somerset Maugham, see his *Vagrant Mood* (New York: Doubleday, 1953), especially "Reflections on a Certain Book." The "certain book" is Part One of the *Critique of Judgment*.

4. For Keats, see his *Letters*, ed. H. E. Rollins (Cambridge: Harvard University Press, 1958). For Liszt, see A. Strelezki, *Conversations with Liszt* (London: E. Dunajowski & Co., 1887). Also see Sacheverell Sitwell, *Liszt*, rev. ed. (New York: Dover, 1967; French translation by Françoise Vernan [Paris: Buchet, Chastal, 1969]).

5. For Baudelaire, see *Curiosités Esthétiques* (Lausanne: Editions de l'Oeil, 1956). See also his introduction to his translation of E. A. Poe, *Nouvelles Histoires Extraordinaires* (1857), in *Oeuvres Complètes*, vol. VII (1933). For Wagner, see *The Art-Work of the Future* (*Das Kunstwerk der Zukunft*, 1850), in *Richard Wagner's Prose Works*, trans. W. A. Ellis (New York: Broude Brothers, 1966), vol. 1.

6. (1897–98). See H. W. Garrod, *Tolstoy's Theory of Art* (London, 1935).

7. First appeared in the *Four Dissertations*, 1757; see also Book III of

the *Treatise on Human Nature* (1739) and the *Inquiry Concerning the Principles of Morals,* app. I, sec. III.

8. (New York, 1934). See also his *Experience and Nature* (Chicago, 1925); and "Aesthetic Experience as a Primary Phase and as an Artistic Development," *Journal of Aesthetics and Art Criticism,* IX (September 1950):56–58.

9. See *The Birth of Tragedy,* tr. Walter Kaufmann (New York: Random House, 1967), and *The Will to Power,* tr. idem, (New York: Random House, 1967).

10. This appears to be Stephen Toulmin's claim in *The Place of Reason in Ethics* (Cambridge: Cambridge University Press, 1950); see especially chap. 1. See by way of corrective Ludwig Wittgenstein, *Lectures and Conversations on Aesthetics, Psychology and Religious Belief,* compiled from notes taken by Yorick Smythies, Rush Rhees, and James Taylor; ed. Cyril Barrett (Berkeley: University of California Press, 1967).

11. See Leo Tolstoy, *What Is Art?* in *What Is Art? and Other Essays on Art,* trans. Aylmer Maude (New York: Bobbs-Merrill, 1960).

12. See T. S. Eliot, *Tradition and the Individual Talent* (London: Methuen, 1917) and *The Sacred Wood: Essays on Poetry and Criticism* (1920; reprint ed., London: Methuen, 1950), for expressions of such a view.

13. See Arnold Isenberg, "Critical Communication," *The Philosophical Review,* 58 (1949), reprinted in *Aesthetics and the Theory of Criticism: Selected Essays of Arnold Isenberg,* ed. Mary Mothersill et al. (Chicago: University of Chicago Press, 1973); and in *Contemporary Studies in Aesthetics,* ed. F. J. Coleman (New York: McGraw-Hill, 1968).

14. See Charles L. Stevenson, *Ethics and Language* (New Haven, 1944) for expressions of such views concerning ethics, with the implication that the same analyses apply to aesthetics.

15. See George Boas, *A Primer for Critics* (Baltimore: Johns Hopkins University Press, 1937) for a statement of aesthetic relativism.

16. A 220, B 267.

17. *CAJ,* preface. *Ak.* V:171; Meredith, p. 6.

18. Maugham, *The Vagrant Mood,* pp. 173–74.

19. See below, p. 62.

20. David Hume, *A Treatise of Human Nature* (1740), ed. L. A. Selby-Bigge (Oxford: Oxford University Press, 1888). This edition has been reprinted often, as have Selby-Bigge's editions of other of Hume's works.

21. A 68–69, B 93–94.

22. A 70, B 95.

23. *CAJ,* §41. *Ak.* V:203; Meredith, p. 41.

24. The reader may perhaps recognize here such views as those of A. J. Ayer in *Language, Truth and Logic* (1936; New York: Dover Press, 1950).

25. Kant does, however, present an interesting dialectical analysis of the history of culture in the appendix to the third *Critique,* which is examined in chapter 5 of the present study. For Marxist criticism of Kant's so-called

formalism, see Georg Lukács, *Die Seele und die Formen* (Berlin, 1911); *Die Theorie des Romans* (Berlin, 1920; English edition, *Theory of the Novel,* trans. Anna Bortock [Cambridge: M.I.T. Press, 1971]); *The Historical Novel,* trans. H. Mitchell and S. Mitchell (London, 1962). See also Lukác's *Realism in Our Time: Literature and the Class Struggle,* trans. J. Mauder and N. Mauder, preface by George Steiner (New York: Harper & Row, 1974).

26. Second ed. (Edinburgh, 1763).

27. *Essai sur le Goût* (Paris, 1766). See Marjorie Grene, "Gerard's 'Essay on Taste,' " *Modern Philological Review,* XLI (August 1943): 45–58.

28. First ed., 1785.

29. *CAJ,* §§1–21; *Ak.* V:203–44; Meredith, pp. 41–89.

30. For discussion of this "antinomy," see the first section of chapter 4.

31. In the next section, I give an analysis of pleasure and its crucial conceptual importance for the Kantian aesthetics.

32. See, *inter alia,* William Elton, ed., *Aesthetics and Language* (Oxford: Blackwell, 1954). Most of the writers in this collection subscribe to "ordinary language" aesthetics.

33. It is such teleological judgments that Kant examines in Part Two of the third *Critique.* I have largely avoided references to such forms of judgment in this study because they do not seem directly related to Kant's conception of aesthetics. There are nonetheless a number of recent German works which attempt to elucidate Kant's aesthetics in the light of the entire *Critique of Judgment,* including Peter Heintel, *Die Bedeutung der Kritik der Aesthetischen Urteilskraft für die transzendentalen Systematik* (Bonn, 1970); Wolfgang Bartuschat, *Zum systematischen Ort von Kants Kritik der Urteilskraft* (Frankfurt, 1972); K. Kuypers, *Kants Kunsttheorie und die Einheit der Kritik der Urteilskraft* (Amsterdam, 1972).

34. Trans. T. M. Greene and H. H. Hudson, with an essay by John R. Silber (La Salle, Ill.: Open Court Publishing Co., 1960), p. 129.

35. Though there are many parallels—as well as profound differences—between Kant's aesthetics and his doctrine of religious belief, I shall touch upon them only in regard to my discussion of metaphorical imagery in Kant's theory of aesthetics and the similarities which Kant conceives to exist between religious language and poetic symbolism; see the first section of chapter 5.

36. I use the more opaque term "person" rather than "perceiver" because it makes no sense to speak of "perceiving" music or poetry, which, for Kant, are clear examples of aesthetic objects.

37. See below, p. 118, for Kant's position in regard to mysticism and "enthusiasm."

38. *CAJ,* §1. *Ak.* V:203; Meredith, p. 41–42.

39. Letter to Marcus Herz, Feb. 21, 1772. *Ak.* X:129–35; *Kant: Philosophical Correspondence, 1759–1799,* trans. Arnulf Zweig (Chicago: University of Chicago Press, 1967), pp. 70–76.

40. I deal with Kant's explanation of "creative" intelligence as it pertains to the fine arts in the first section of chapter 5.

41. I.e., such a judgment would not be what Kant calls "a judgment of taste."

42. A similar point might be made in regard to ethical theory, though Kant himself does not explicitly make it. Although moral terms cannot be defined in terms of feelings and attitudes, a morality that makes no reference to human nature and human feelings would be patently incomplete as an ethical theory. It is unfortunate that Kant's ethical system is generally equated with his very formal account in *Foundations of the Metaphysics of Morals*. In the second *Critique* and in the *Metaphysics of Morals*, Kant greatly expands his conception of the Categorical Imperative and enriches it with theories concerning self-preservation, rational benevolence, and the unlimited development of human potential—from the point of view of both the individual and society.

43. *CAJ*, §4. *Ak.* V:207; Meredith, p. 46.

44. *CAJ*, §4. *Ak.* V:209; Meredith, p. 48.

45. *G*, 2nd sec. *Ak.* IV:434; Beck, p. 52.

46. *CAJ*, §16. *Ak.* V:229; Meredith, p. 72.

47. *CAJ*, §41. *Ak.* V:297; Meredith, p. 155.

48. *CAJ*, §54. *Ak.* V:332; Meredith, p. 199.

49. *CAJ*, §1. *Ak.* V:204; Meredith, p. 42.

50. Readers acquainted with the aesthetic theories of Schopenhauer will recognize here his conception of art as the vehicle of "will-less" perception. For Schopenhauer's development of "disinterested pleasure," see "The World as Idea," Second Aspect, in *The World as Will and Idea*, trans. R. B. Haldane and J. Kemp (1883; 11th impression, London: Routledge and Kegan Paul, 1964). One of the few good essays on Schopenhauer is the introduction by Thomas Mann in his *Living Thoughts of Schopenhauer* (London, 1939). See also Patrick Gardiner, *Schopenhauer* (Baltimore: Penguin Books, 1971).

51. *G*, 2nd sec. *Ak.* IV:407; Beck, p. 23.

52. See pp. 79–84.

53. *CAJ*, §6. *Ak.* V:211; Meredith, p. 50.

54. *CAJ*, §7. *Ak.* V:212; Meredith, pp. 51–52.

55. *CAJ*, §14. *Ak.* V:225; Meredith, p. 67.

56. *CAJ*, §14. *Ak.* V:224; Meredith, pp. 66–67.

57. *CAJ*, §14. *Ak.* V:224; Meredith, p. 66.

58. The problematic passage (*Ak.* V:224; Meredith, p. 66) involves two phrases: "*gar sehr zweifle*" or "*nicht zweifle.*" Whether Kant is simply using Euler's theory of color as an example or illustration of his own philosophical point concerning the formal beauty of "pure" sensations, or whether he is actually subscribing to Euler's theory cannot, to the best of my knowledge, be resolved on textual grounds from Kant's other writings. See Theodore E. Vehling, Jr., *The Notion of Form in Kant's Critique of Aesthetic Judgment* (The Hague/Paris: Mouton, 1971).

59. *CAJ*, introduction. *Ak.* V:189; Meredith, p. 29.

60. *CAJ*, §3. *Ak.* V:206; Meredith, p. 45.

61. For Kant's views concerning purposefulness in the *Erste Einleitung in die Kritik der Urteilskraft*, consult *Ak.* XX:193–251; English translation by James Haden, *Immanuel Kant: The First Introduction to the Critique of Judgment* (New York: Bobbs-Merrill, 1965). Although Kant discarded his "First Introduction," there do not appear to be any philosophical differences between it and the second "Introduction" on the topic of purposefulness. In general, the second is more perspicuous and less convoluted than the first.

62. G, 1st sec. *Ak.* IV:393; Beck, p. 11.

63. *CAJ*, §16. *Ak.* V:229; Meredith, p. 72.

64. Natural objects, such as a sea-weathered stone or log, are called "works of art" elliptically; it is as if they were fashioned by an artist. Kant does not explicitly state this view but indicates it when he speaks of "nature's *style*": "Simplicity (artless finality) is, as it were, the style adopted by nature in the sublime" (*CAJ*, §29. *Ak.* V:275; Meredith, p. 128).

65. *CAJ*, §10. *Ak.* V:220; Meredith, pp. 61–62.

66. *CAJ*, §11. *Ak.* V:221; Meredith, pp. 62–63.

67. *CAJ*, §22. *Ak.* V:241; Meredith, p. 86.

68. *CAJ*, §13. *Ak.* V:222–23; Meredith, pp. 64–65.

69. A 70 ff., B 95 ff.

70. G, 1st sec. *Ak.* IV:389; Beck, p. 5.

71. *CAJ*, §22. *Ak.* V.239; Meredith, p. 84.

72. *CAJ*, §21. *Ak.* V:238; Meredith, p. 83.

73. *CAJ*, §15. *Ak.* V:228; Meredith, p. 71.

74. E. H. Gombrich, *Art and Illusion*, 2nd ed. rev. (Princeton: Princeton University Press, Bollingen Series, 1961), p. 199.

75. Ibid., p. 157.

76. Ibid., p. 200. In the same passage quoted by Gombrich, Reynolds warns of the danger of Gainsborough's highly indeterminate style: "For unless the perceiver approaches the paintings of Gainsborough's with a conception of whom or of what the painting represents . . . all would be disappointed at not finding the original correspond with their own conceptions, under the great latitude which indistinctness gives to the imagination to assume almost what character or form it pleases."

77. Ibid., p. 293.

78. Ibid., p. 216.

79. Ibid., p. 221.

80. Ibid., p. 225.

81. *CAJ*, §29. *Ak.* V:275; Meredith, p. 128.

82. For Constable's view, see Gombrich, *Art and Illusion*, pp. 33, 34, 48, 49, 175, 319, 322.

83. A 137 ff., B 176 ff.

84. A 78, B 103.

85. *CAJ*, §22, *Ak.* V:241; Meredith, p. 87.

86. In the Galleria Borghese.
87. *CAJ*, §16. *Ak.* V:229; Meredith, p. 72.
88. *CAJ*, §16. *Ak.* V:230; Meredith, p. 73.
89. A 137 ff., B 176 ff.
90. A 146, B 185–86.
91. *CAJ*, §29. *Ak.* V:218; Meredith, p. 59.
92. *CAJ*, §29. *Ak.* V:269; Meredith, p. 121.
93. E. H. Gombrich, *Art and Illusion*, p. 116.
94. Ibid., p. 365.
95. Ibid., p. 321.
96. Ibid., p. 73.
97. Ibid.
98. Ibid., p. 147.
99. Ibid., p. 272.
100. Ibid., p. 87.
101. Ibid., p. 30.
102. Ibid., p. 83.
103. Ibid., p. 342.
104. *Summa Theologica*, I, question 5, art. 4.
105. *MEJ*, introduction. *Ak.* VI:211; Ladd, p. 10.
106. *Anthropologie in Pragmatischer Hinsicht*, 1st part, 2nd bk., "Vom Gefühl der Lust and Unlust," section B; "Vom Gefühl für das Schöne." *Ak.* VII:239.
107. *CAJ*, §14. *Ak.* V:223 ff.; Meredith, pp. 65–67. See also *CAJ* §3. *Ak.* V:205 ff.; Meredith, pp. 44–45.
108. *CAJ*, §29. *Ak.* V:277–78; Meredith, p. 131.
109. *CAJ*, §4. *Ak.* V:207–08; Meredith, p. 46.
110. See chapter 3 for Kant's theory of the sublime.
111. *CAJ*, §14. *Ak.* V:225–26; Meredith, p. 68.
112. *CAJ*, §29. *Ak.* V:272–73; Meredith, p. 125.
113. Kant's particular dislike of writers of the "sentimental school," such as Klopstock, Richardson, and Bellert, is apparent in the *Anthropology*. See also Otto Schlapp, *Kants Lehre Vom Genie* (Göttingen, 1901).
114. See chapter 5.
115. *Art and Illusion*, p. 366. See also Gombrich's discussion of "reading" faces, ibid., pp. 331–58, 360.
116. *CAJ* §29. *Ak.* V:272–73; Meredith, p. 125.
117. *CAJ* §29. *Ak.* V:273; Meredith, p. 126.
118. Ibid.
119. P. A. Schilpp, *Kant's Pre-Critical Ethics* (1938; Evanston, Ill.: Northwestern University Press, 1960), p. 128.
120. *CAJ*, §60. *Ak.* V:356; Meredith, p. 227.
121. *CAJ*, §60. *Ak.* V:355; Meredith, p. 226.
122. "Principles of Nature and Grace," in *The Philosophic Works of*

Leibniz, trans. George Martin Duncan (New Haven: Yale University Press, 1908), pp. 306–07.

123. *CAJ,* §29. *Ak.* V:277; Meredith, p. 131.
124. *CAJ,* §54. *Ak.* V:330 ff.; Meredith, p. 196 ff.
125. *CAJ,* §57. *Ak.* V:217; Meredith, p. 57.
126. *Art and Illusion,* p. 103.
127. *CAJ,* §9. *Ak.* V:217; Meredith, p. 58.
128. *CAJ,* §16. *Ak.* V:231; Meredith, p. 74.
129. *CAJ,* §17. *Ak.* V:231–32; Meredith, pp. 75–76.
130. *CAJ,* §33. *Ak.* V:284; Meredith, p. 140.
131. *CAJ,* §16. *Ak.* V:229; Meredith, p. 72.
132. *G,* 2nd sec. *Ak.* IV:407; Beck, p. 23.
133. Ibid.

3. The Analysis of the Sublime

1. *General History of Nature and Theory of the Heavens,* trans. W. D. Hastie (Glasgow: Maclehose, 1900), pp. 54–55. Kant first published this treatise anonymously in 1755.
2. "The Meaning of 'Romanticism' for the Historian of Ideas," *Journal of the History of Ideas,* II (1941):257–78.
3. *CAJ,* §26. *Ak.* V:252–53; Meredith, p. 100.
4. *CAJ,* §29. *Ak.* V:270; Meredith, p. 122.
5. *General History of Nature,* p. 144 ff.
6. See *Characteristics of Men, Manners, Opinions, Times, Etc.,* ed. J. M. Robertson, 2 vols. (London, 1900).
7. *CAJ,* §29. *Ak.* V:277; Meredith, pp. 130–31.
8. See Edmond and Jules de Goncourt, *La Femme au dix-huitième siècle* (Paris: Firmin-Didot & Co., 1887).
9. *MEJ,* introduction. *Ak.* VI:212; Ladd, p. 11.
10. Ibid.
11. *Anthropologie in Pragmatischer Hinsicht.* Ak. VII:239 ff.
12. *CAJ,* §23. *Ak.* V:244; Meredith, p. 90.
13. *CAJ,* §23. *Ak.* V:245; Meredith, p. 91.
14. *CAJ,* §29. *Ak.* V:275; Meredith, p. 128.
15. *CAJ,* §23. *Ak.* V:246; Meredith, p. 92.
16. *CAJ,* §23. *Ak.* V:246; Meredith, p. 93.
17. *CAJ,* §26. *Ak.* V:253–54; Meredith, p. 101.
18. *CAJ,* §26. *Ak.* V:252; Meredith, p. 100.
19. *CAJ,* §26. *Ak.* V:254–55; Meredith, p. 103.
20. *CAJ,* §24. *Ak.* V:247; Meredith, p. 94.
21. Canto LXXXI, *The Pisan Cantos.*
22. *CAJ,* §25. *Ak.* V:250; Meredith, p. 98.

23. See the first section of chapter 5.
24. *Anthropologie. Ak.* VII:239 ff.
25. *Anthropologie. Ak.* VII:241.
26. *CAJ*, §60. *Ak.* V:356; Meredith, p. 227.
27. *CAJ*, §17. *Ak.* V:231 ff.; Meredith, pp. 75, 80.
28. *CAJ*, §26. *Ak.* V:251–52; Meredith, p. 99.
29. " 'Psychical Distance' as a Factor in Art and an Aesthetic Principle," in *Aesthetics: Lectures and Essays*, ed. E. M. Wilkinson (Stanford: Stanford University Press, 1957).
30. *CAJ*, §26. *Ak.* V:252; Meredith, p. 99.
31. See the first section of chapter 5.
32. *CAJ*, §26. *Ak.* V:252; Meredith, p. 100.
33. *The Enneads*, trans. Stephen MacKenna, rev. B. S. Page (London, 1956). See especially VI, vii, viii.
34. *CAJ*, §26. *Ak.* V:252; Meredith, p. 100.
35. *CAJ*, §29. *Ak.* V:270; Meredith, p. 122.
36. *CAJ*, §26. *Ak.* V:253; Meredith, p. 100.
37. *CAJ*, §28. *Ak.* V:264; Meredith, p. 114.
38. *CAJ*, §26. *Ak.* V:255; Meredith, p. 104.
39. *CAJ*, §27. *Ak.* V:260; Meredith, p. 109.
40. *CAJ*, §27. *Ak.* V:257; Meredith, p. 106.
41. *CAJ*, §28. *Ak.* V:261; Meredith, p. 110.
42. *CAJ*, §28. *Ak.* V:264; Meredith, p. 114.
43. *CAJ*, §29. *Ak.* V:271; Meredith, p. 124.
44. *Religion Within the Limits of Reason Alone. Ak.* VI:30; trans. T. M. Greene and H. H. Hudson (La Salle, Ill.: Open Court, 1960), p. 25.
45. "Was Ist Aufklärung?" (first published in 1784). English translation in Immanuel Kant, *On History*, ed. L. W. Beck, trans. L. W. Beck, R. E. Anchor, and E. L. Fackenheim (New York: Bobbs-Merrill, 1963), pp. 3–10.
46. *O*, 1st pt. *Ak.* II:208; Goldthwait, p. 46.
47. *CAJ*, §29. *Ak.* V:265; Meredith, p. 116.
48. *CAJ*, §30. *Ak.* V:280; Meredith, p. 134. See also Rudolf Odebrecht, *Form und Geist: Der Aufsteig des dialektischen Denkens in Kants Aesthetik* (Berlin, 1930).
49. For an earlier essay reflecting Swedenborg's influence upon Kant, see Kant's *Träume eines Geistersehers* (1766). *Ak.* II:315–68; *Dreams of a Spirit-Seer*, trans. E. F. Goerwitz, ed. F. Sewall (London: Swann Sonnenschein, 1900).
50. *Dreams. Ak.* II:317–18; Goerwitz, p. 39.
51. See A 695 ff., B 723 ff.
52. Also quoted by J. C. Meredith on the title page of his 1911 translation of *CAJ*.
53. *CAJ*, §28. *Ak.* V:264; Meredith, p. 114.
54. Monroe Beardsley, *Aesthetics from Classical Greece to the Present*

(New York: Macmillan, 1966), p. 221. Beardsley's account of Kant's aesthetics is one of the best in English, though brief and incomplete.

55. *CAJ*, §52. *Ak*. V:325; Meredith, p. 190.
56. *CAJ*, §16. *Ak*. V:229; Meredith, p. 72.
57. B 164.
58. *CAJ*, §29. *Ak*. V:265; Meredith, p. 115.
59. *CAJ*, §28. *Ak*. V:260; Meredith, p. 110.
60. *CAJ*, §28. *Ak*. V:262; Meredith, p. 112.
61. *CAJ*, §26. *Ak*. V:252; Meredith, p. 100.
62. *CAJ*, §29. *Ak*. V:270; Meredith, p. 122.
63. *CAJ*, §29. *Ak*. V:275; Meredith, p. 128.
64. See below, p. 170, for a discussion of Kant's notion of "art as exhibiting exemplary validity."
65. *CAJ*, §29. *Ak*. V:275; Meredith, p. 128.
66. Ibid.
67. *CAJ*, §29. *Ak*. V:274; Meredith, p. 127.
68. First published in 1800.
69. *CAJ*, §29. *Ak*. V:275; Meredith, p. 128.
70. *CAJ*, §43. *Ak*. V:304; Meredith, p. 164.
71. See the first section of chapter 4.
72. *CAJ*, §29. *Ak*. V:274; Meredith, p. 127.
73. Authorship of the treatise is sometimes attributed to Dionysius of Halicarnassus, but given the pedantry and lack of enthusiasm generally found in Dionysius' works, it is unlikely that he was the author of "On the Sublime." Gibbon attributes it to Longinus of Palmyra, who was the counselor to Queen Zenobia. Though the work is sometimes placed in the third century, it mentions no writer later than the first century, in which many Greek scholars prefer to place it. Since nothing of the author is known, his name is often italicized, but I shall not follow that practice here. The text was first published in 1554 but did not become well known until a French translation by Boileau appeared in 1674.
74. D. A. Russell, trans., *'Longinus' on Sublimity* (Oxford, The Clarendon Press, 1965), pp. 9–10, 7.
75. I have not attempted to give more than the salient philosophical ideas related to the sublime that have evident parallels to Kant's thought. For greater detail consult Samuel H. Monk, *The Sublime: A Study of Critical Theories in Eighteenth-Century England* (Ann Arbor, 1960).
76. Thomas Burnet, *Sacred Theory of the Earth* (1681), I, xi, quoted from Beardsley, *Aesthetics from Classical Greece to the Present*, p. 182.
77. See nos. 409, 411–21, June and July, 1712.
78. *O*, 4th pt. *Ak*. II:255; Goldthwait, p. 114. I have used Professor T. M. Greene's translation of this passage from *The Heritage of Kant*, ed. G. T. Whitney and D. F. Bowers (New York: Russell and Russell, 1962), p. 325.
79. *Spectator*, VI, no. 412.

80. First published in 1757.

81. *CAJ*, §29. *Ak.* V:277; Meredith, p. 130.

82. Kant's third *Critique* was published thirty-three years after Burke's *Enquiry*, with which Kant was familiar as early as 1764, when his *Observations on the Feeling of the Beautiful and the Sublime* was published.

83. Edmund Burke, *A Philosophical Enquiry into the Origin of Our Ideas of the Sublime and Beautiful*, ed. J. T. Boulton, 2nd ed. (1759; New York, 1958).

84. Burke, *Enquiry*, p. 13.

85. Ibid.

86. Ibid.

87. Ibid., p. 52.

88. Ibid., p. 57.

89. Ibid., p. 39.

90. Ibid., p. 63.

91. *CAJ*, §29. *Ak.* V:277; Meredith, p. 131.

92. *CAJ*, §29. *Ak.* V:276; Meredith, pp. 131–32.

93. Burke, *Enquiry*, p. 23.

4. The Metaphysics of Criticism

1. Sections 55–60 of Part One of the third *Critique* concern the "Dialectic of Aesthetic Judgment."

2. *CAJ*, §57. *Ak.* V:341; Meredith, p. 209.

3. *CAJ*, §55. *Ak.* V:337; Meredith, p. 204.

4. Ibid.

5. *CAJ*, §58. *Ak.* V:347; Meredith, p. 217.

6. See below, pp. 170–78.

7. A 320, B 376.

8. A 106.

9. See A 115–30, B 130–69.

10. *CAJ*, §3. *Ak.* V:206; Meredith, p. 45.

11. I prefer not to use "data" because of its empirical associations.

12. A 320, B 376.

13. *CAJ*, §16. *Ak.* V:230; Meredith, p. 73.

14. *CAJ*, §17. *Ak.* V:233; Meredith, p. 76.

15. Ibid.

16. *CAJ*, §17. *Ak.* V:235; Meredith, p. 80.

17. *CAJ*, §17. *Ak.* V:234–35; Meredith, pp. 77–78.

18. *CAJ*, §17. *Ak.* V:235; Meredith, p. 79.

19. *CAJ*, §17. *Ak.* V:236; Meredith, p. 80.

20. *CAJ*, §5. *Ak.* V:211; Meredith, p. 50.

21. *CAJ*, §9. *Ak.* V:219; Meredith, p. 60.

22. *CAJ*, §17. *Ak.* V:236; Meredith, p. 80.
23. *CAJ*, §22. *Ak.* V:240; Meredith, p. 85.
24. A 20, B 34.
25. A 67 ff., B 92 ff.
26. *CAJ*, §57. *Ak.* V:340; Meredith, p. 208.
27. See Marie Jean Antoine Nicolas Caritat, Marquis de Condorcet, *Esquisse d'un tableau historique du progrès de l'esprit humain* (first published 1794; 3rd ed. [Paris: Brissot-Thivars, 1823]; English ed., *Outlines of an Historical View of the Progress of the Human Mind*, trans. unknown [Philadelphia, 1795]).
28. *CAJ*, §57. *Ak.* V:341; Meredith, pp. 208–09.
29. *CAJ*, §57. *Ak.* V:340; Meredith, p. 208.
30. *CAJ*, §57. *Ak.* V:346; Meredith, p. 215.
31. A better rendering of *Ding-an-sich* might be "thing *by* itself."
32. A 235, B 310–11.
33. *CAJ*, §5. *Ak.* V:210; Meredith, p. 50. *CAJ*, §52. *Ak.* V:326; Meredith, p. 191. *CAJ*, §44. *Ak.* V:335; Meredith, p. 202. *CAJ*, §59. *Ak.* V:351–52; Meredith, pp. 221–22. *CAJ*, §60. *Ak.* V:355–56; Meredith, p. 227.
34. *CAJ*, §49. *Ak.* V:313; Meredith, p. 175.
35. *CAJ*, §49. *Ak.* V:318–19; Meredith, p. 182.
36. *CAJ*, §59. *Ak.* V:351; Meredith, p. 221.
37. *CAJ*, §12. *Ak.* V:221–22; Meredith, p. 63.
38. *CAJ*, §34. *Ak.* V:286; Meredith, p. 142.
39. *CAJ*, §57. *Ak.* V:340; Meredith, p. 207.
40. See the first section of chapter 2 for the distinction between "substantive" and "analytic" aesthetics.
41. *CAJ*, §33. *Ak.* V:284; Meredith, p. 140.
42. Trans. Louis Infield and J. Macmurray (New York: Harper Torchbooks, 1963), p. 78.
43. *G*, 2nd sec. *Ak.* IV:409; Beck, p. 25.
44. *CAJ*, §32. *Ak.* V:283; Meredith, p. 139.
45. *CAJ*, §33. *Ak.* V:284; Meredith, p. 139.
46. *G*, 2nd sec. *Ak.* IV:422; Beck, p. 39.
47. See *CAJ*, §30. *Ak.* V:279–303; Meredith, pp. 133–62, for the essential statements of the "Deduction."
48. *CAJ*, §34. *Ak.* V:285; Meredith, p. 141.
49. *CAJ*, §17. *Ak.* V:235; Meredith, p. 79.
50. *CAJ*, §36. *Ak.* V:288; Meredith, pp. 144–45.
51. *CAJ*, §42. *Ak.* V:299; Meredith, p. 158.
52. First published in 1750.
53. First published in 1762.
54. It might be of interest to note that many of the so-called New Critics, such as John Crowe Ransom, René Wellek, Alan Tate, and Cleanth Brooks, claim a certain parentage from Kant's aesthetics. In "The Concrete

Universal" (*The Kenyon Review*, XVI [Autumn 1954]:554–64), Ransom says, "But Hegel's thought is a special development of Kant's and the fact is that I am obliged to think of Kant as my own mentor. Kant is closer to our critical feeling than Hegel is! So I shall talk of Kant's understanding of poetry." For the discussions of autonomy and form by certain of the new critics (i.e., 1950–60), see William J. Handy, *Kant and the Southern New Critics* (Austin: University of Texas Press, 1963).

55. *CAJ*, §34. *Ak*. V:286; Meredith, p. 141.
56. Ibid.
57. *CAJ*, §34. *Ak*. V:286; Meredith, p. 142.
58. Ibid.
59. Ibid.
60. *CAJ*, §38. *Ak*. V:291; Meredith, p. 147.
61. *CAJ*, §38, fn. *Ak*. V:291; Meredith, p. 147.
62. *CAJ*, §17. *Ak*. V:234; Meredith, p. 78.
63. *CAJ*, §40. *Ak*. V:295; Meredith, p. 153.
64. *CAJ*, §22. *Ak*. V:239; Meredith, p. 84.
65. *CAJ*, §40. *Ak*. V:293 ff.; Meredith, pp. 150–54.
66. *Philosophical Writings*, trans. Norman Kemp Smith (New York: Modern Library, 1958), p. 93.
67. *CAJ*, §41. *Ak*. V:297; Meredith, p. 156.
68. *CAJ*, §40. *Ak*. V:293; Meredith, p. 151.
69. Ibid.
70. *CAJ*, §40. *Ak*. V:294; Meredith, p. 152.
71. *CAJ*, §40. *Ak*. V:295; Meredith, p. 153.
72. *CAJ*, §40. *Ak*. V:296; Meredith, p. 154.

5. The Cognitive and Pedagogical Roles of the Aesthetic

1. *A Treatise of Human Nature*, ed. L. A. Selby-Bigge (1888; reprint ed., Oxford: The Clarendon Press, 1972), p. 469.
2. An interesting, though I believe mistaken, interpretation of the relationship between the noumenal and the phenomenal in aesthetic judgment is given by Robert L. Zimmerman, "Kant: The Aesthetic Judgment," *Journal of Aesthetics and Art Criticism*, 24 (1962–63): "It is necessary to bear in mind that aesthetic experience, i.e., the experience of natural beauty, is experience of the noumenal world as it filters through the phenomenal world" (pp. 333–34). There are some passages (discussed in this section) which might bear out the thesis that for Kant it is *as if* aesthetic experience could be construed as the "noumenal filtering through the phenomenal." But Kant himself warns against such supposed insights into or experiences of the noumenon (see *CAJ*, §29. *Ak*. V:275; Meredith, p. 128). For Kant, moreover, the noumenon by definition cannot be the object of any experience, even aesthetic experience. The metaphor of "filtering" is highly misleading.

3. Loeb Classical Library (Cambridge: Harvard University Press, 1965), pp. 16–18.

4. Hobbes, *Leviathan*, ed. Michael Oakeshott (Oxford: Blackwell, 1958), p. 26.

5. John Locke, *Essay Concerning Human Understanding*, 2 vols. (1690; New York: Dover, 1959), II:146 (bk. II, chap. x).

6. For Bacon, see *Advancement of Learning* (1605), in *Bacon's Essays*, ed. J. M. McNeill (London: Macmillan, 1964) and in *Essays, Advancement of Learning, New Atlantis, and Other Pieces*, selected and edited by Richard Foster Jones (New York: Odyssey Press, 1937). For Hobbes, see *Leviathan*, I, ii. For Locke, see "Of the Association of Ideas," added to the fourth edition (1700) of the *Essay Concerning Human Understanding*, bk. II, chap. xxxiii (Dover ed., I:527–35).

7. *CAJ*, §57. *Ak.* V:341; Meredith, p. 209.

8. A 674, B 702.

9. *CAJ*, §49. *Ak.* V:314; Meredith, p. 176.

10. *CAJ*, §48. *Ak.* V:313; Meredith, p. 175.

11. *CAJ*, §49. *Ak.* V:314; Meredith, p. 176.

12. *CAJ*, §47. *Ak.* V:309; Meredith, p. 170.

13. *CAJ*, §42. *Ak.* V:300; Meredith, p. 159.

14. *CAJ*, §49. *Ak.* V:316; Meredith, p. 179.

15. *CAJ*, §49. *Ak.* V:315; Meredith, p. 178.

16. *CAJ*, §49. *Ak.* V:316; Meredith, p. 178.

17. Ibid.

18. *Religion Within the Limits of Reason Alone*. *Ak.* VI:62; trans. T. M. Greene and H. H. Hudson (La Salle, Ill.: Open Court Publishing Co., 1960), p. 55; *Ak.* VI:137; Greene and Hudson, p. 129.

19. *Religion*. *Ak.* VI:137; Greene and Hudson, p. 129.

20. "The Legacy," stanza 1; "An Anatomy of the World. The First Anniversary of the Death of Mistress Elizabeth Drury" (1. 205).

21. *CAJ*, §46. *Ak.* V:307; Meredith, p. 168.

22. *CAJ*, §49. *Ak.* V:317; Meredith, pp. 179–80.

23. *CAJ*, §59. *Ak.* V:320–21; Meredith, p. 183.

24. *CAJ*, §47. *Ak.* V:309; Meredith, p. 170.

25. *Anthropologie*. *Ak.* VII:224 ff.

26. This essay is included in *On History*, ed. L. W. Beck, trans. L. W. Beck, R. E. Anchor, and E. L. Fackenheim (New York: Bobbs-Merrill, 1963), pp. 3–10.

27. It will be recalled from the *Critique of Pure Reason* that "regulative" is a term applied by Kant to any idea or principle that is useful as a heuristic or organizing ideal of knowledge or experience. "Constitutive" is ordinarily applied by Kant to any idea or principle that makes a necessary or formal contribution to knowledge. For example, the categories are constitutive of knowledge, whereas the transcendental ideas—of the self, the cosmos, and God—when taken as constitutive rather than as regulative, are the

sources of metaphysics. As applied to the ways in which an exemplary work of art might be employed, the usage of the two terms is analogical. Kant himself does not use the two terms in regard to "exemplary" art, but they might make clear the important distinction between merely imitating a great work and having either one's own taste or one's own creative power regulated and enriched by it. An artist, then, can be influenced in either a "constitutive" or a "regulative" way by the history of art.

28. Probably written by Petronius, ca. 50 A.D.

29. *Phaedrus*, 245A.

30. *CAJ*, §49. *Ak.* V:318; Meredith, p. 181.

31. *CAJ*, §47. *Ak.* V:310; Meredith, p. 171.

32. *CAJ*, §51. *Ak.* V:321; Meredith, p. 185.

33. Ibid.

34. *CAJ*, §53. *Ak.* V:330; Meredith, p. 196.

35. Ibid.

36. *CAJ*, §52. *Ak.* V:326; Meredith, p. 191.

37. *CAJ*, §53. *Ak.* V:326; Meredith, p. 191.

38. *CAJ*, §53. *Ak.* V: 329; Meredith, p. 195.

39. *CAJ*, §59. *Ak.* V:353; Meredith, p. 223.

40. *CAJ*, §59. *Ak.* V:352; Meredith, p. 223.

41. Ibid.

42. Ibid.

43. See *Analytica Priora*, 89, b9; and *Politica*, 1261.

44. *CAJ*, §52. *Ak.* V:326; Meredith, p. 191.

45. *CAJ*, §59. *Ak.* V:354; Meredith, p. 225.

46. Ibid.

47. *CTJ*, §22. *Ak.* V:429 ff.; Meredith, p. 92 ff.

48. *CTJ*, §22. *Ak.* V:431 ff.; Meredith, p. 94 ff.

49. *On History*, ed. Beck, pp. 11–26.

50. *On History*, ed. Beck, pp. 15–22.

51. "O felix culpa, quae talem ac tantum meruit habere Redemptorem" ["O happy fault, which has deserved to have such and so mighty a Redeemer"] ("Exultet on Holy Sunday," attributed both to St. Augustine and to St. Ambrose, in *The Missal*, 1570).

52. *On History*, ed. Beck, p. 59 ff. "The Conjectural Beginning of Human History" was first published in 1786.

53. *G*, 3rd sec. *Ak.* IV:446 ff.; Beck, p. 64 ff.

54. A good translation is the one by Reginald Snell (New Haven: Yale University Press, 1954).

55. E. H. Gombrich, *Art and Illusion*, 2nd ed. rev. (Princeton: Princeton University Press, Bollingen Series, 1961), p. 141.

56. Ibid., p. 385.

57. Ibid., p. 287.

58. See Max Black, "Metaphor," in *Contemporary Studies in Aesthetics*, ed. F. J. Coleman (New York: McGraw-Hill, 1968), p. 216–32.

59. Frank Sibley, "Aesthetics and the Looks of Things," in *Contemporary Studies in Aesthetics,* ed. Coleman, pp. 335–45.

60. See Stuart Hampshire, "Logic and Appreciation," in *Aesthetics and Language,* ed. William Elton (New York: Philosophical Library, 1954), pp. 161–69.

61. For an example of the "good reasons" approach to aesthetics, see Paul Ziff, "Reasons in Art Criticism," in *Art and Philosophy,* ed. W. W. Kennick (New York: St. Martin's Press, 1964). "That a painting is not too large, not too small, is not apt to seduce and is even apt to improve one, has splendid subject matter, etc., are not, in themselves, or in isolation, reasons why a work is a good work, why the work is worth contemplating" (p. 616).

62. See Ludwig Wittgenstein, *Lectures and Conversations on Aesthetics, Psychology and Religious Belief,* compiled from notes taken by Yorick Smythies, Rush Rhees, and James Taylor; ed. Cyril Barrett (Berkeley: University of California Press, 1967). See also George Dickie, "Is Psychology Relevant to Aesthetics?" in *Contemporary Studies in Aesthetics,* ed. Coleman, pp. 321–35.

63. See Michael Podro, *The Manifold in Perception* (London: Oxford University Press, 1972). "We must therefore assume that to adopt an aesthetic attitude, if it means anything, must imply that we use ordinary concepts, but that we use them with a special attitude and purpose, to sustain ourselves in perception" (p. 124).

Bibliography

Primary Sources

Kant, Immanuel. *Anthropologie. Gesammelte Schriften,* vol. VII. Berlin, 1900–34.
———. *Beobachtungen über das Gefühl des Schönen und Erhaben. Gesammelte Schriften,* vol. II. Berlin, 1900–34.
———. *Briefwechsel. Gesammelte Schriften,* vols. X–XIII. Berlin, 1900–34.
———. *Critique of Judgement.* Translated by J. H. Bernard. London, 1951.
———. *Critique of Judgement.* Translated by James Creed Meredith. 1911. New York: Oxford University Press, 1952.
———. *Critique of Practical Reason, and Other Works on the Theory of Ethics.* Translated by Thomas Kingsmill Abbott. 6th ed. London, 1914.
———. *Critique of Pure Reason.* Translated by Norman Kemp Smith. London: Macmillan and Co., 1929.
———. *Die drei Kritiken, in ihrem Zusammenhang mit dem Gesamtwerk.* (Mit verbindendem Text Zusammengefasst, von Raymond Schmidt.) Leipzig, 1933.
———. *The Educational Theory of Immanuel Kant.* Translated and with an introduction by E. F. Buchner. London and Philadelphia, 1908.
———. *Foundations of the Metaphysics of Morals.* Translated by Lewis White Beck. New York: Bobbs-Merrill, 1959.
———. *On History.* Edited by L. W. Beck. Translated by L. W. Beck, R. E. Anchor, and E. L. Fackenheim. New York: Bobbs-Merrill, 1963.
———. *Kant: Philosophical Correspondence, 1759–1799.* Translated by Arnulf Zweig. Chicago: University of Chicago Press, 1967.
———. *Kant's Critique of Aesthetic Judgement* (Part One of the *Critique of Judgement*). Translated and with seven introductory essays by James Creed Meredith. Oxford: The Clarendon Press, 1911.
———. *Kant's Critique of Teleological Judgement* (Part Two of the *Critique of Judgement*). Translated and with an introduction by James Creed Meredith. Oxford: The Clarendon Press, 1928.
———. *Kant: Selected Pre-Critical Writings.* Translated by G. B. Kerferd and D. E. Walford. Manchester: Manchester University Press, 1968.
———. *Lectures on Ethics.* Translated by Louis Infield and J. Macmurray. 1930. New York: Harper Torchbooks, 1963.

———. *The Metaphysical Elements of Justice* (Part One of the *Metaphysics of Morals*). Translated by John Ladd. New York: Bobbs-Merrill, 1965.
———. *The Metaphysical Principles of Virtue* (Part Two of the *Metaphysics of Morals*). Translated by James Ellington. New York: Bobbs-Merrill, 1964.
———. *Observations on the Feeling of the Beautiful and the Sublime.* Translated by J. T. Goldthwait. Berkeley: University of California Press, 1960.
———. *Prolegomena to Any Future Metaphysics.* Translated by L. W. Beck. New York: Liberal Arts Press, 1951.
———. *Religion Within the Limits of Reason Alone.* Translated and with an introduction by Theodore M. Greene and Hoyt H. Hudson. La Salle, Ill.: Open Court Publishing Co., 1960.
———. *Selections.* Edited by Theodore M. Greene. New York: Scribners, 1957.

Secondary Sources

Aldrich, Virgil. *Philosophy of Art.* Englewood Cliffs, N.J.: Prentice-Hall, 1963.
Alexander, Samuel. *Art and Instinct.* Oxford: The Clarendon Press, 1927.
———. *Art and the Material.* London and New York: Oxford University Press, 1925.
———. *Artistic Creation and Cosmic Creation.* London: Oxford University Press, 1927.
———. *Beauty and Other Forms of Value.* 1933. New York: Apollo, 1968.
———. *Space, Time and Deity.* 2 vols. 1920. New York: Dover Press, 1966.
Alison, Archibald. *Essays on the Nature and Principles of Taste.* 4th ed. 1815. New York: Adler, 1968.
Allen, Grant. *Physiological Aesthetics.* New York, 1877.
Aristotle. *The Poetics.* Translated by Gerald F. Else. Ann Arbor: University of Michigan Press, 1967.
Arnold, Matthew. *Essays in Criticism* (first and second series). 1902. New York: Dutton, 1971.
———. *Selected Essays.* Introduction by Noel Annan. London: Oxford University Press, 1964.
Aschenbrenner, K., and Isenberg, A., eds. *Aesthetic Theories: Studies in the Philosophy of Art.* Englewood Cliffs, N.J.: Prentice-Hall, 1965.
Barrows, Dunham. "Kant's Theory of Aesthetic Form." In G. T. Whitney and D. F. Bowers, eds. *The Heritage of Kant.* 1939. Reprint. New York: Russell, 1962.
Bartuschat, Wolfgang. *Zum systematischen Ort von Kants Kritik der Urteilskraft.* Frankfurt, 1972.
Basch, Victor. *Essai critique sur l'esthétique de Kant.* 2nd ed. Paris, 1927.
Baumgarten, Alexander Gottlieb. *Die Aesthetik Alexander Gottlieb Baumgartens, unter besonderer Berucksichtigung der Meditationes Philophi-*

cae de nonnulis ad Poema Pertinentibus, nebst einer Übersetzung dieser Schrift, von Albert Riemann. Halle, 1928.

Beardsley, Monroe. *Aesthetics.* New York: Harcourt, Brace, 1958.

————. *Aesthetics from Classical Greece to the Present.* New York: Macmillan, 1966.

————, and Schueller, H., eds. *Aesthetic Inquiry: Essays on Art Criticism and the Philosophy of Art.* Belmont, Calif.: Dickerson, 1967.

Beck, Lewis White. *A Commentary on Kant's Critique of Practical Reason.* Chicago: University of Chicago Press, 1960.

Bell, Clive. *Art.* 1914. New York: Capricorn Books, 1958.

Berenson, Bernard. *The Italian Painters of the Renaissance.* Rev. ed. 1930. New York: Phaidon Publishers, 1968.

Bergson, Henri, *An Introduction to Metaphysics.* Translated by T. E. Hulme. 1912. New York: Liberal Arts Press, 1949.

————. *Laughter.* Translated by Cloudesley Brereton and Fred Rothwell. New York, 1912. Also, Wylie Sypher, ed. Garden City, N.Y.: Doubleday, 1956.

Bird, Graham. *Kant's Theory of Knowledge.* New York: Humanities Press, 1962.

Blocker, Harry. "Kant's Theory of the Relation of Imagination and Understanding In Aesthetic Judgments of Taste." *British Journal of Aesthetics,* V (1965):37–45.

Boas, Franz. *Primitive Art.* 1927. New York: Peter Smith, 1962.

Bodkin, Thomas. *The Approach to Painting.* New York: Harcourt, Brace, 1927.

Bohning, Elizabeth E. "Goethe's and Schiller's Interpretation of Beauty." *German Quarterly,* XXII (1949).185–94.

Bosanquet, Bernard. *Three Lectures on Aesthetic.* 1915. Edited by Ralph G. Ross. New York and Indianapolis: Bobbs-Merrill, 1963.

Bradley, Andrew Cecil. *Oxford Lectures on Poetry.* 2nd ed. London: Macmillan and Co., 1909.

Bretall, R. W. "Kant's Theory of the Sublime." In G. T. Whitney and D. F. Bowers, eds. *The Heritage of Kant.* 1939. Reprint. New York: Russell, 1962.

Burke, Edmund. *A Philosophical Enquiry into the Origin of Our Ideas of the Sublime and the Beautiful.* Edited by J. T. Boulton. New York: Columbia University Press, 1958.

Butcher, S. H. *Aristotle's Theory of Poetry and Fine Art: A Translation and a Long Essay on the 'Poetics.'* 1911. 4th ed. New York: Dover, 1955.

Bywater, Ingram. *Aristotle, on the Art of Poetry: Greek Text, an Introduction, and a Commentary.* 1909. London: Oxford University Press, 1920.

Caird, Edward. *The Critical Philosophy of Immanuel Kant.* 2 vols. 1889. Reprint. Millwood, N.Y.: Kraus, 1968. Book III.

————. *Essays on Literature and Philosophy,* vol. I. 1892. Reprint, 2 vols. in 1. Millwood, N.Y.: Kraus, 1968.

Campbell, Lewis. *Tragic Drama in Aeschylus, Sophocles, and Shakespeare.* 1904. Reprint. New York: Russell, 1965.

Carpenter, Rhys. *The Aesthetic Basis of Greek Art of the Fifth and Fourth Centuries B.C.* 1921. Bloomington: Indiana University Press, 1959.

Carritt, E. F. *The Theory of Beauty.* 1914. 2nd ed., enlarged. London: Methuen, 1923.

————. *What Is Beauty?* Oxford: The Clarendon Press, 1932.

————, ed. *Philosophies of Beauty, from Socrates to Robert Bridges.* New York and London: Oxford University Press, 1931.

Cassirer, H. W. *A Commentary on Kant's Critique of Judgment.* 1938. Reprint. New York: Barnes and Noble, 1970.

Chambers, Frank P. *The History of Taste.* 1932. Reprint. Westport, Conn.: Greenwood, 1971.

Cohen, Hermann. *Kants Begründung der Asthetik.* Berlin: Bruno and Cassirer, 1910.

Coleman, Francis X. J. *The Aesthetic Thought of the French Enlightenment.* Pittsburgh: University of Pittsburgh Press, 1971.

————, ed. *Contemporary Studies in Aesthetics.* New York: McGraw-Hill, 1968.

Collingwood, Robin G. *Outlines of a Philosophy of Art.* 1925. Reprint. New York: Somerset, 1925.

————. *The Principles of Art.* New York: Oxford University Press, 1958.

————. *Speculum Mentis.* Oxford: The Clarendon Press, 1924.

Croce, Benedetto. *Aesthetic.* Translated by Douglas Ainslee. 2nd ed. New York: Macmillan, 1922.

————. *The Essence of Aesthetic.* Translated by Douglas Ainslee. 1921. Rev. ed. New York: Noonday Press, 1953.

Daval, R. *La Métaphysique de Kant.* Paris: Presses Universitaires de France, 1951.

Delacroix, Henri. *Psychologie de l'Art.* Paris: F. Alcan, 1927.

Denckmann, Gerhard. *Kants Philosophie des Asthetischen.* Heidelberg: C. Winter, 1947.

Dewey, John. *Art as Experience.* 1934. New York: Putnam, 1953.

————. *Experience and Nature.* La Salle, Ill.: Open Court Publishing Co., 1925.

————. *Human Nature and Conduct.* 1922. New York: Modern Library, 1930.

————. *Philosophy and Civilization.* 1931. New York: Peter Smith, 1968.

Ducasse, Curt John. *The Philosophy of Art.* 1929. Rev. and enlarged ed. New York: Dover, 1963.

Duncan, A. R. C. *Practical Reason and Morality.* New York and London: Nelson, 1957.

Dunham, Barrows. *A Study in Kant's Aesthetics.* Lancaster, Pa., 1934.

Eliot, T. S. *Selected Essays.* 1932. Rev. ed. New York: Harcourt, Brace, 1950.

————. *The Use of Poetry and the Use of Criticism.* 1933. 2nd ed. New York: Barnes and Noble, 1970.

Ellis, Havelock. *The Dance of Life.* 1923. Reprint. Westport, Conn.: Greenwood, 1973.

Elton, William, ed. *Aesthetics and Language.* New York: Philosophical Library, 1954.

Ewing, A. C. *Kant's Treatment of Causality.* 1924. Reprint. New York: Anchor, 1969.

————. *A Short Commentary on Kant's Critique of Pure Reason.* 1938. 2nd ed. Chicago: University of Chicago Press, 1950.

Fackenheim, Emil L. "Schelling's Philosophy of the Literary Arts." *Philosophical Quarterly,* IV (1954):310–26.

Fechner, Gustav Theodor. *Vorschule der Asthetik.* Leipzig: Breitkopf an Häntel, 1876.

Freud, Sigmund. *Wit and Its Relation to the Unconscious.* Translated and with an introduction by A. A. Brill. *The Standard Edition of the Complete Psychological Works of Sigmund Freud.* James Strachey, ed. 1916. Reprint. London: Hogarth Press, 1968. Vol. VIII.

Fry, Roger. *Transformations.* New York: Brentano's, 1926.

————. *Vision and Design.* New York: Brentano's, 1924.

Gérard, Alexander. *An Essay on Genius.* 1774. Reprint. Havertown, Pa.: Richard West, 1973.

Gibelin, Jean. *L'esthétique de Schelling d'après la philosophie de l'art.* Paris, J. Vrin, 1934.

Gilbert, Katherine Everett. *Studies in Recent Aesthetics.* Chapel Hill: University of North Carolina Press, 1927.

Gombrich, E. H. *Art and Illusion.* Princeton: Princeton University Press, Bollingen Series, 1960.

Greene, T. M. *The Arts and the Art of Criticism.* 1947. Reprint. Staten Island, N.Y.: Gordian, 1973.

————. "A Reassessment of Kant's Aesthetic Theory." In G. T. Whitney and D. F. Bowers, eds. *The Heritage of Kant.* 1939. Reprint. New York: Russell, 1962.

Gross, Karl. *The Play of Man.* Translated by Elizabeth D. Baldwin. New York: D. Appleton and Company, 1901.

Grosse, Ernst. *The Beginnings of Art.* Translator unknown. New York: D. Appleton and Co., 1897.

Grudin, Louis. *A Primer of Aesthetics.* New York: Covici, Friede, 1930.

Guyau, Marie Jean. *L'Art au point de vue sociologique.* 15th ed. Paris: F. Alcan, 1930.

————. *Les Problèmes de l'esthétique contemporaine.* 13th ed. Paris: F. Alcan, 1935. Translated by Helen L. Mathews as *Problems of Contemporary Aesthetics.* Los Angeles: De Vorss, 1947.

Handy, William J., ed. *Kant and the Southern New Critics.* Austin: University of Texas Press, 1963.

Hanslick, Eduard. *The Beautiful in Music.* Translated by Gustav Cohen. 1891. New York: Bobbs-Merrill, 1957.

Hartmann, Eduard von. *Philosophie des Schönen.* Berlin: Dunckner, 1887.

Hazlitt, Henry. *The Anatomy of Criticism.* New York: Simon and Schuster, 1933.

Hegel, G. W. F. *The Introduction to Hegel's Philosophy of Fine Art.* Translated by Bernard Bosanquet. 1886. London: K. Paul, Trench, and Co., 1905.

————. *Philosophy of Fine Art.* Translated by F. P. B. Osmaston. 4 vols. 1920. Reprint. New York: Hacker, 1973.

Heintel, Peter. *Die Bedeutung der Kritik des Aesthetischen Urteilskraft für die transzendentalen Systematik.* Bonn, 1970.

Herder, Johann Gottlieb von. *Geschichte der Kunst des Altertums.* Berlin: Safari, 1942.

Hermerén, Gören. *Representation and Meaning in the Visual Arts.* Lund: Berlingska, Boktryckeriet, 1969.

Heyl, Bernard. *New Bearings in Esthetics and Art Criticism.* 1943. Reprint. Westport, Conn.: Greenwood, 1971.

Hildebrand, Adolf. *The Problem of Form in Painting and Sculpture.* Translated by Max Meyer and Robert Morris Ogden. London and New York: 1932.

Hipple, Walter John, Jr. *The Beautiful, the Sublime, and the Picturesque in Eighteenth Century British Aesthetic Theory.* Carbondale: Southern Illinois University Press, 1957.

Hirn, Yrjo. *The Origins of Art: A Psychological and Sociological Inquiry.* 1900. Reprint. New York: B. Blom, 1971.

Hofstader, A., and Kuhns, Richard, eds. *Philosophies of Art and Beauty.* New York: Modern Library, 1964.

Horace. *Art of Poetry.* Edited and with an introduction and notes by Albert S. Cook. 1926. *Collected Works.* Translated by Lord Dunsany and Michael Oakley. New York: Dutton, 1961.

Hospers, John. *Meaning and Truth in the Arts.* Chapel Hill: University of North Carolina Press, 1946.

————, ed. *Introductory Readings in Aesthetics.* New York: Free Press, 1969.

Hulme, Thomas Ernest. *Speculations.* 1924. Edited by Herbert Read. 2nd ed. New York: Humanities Press, 1963.

Hume, David. *An Enquiry Concerning the Human Understanding, and an Enquiry Concerning the Principles of Morals.* Edited by L. A. Selby-Bigge. 1894. Reprint. Oxford: The Clarendon Press, 1957.

————. *Essays, Moral, Political and Literary.* 1882. London: Oxford University Press, 1963.

————. *A Treatise of Human Nature.* Edited by L. A. Selby-Bigge. 1888. Reprint. Oxford: The Clarendon Press, 1972.

Hutcheson, Francis. *An Inquiry into the Original of Our Ideas of Beauty and Virtue.* 2nd ed. 1726. New York: Garland Publishers, 1971.

Jacoby, Günther. *Herders and Kants Aesthetik.* Leipzig: Dürr, 1907.

Jones, Edmund D., ed. *English Critical Essays: 19th Century.* London: Oxford University Press, 1971.

———. *English Critical Essays: 16th, 17th, and 18th Centuries.* London: Oxford University Press, 1922.

Kabir, Humayun. *Immanuel Kant on Philosophy in General.* Introductory essays on the first introduction to the *Critique of Judgment.* Calcutta, 1935.

Kames, Henry H. *Elements of Criticism.* 1762. Reprint. New York: Johnson Reprint, 1971.

Kemp Smith, Norman. *A Commentary to Kant's Critique of Pure Reason.* 1918. 2nd ed. New York: Humanities Press, 1962.

Kennick, W. E., ed. *Art and Philosophy.* New York: St. Martin's, 1964.

Kerry, S. S. "The Artist's Intuition in Schiller's Aesthetic Philosophy." *Publications of the English Goethe Society.* Vol. XXVIII (N.S.). Leeds, 1959.

Knox, I. *The Aesthetic Theories of Kant, Hegel, and Schopenhauer.* 1936. New York: Humanities Press, 1958.

Körner, Stephen. *Kant.* Harmondsworth: Penguin Books, 1955.

Kroner, Richard. *Kant's Weltanschauung.* Translated by John E. Smith. Chicago: University of Chicago Press, 1956.

Krutch, Joseph Wood. *Experience and Art.* New York: H. Smith and R. Hass, 1932.

Kuypers, K. *Kants Kunsttheorie und die Einheit der Kritik der Urteilskraft.* Amsterdam: North-Holland Publishing Co.. 1972.

Lalo, Charles. *L'Art et la vie sociale.* Paris: G. Doin, 1921.

Lange, Konrad von. *Das Wesen der Kunst.* 2nd ed. Berlin: G. Grote, 1907.

Langer, Suzanne. *Feeling and Form.* New York: Scribners, 1953.

———. *Philosophy in a New Key.* 1948. 3rd ed. Cambridge: Harvard University Press, 1957.

———. *Problems of Art.* New York: Scribners, 1957.

Langfeld, Herbert S. *The Aesthetic Attitude.* 1920. Reprint. Port Washington, N.Y.: Kennikat, 1967.

Lee, Harold N. "Kant's Theory of Aesthetics." *Philosophical Review,* XL (1931):537–48.

Lee, Vernon, and Anstruther-Thomson, C. *Beauty and Ugliness.* 1912. Translated by G. Waterhouse. Cambridge: Cambridge University Press, 1926.

Lessing, G. Ephraim. *Hamburgischen Dramaturgie.* Münster: Aschendorff, 1907. *Hamburg Dramaturgy.* New introduction by Victor Lange. New York: Dover, 1962.

———. *Laocoön.* Translated by Ellen Frothingham. 1910. New York: Noonday Press, 1957.

———. *Selected Prose Works.* Translated by Helen Zimmerman and E. C. Beasley. London: G. Bell and Sons, 1900.

Levich, Marvin, ed. *Aesthetics and the Philosophy of Criticism.* New York: Random House, 1963.

Lindsay, A. D. *Kant*. London: Oxford University Press, 1936.

Lipps, Theodor. *Aesthetik*. 2 vols. 1903. Reprint. Leipzig and Hamburg: L. Voss, 1920–23.

Listowel, W. A. *A Critical History of Modern Aesthetic*. 1933. New York: Gordon Press, 1972.

'Longinus' On Sublimity. Translated and with an introduction by D. A. Russell. Oxford: The Clarendon Press, 1965.

Lotze, Hermann. *Microcosmos*. Translated by Elizabeth Hamilton and E. E. Constance Jones. 1886. Reprint. Freeport, N.Y.: Books for Libraries, 1973.

Lovejoy, A. O. *The Great Chain of Being*. New York: Harper Torchbooks, 1960.

———. "The Meaning of Romanticism for the Historian of Ideas." *Journal of the History of Ideas*, II (1941):257–78.

———. " 'Nature' as Aesthetic Norm." *Modern Language Notes*, XLII (1927):444–50.

Macmillan, R. A. C. *The Crowning Phase of the Critical Philosophy*. London: Macmillan and Co., 1912.

Marc-Wogau, Konrad. *Vier Studien zu Kants Kritik der Urteilskraft*. Uppsala, Sweden: Uppsala Universitets årrokrift, 1938.

Margolis, Joseph. *The Language of Art and Art Criticism*. Detroit: Wayne State University Press, 1965.

———. "Recent Work in Aesthetics." *American Philosophical Quarterly*, II (1965):182–92.

Maritain, Jacques. *Art and Scholasticism*. 1930. Translated by J. F. Scanlan. Reprint. Freeport, N.Y.: Books for Libraries, 1970.

Mead, Hunter. *An Introduction to Aesthetics*. New York: Ronald Press, 1952.

Menzer, P. *Kants Asthetik in ihrer Entwicklung*. Berlin, 1952.

Mercier, Louis Joseph Alexander. *The Challenge of Humanism*. New York, 1933.

Meredith, George. *An Essay on Comedy*. 1903. Reprint. Port Washington, N.Y.: Kennikat, 1971.

Meredith, James C. Introductory essays in Kant, *Critique of Aesthetic Judgement*. Translated idem. 1911. New York: Oxford University Press, 1961.

Meumann, Ernst. *Einführung in die Aesthetik der Gegenwart*. 3rd ed. Leipzig, 1919.

Monk, Samuel H. *The Sublime: A Study of Critical Theories in Eighteenth-Century England*. Rev. ed. Ann Arbor: University of Michigan Press, 1960.

Moore, George Edward. *Principia Ethica*. 1903. Cambridge: Cambridge University Press, 1959.

Morris, William. *Art, Labour, and Socialism*. 1884. Reprint. London: Socialist Party of Great Britain, 1962.

———. *Hopes and Fears for Art. Collected Works of William Morris*, vol. 22. New York: Russell, 1910–15.

Mumford, Lewis. *Technics and Civilization.* 1934. New York: Harcourt, Brace, 1972.
Mundt, Ernest K. "Three Aspects of German Aesthetic Theory." *Journal of Aesthetics and Art Criticism,* XVII (March 1959):287–310.
Munro, Thomas. *Scientific Method in Aesthetics.* New York: W. W. Norton, 1928.
Murray, Gilbert. *The Classical Tradition in Poetry.* 1927. Reprint. New York: Russell, 1968.
Neumann, Karl. *Gegenständlichkeit und Existenzbedeutung des Schönen.* Bonn, 1973.
Newman, John Henry. *Poetry with Reference to Aristotle's Poetics.* Boston, 1891.
Odebrecht, Rudolf. *Form und Geist: Der Aufsteig des dialektischen Denkens in Kants Aesthetik.* Berlin, 1930.
Osborne, Harold. *Aesthetics and Criticism.* 1955. Reprint. Westport, Conn.: Greenwood, 1973.
———. *Theory of Beauty.* New York: Philosophical Library, 1953.
Parker, DeWitt Henry. *The Analysis of Art.* New Haven and London, 1926.
———. *The Principles of Aesthetics.* 1920. 2nd ed. New York: Appleton, 1946.
Pater, Walter. *The Renaissance.* New York: New American Library, 1959.
Paton, H. J. *The Categorical Imperative.* 1947. Philadelphia: University of Pennsylvania Press, 1971.
———. *Kant's Metaphysic of Experience.* 2 vols. 1936. New York: Macmillan, 1961.
Pepper, Stephen. *The Basis of Criticism in the Arts.* Cambridge: Harvard University Press, 1949.
Philipson, Morris, ed. *Aesthetics Today.* New York: Meridan Books, 1961.
Plato, "Ion." In *The Collected Dialogues of Plato.* Translated by Edith Hamilton and Huntington Cairns. New York: Pantheon Books, 1961.
———. *Phaedrus.* Translated by Benjamin Jowett. 4th ed. Oxford: The Clarendon Press, 1953.
———. *The Republic.* Translated by Benjamin Jowett. Cleveland: Fine Editions Press, 1946.
———. "The Symposium." In *The Collected Dialogues of Plato.* Translated by Edith Hamilton and Huntington Cairns. New York: Pantheon Books, 1961.
Plotinus. *The Enneads.* Translated by Stephen MacKenna. 5 vols. 1917–30. New York: Pantheon Books, 1957.
Podro, Michael. *The Manifold in Perception.* London: Oxford University Press, 1972.
Pole, William. *The Philosophy of Music.* 6th ed. rev. New York: Harcourt, Brace, 1924.
Powell, A. E. *The Romantic Theory of Poetry.* London, 1926.
Prall, David W. *Aesthetic Analysis.* New York: Crowell, 1936.

(214) BIBLIOGRAPHY

————. *Aesthetic Judgment*. New York: Crowell, 1929.

Prichard, H. A. *Kant's Theory of Knowledge*. Oxford: The Clarendon Press, 1909.

Proudhon, Pierre-Joseph. *Du principe de l'art et de sa destination sociale*. 1865. Westmead, England: Gregg International Publishers, 1971.

Rader, Melvin M. *A Modern Book of Aesthetics*. 1935. 4th ed. New York: Holt, Rinehart and Winston, 1973.

Rank, Otto. *Art and Artist*. Translated by Charles Francis Atkinson. New York, 1932.

Raymond, George Lansing. *The Essentials of Aesthetics (in Music, Poetry, Painting, Sculpture and Architecture)*. 3rd ed. New York, 1921.

Reid, Louis A. *A Study in Aesthetics*. 1931. Reprint. Westport, Conn.: Greenwood, 1973.

Richards, I. A. *Coleridge on Imagination*. 1935. Edited by Kathleen Coburn. Bloomington: Indiana University Press, 1960.

————. *Practical Criticism*. New York: Harcourt, Brace, 1929.

————. *Principles of Literary Criticism*. 1925. New York: Harcourt, Brace, 1950.

————. *Science and Poetry*. 1926. 2nd ed. rev. London: K. Paul, Trench and Trubner, 1935.

————, Ogden, C. K., and Wood, James. *The Foundations of Aesthetics*. 1922. 2nd ed. New York: Lear Publishers, 1925.

Ritcher, Peyton, ed. *Perspectives in Aesthetics*. New York: Odyssey, 1967.

Ross, W. D. *Kant's Ethical Theory*. Oxford: The Clarendon Press, 1954.

Ruskin, John. *Modern Painters*. New York: Dutton, 1907.

————. *The Seven Lamps of Architecture*. New York: Dutton, 1907.

Russell, Bertrand. *Selected Papers*. New York: Modern Library, 1927.

Santayana, George. *Interpretations of Poetry and Religion*. 1900. Magnolia, Mass.: Peter Smith, 1960.

————. *The Realm of Essence*. 1927. Reprint. Westport, Conn.: Greenwood, 1962.

————. *Reason in Art*. 1905. New York: Macmillan, 1962.

————. *The Sense of Beauty*. 1896. New York: Modern Library, 1955.

————. *Three Philosophical Poets*. 1910. Havertown, Pa.: Richard West, 1973.

Schaper, Eva. "Friedrich Schiller: Adventures of a Kantian." *British Journal of Aesthetics*, IV (1964):348–62.

Schelling, Friederich von. "Concerning the Relation of the Plastic Arts to Nature" (*Uber das Verhältnis der bildenen Künste zu der Natur*). 1807. Translated by Michael Bullock. In Herbert Read, *The True Voice of Feeling*. New York: Pantheon Books, 1953.

————. *Sammtliche Werke*. 14 vols. 1856–61. *Ausgewählte Werke*. Darmstadt: Wissenschaftliche Buchgesellshaft, 1966–68.

————. *System des Transzendentalen Idealismus*. Hamburg: Meiner, 1957.

————. *On University Studies (Vorlesung über die Methode des akademi-*

schen Studiums). 1803. 14th lecture. Translated by Ella S. Morgan. Athens: Ohio University Press, 1966.

Schilpp, P. A. *Kant's Pre-Critical Ethics.* 1938. Evanston, Ill.: Northwestern University Press, 1960.

Schlapp, O. *Kants Lehre vom Genie und die Entstehung der "Kritik der Urteilskraft."* Göttingen, 1901.

Schueller, Herbert M. "Immanuel Kant and the Aesthetics of Music." *Journal of Aesthetics and Art Criticism,* XIV (December 1955):218–47.

————. "Schelling's Theory of the Metaphysics of Music." *Journal of Aesthetics and Art Criticism,* XV (June 1957):461–76.

Sesonske, Alexander, ed. *What is Art? Aesthetic Theory from Plato to Tolstoy.* New York: Oxford University Press, 1965.

Shaftesbury, Anthony. *Characteristics of Men, Manners, Opinions, Times, Etc.* 1900. Edited by J. M. Robinson. New York: Bobbs-Merrill, 1964.

Sidney, Philip. *The Defense of Poetry.* Edited and with an introduction and notes by Albert S. Cook. 1890. In idem., *Selected Poetry and Prose.* New York: Holt, Rinehart and Winston, 1969.

Stace, W. T. *The Philosophy of Hegel.* New York: Dover, 1923. Pt. IV, 3rd div., chap. 1.

Stein, Leo. *The ABC of Aesthetics.* New York: Boni and Liveright, 1927.

Stolnitz, Jerome. *Aesthetics and Philosophy of Art Criticism.* Boston: Houghton Mifflin, 1960.

Strachey, John. *Literature and Dialectical Materialism.* New York: Covici, Friede, 1934.

Sully, James. *An Essay on Laughter.* London and New York, 1902.

Taine, Hippolyte Adolphe. *A History of English Literature.* Translated by H. von Laun. 4 vols. 1871. Reprint. New York. F. Ungar, 1965.

————. *Lectures on Art.* Translated by John Durand. 2 vols. 1875. Reprint. New York: AMS, 1971.

Tillman, Frank, and Kahn, Steven, eds. *Philosophy of Art and Aesthetics.* New York: Harper and Row, 1969.

Tolstoy, Leo. *What Is Art? and Other Essays on Art.* Translated by Aylmer Maude. New York: Bobbs-Merrill, 1960.

Uehling, Theodore E., Jr. *The Notion of Form in Kant's Critique of Aesthetic Judgment.* The Hague/Paris: Mouton, 1971.

Vaihinger, Hans. *Kommentar zur Kritik der reinen Vernunft.* 2 vols. Stuttgart, 1881–92.

Véron, Eugène. *L'Esthétique.* 1876. Translated by W. H. Armstrong. London: Library of Contemporary Science, 1879.

Vivas, Eliseo, and Krieger, Murray, eds. *The Problems of Aesthetics.* New York: Rinehart, 1953.

Walsh, W. H. *Reason and Experience.* New York: Oxford University Press, 1947.

Ward, Keith. *The Development of Kant's View of Ethics.* New York: Humanities Press, 1972.

Weitz, Morris. *Philosophy of the Arts.* 1950. Reprint. New York: Russell, 1964.

Weldon, T. D. *Introduction to Kant's Critique of Pure Reason.* 1945. 2nd ed. Oxford: The Clarendon Press, 1958.

Wellek, René. "[Kant's] Aesthetics and Criticism." In C. W. Hendel, ed. *The Philosophy of Kant and Our Modern World.* New York, 1957.

Wells, Henry. *The Judgment of Literature.* New York: W. W. Norton, 1928.

Whitehead, Alfred North. *Adventure of Ideas.* 1933. New York: New American Library, 1959.

————. *The Aim of Education and Other Essays.* 1929. New York: New American Library, 1956.

————. *Science and the Modern World.* 1929. New York: New American Library, 1959.

————. *Symbolism.* 1927. New York: Putnam, 1959.

Will, Frederic. *Intelligible Beauty in Aesthetic Thought from Winckelmann to Victor Cousin.* Tübingen: M. Niemeyer, 1958.

Winckelmann, John Joachim. *The History of Ancient Art.* Translated by G. Henry Lodge. 1880. New York: Ungar, 1968.

Wittgenstein, Ludwig. *Philosophical Investigations.* Translated by G. E. M. Anscombe. New York: Macmillan, 1953.

Wolff, Robert Paul, ed. *Kant: A Collection of Critical Essays.* New York: Doubleday, 1967.

————. *Kant's Theory of Mental Activity.* Cambridge: Harvard University Press, 1963.

Zimmerman, Robert L. "Kant: The Aesthetic Judgment." *Journal of Aesthetics and Art Criticism,* XXI (Spring 1963):333–44.

Index

(217)